Cisco® Router Configuration & Troubleshooting
Second Edition

New Riders

Other Books by New Riders Publishing

Inside Windows 2000 Server
William Boswell, 1-56205-929-7

Windows 2000 Active Directory
*Edgar Brovick, Doug Hauger, and
William C. Wade III, 0-7357-0870-3*

Windows 2000 Deployment and
Desktop Management
Jeffrey Ferris, 0-7357-0975-0

Windows 2000 Routing and Remote
Access Service
Kackie Charles, 0-7357-0951-3

Windows 2000 Professional
Jerry Honeycutt, 0-7357-0950-5

Planning for Windows 2000
*Eric Cone, Jon Boggs, and Sergio Perez,
0-7357-0048-6*

Windows NT Power Toolkit
*Stu Sjouwerman and Ed Tittel,
0-7357-0922-X*

Windows NT DNS
*Michael Masterson, Herman Kneif, Scott
Vinick, and Eric Roul, 1-56205-943-2*

Windows NT Network Management:
Reducing Total Cost of Ownership
Anil Desai, 1-56205-946-7

Windows NT Performance:
Monitoring, Benchmarking, and Tuning
*Mark Edmead and Paul Hinsburg,
1-56205-942-4*

Windows NT Registry: A Settings
Reference
Sandra Osborne, 1-56205-941-6

Windows NT TCP/IP
Karanjit Siyan, 1-56205-887-8

Windows NT Terminal Server & Citrix
MetaFrame
Ted Harwood, 1-56205-944-0

Exchange System Administration
Janice Rice Howd, 0-7357-0081-8

Implementing Exchange Server
*Doug Hauger, Marywynne Leon, and
William C. Wade III, 1-56205-931-9*

SQL Server Essential Reference
Sharon Dooley, 0-7357-0864-9

Network Intrusion Detection:
An Analyst's Handbook
Stephen Northcutt, 0-7357-0868-1

Understanding Data Communications,
Sixth Edition
Gilbert Held, 0-7357-0036-2

SQL Server System Administration
*Sean Baird, Chris Miller, et al.,
1-56205-955-6*

Domino System Administration
Rob Kirkland, 1-56205-948-3

Understanding Directory Services
Beth and Doug Sheresh, 0-7357-0910-6

Understanding the Network:
A Practical Guide to Internetworking
Michael Martin, 0-7357-0977-7

Internet Information Services
Administration
Kelli Adam, 0-7357-0022-2

SMS 2 Administration
*Michael Lubanski and Darshan Doshi,
0-7357-0082-6*

Cisco® Router Configuration & Troubleshooting
Second Edition

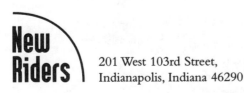

New Riders
201 West 103rd Street,
Indianapolis, Indiana 46290

Mark Tripod

Cisco® Router Configuration & Troubleshooting

Second Edition

Copyright® 2000 by New Riders Publishing

SECOND EDITION: *June, 2000*

International Standard Book Number: 0-7357-0999-8

Library of Congress Catalog Card Number: 00-100504

04 03 02 01 00 7 6 5 4 3 2 1

Interpretation of the printing code: The rightmost double-digit number is the year of the book's printing; the rightmost single-digit number is the number of the book's printing. For example, the printing code 00-1 shows that the first printing of the book occurred in 2000.

Composed in Bembo and MCPdigital by New Riders Publishing

Printed in the United States of America

Trademarks

Warning and Disclaimer

Publisher
David Dwyer

Executive Editor
Al Valvano

Managing Editor
Gina Brown

Product Marketing Manager
Stephanie Layton

Acquisitions Editor
Theresa Gheen

Development Editor
Lisa M. Thibault

Senior Editor
Kristy Knoop

Copy Editor
Scott MacLean

Indexer
Cheryl Landis

Manufacturing
Chris Moos
Jim Conway

Book Designer
Louisa Klucznik

Cover Designer
Aren Howell

Proofreader
Debbie Williams

Composition
Amy Parker

Contents

About the Author

Mark Tripod is Manager of the Internetworking Engineering Group at Exodus Communications, a leading provider of Internet systems and network management solutions for companies with mission-critical Internet operations. As part of his job, Mark designs, deploys, and maintains the national network infrastructure linking all of the Exodus Internet Data Centers; maintains and configures all external BGP peers; and advises on all backbone routing policies. Previously, Mark was a Senior Network Engineer for Pacific Bell where he designed and deployed its regional network infrastructure. He has worked in the Internet industry and with Cisco routers for more than six years. Mark likes to spend his spare time water skiing, swimming, and racing go-carts.

About the Technical Reviewers

These reviewers contributed their considerable hands-on expertise to the entire development process for *Cisco Router Configuration & Troubleshooting*, Second Edition. As the book was being written, these dedicated professionals reviewed all the material for technical content, organization, and flow. Their feedback was critical to ensuring that *Cisco Router Configuration & Troubleshooting*, Second Edition fits our reader's need for the highest quality technical information.

Lance Skok is a Network Technical Expert with SBC in San Antonio, TX. Before going to work for SBC, he held a position of Senior Systems Engineer at Inacom Information Systems. In addition to having obtained CCIE # 4480, he holds numerous other industry certifications including MCSE, Novell Master CNE, and Compaq ASE. He has been heavily involved with PCs since 1980 and has skills in programming, networking, and systems integration. You can reach him at lskok@netfix.com.

Evan Wagner is MIS Director for a software development company based in Vienna, Virginia, with offices in the U.S. and Europe. He is responsible for the direction and hands-on management of all aspects of the company's information, system, and voice services architecture worldwide. He has 15 years of experience in the IT industry and possesses a wide variety of skills in the areas of network integration and management in diverse environments, troubleshooting, technical training, and computer programming. Evan is a CCIE candidate with technical certifications including Cisco CCDA, MCSE/MCT, and Sun Microsystems Enterprise SE among others. (His internetworking adventures began more than a decade ago with big boxes that took 8-inch floppy disks.) He also has extensive network operating system experience with Microsoft Windows NT, Novell NetWare, and multiple UNIX variants including Linux. In his spare time, Evan is preparing for the CCIE routing and switching lab practical exam. Above all, Evan enjoys spending time with his wife and two daughters, hiking, playing soccer, and playing guitar.

For my loving wife Melissa who continues to allow me the self-indulgence to continue doing what I love. Also, for my two beautiful daughters who bring a smile to my face with every thought. I'd also like to dedicate this book to my parents Jerry and Christine. I love you all very much.

Acknowledgments

I'd like to acknowledge both Paul Steiger and Jim McInerney. I would never have been able to continue on this project if the people whom I work with at Exodus had not been so accommodating. Their guidance and support have been invaluable.

Tell Us What You Think

As the reader of this book, you are the most important critic and commentator. We value your opinion and want to know what we're doing right, what we could do better, what areas you'd like to see us publish in, and any other words of wisdom you're willing to pass our way.

As the Executive Editor for the Networking team at New Riders Publishing/MTP, I welcome your comments. You can fax, email, or write me directly to let me know what you did or didn't like about this book—as well as what we can do to make our books stronger.

Please note that I cannot help you with technical problems related to the topic of this book, and that due to the high volume of mail I receive, I might not be able to reply to every message.

When you write, please be sure to include this book's title and author as well as your name and phone or fax number. I will carefully review your comments and share them with the author and editors who worked on the book.

Fax: 317-581-4663
Email: nrfeedback@newriders.com
Mail: Al Valvano
            Executive Editor
            New Riders Publishing
            201 West 103rd Street
            Indianapolis, IN 46290 USA

Introduction

Welcome to the second edition of *Cisco Router Configuration & Troubleshooting,* Second Edition. Through the course of reading this book, it is my hope that you will gain some insight into how to design and maintain an IP network and why some networks that you may have worked on in the past were built the way they were.

This edition builds upon the first by updating the product information as well as introducing many new commands that Cisco has added to its latest revision of IOS, 12.0. This second edition also adds information for virtual LANs, virtual private networks, and multicast. The OSPF portion of Chapter 6 has been made much more robust.

Cisco Systems is the dominant router vendor for Enterprise and Internet applications. You will no doubt encounter them at some point in your networking career. This book aims to familiarize you with how Cisco routers can be used to help troubleshoot network problems. This book also offers suggestions on how to monitor your network equipment to prevent problems from occurring.

Who Should Read This Book?

You should read this book if you are responsible for monitoring or maintaining a network that contains Cisco routers. You should also read this book if you are looking to find out more about Cisco routers than what is contained in the Cisco documentation. If you have not yet encountered Cisco routers in your workplace, you will gain a basic familiarity which will ease your introduction to the routers when you do encounter them. If you already work with Cisco routers, you will gain a better understanding of how to utilize the tools available in the Cisco IOS to troubleshoot network problems.

This book will also help the general network operator in monitoring his/her network devices.

Contents of the Book

This book is arranged into four parts. The parts and chapters can be summarized as follows:

Part I: Getting Started

Part I acts as a refresher of TCP/IP and introduces the various router products offered by Cisco. The Cisco products mentioned are the basis for the remaining text of the book. If you are comfortable with the Cisco product line and have a moderate level of IP networking experience, you can skip this part of the book and proceed directly to Part II.

Chapter 1: Networking and TCP/IP

Chapter 1 introduces networking principles and lays the foundation for the rest of the book. A full discussion of the OSI model and TCP/IP addressing basics is provided.

Chapter 2: Cisco Routers: An Overview

Cisco makes products that span the spectrum of networking technology. This chapter explores the high-end routers and remote access devices you may be working with.

Part II: Router Configuration

Part II jumps right into the configuration of Cisco routers. It starts off explaining the Cisco IOS command-line interface and moves into specific examples of interface configuration. Interior and exterior routing protocols are discussed. Managing the user base for your routers is explored, as well as the functionality of filter-lists. Finally, IP multicast communication is explored along with multicast routing protocols.

Chapter 3: Initial Router Setup

Cisco routers come with no default configuration, which means you must configure them to accomplish your predefined tasks. Chapter 3 discusses the various programming options and command-line programming modes you can use.

Chapter 4: Local Area Networking

Chapter 4 discusses a few of the most common protocols used to connect local area networks. These are Ethernet, Fiber Distributed Data Interface (FDDI), and Token Ring.

Chapter 5: Wide Area Networking

A wide area network (WAN) is generally considered to be any network that incorporates links that are supplied by a telecommunications company (telco) of some sort. Chapter 5 discusses the issues related to configuring and troubleshooting WANs.

Chapter 6: Configuring Dynamic Routing Protocols

Chapter 6 discusses the differences between static routing and dynamic routing. The primary focus is on the different dynamic routing protocols and how they are usually implemented.

Chapter 7: Multicast

Chapter 7 introduces the concept of multicast IP communication. Discussions of the origin, uses, and current development of multicast protocols are included. Multicast routing protocols are also covered.

Chapter 8: Access and Traffic Management

Chapter 8 concentrates on ways to limit access to and manage the traffic flowing through the routers in your network.

Part III: Router Monitoring

Part III introduces the various methods available to collect data from your Cisco routers. In addition to collecting the data, suggestions are made on the processing of the data into a usable format. This includes graphical displays and automated text reports. Some of the facilities that you should use for proactive monitoring of your network equipment are introduced here as well.

Chapter 9: Collecting Data via SNMP

Collecting data from your routers is the key to understanding the growth patterns of your network. Chapter 9 focuses on collecting data with SNMP.

Chapter 10: Collecting Data via Other Means

Chapter 10 covers the most basic and useful of the many data-collection options available to a network operator: automated telnet sessions, rsh and rcp, and the syslog facilities built into the Cisco IOS.

Part IV: Router Troubleshooting

Part IV provides an outline for proper troubleshooting of network problems. Proactive monitoring of network equipment is also discussed so possible problems can be corrected before a network outage. The most common diagnostic tools and their uses are discussed. Finally, specific examples of the use of troubleshooting commands are given for each of the first three layers of the OSI model.

Chapter 11: Troubleshooting

Chapter 11 focuses on methods and techniques for isolating and troubleshooting problems on your network systems.

Chapter 12: Tools of the Trade

Chapter 12 discusses the tools you can use as you begin to troubleshoot systems. Specifically, PING and traceroute are discussed in detail.

Chapter 13: Case Study

This chapter introduces the case study and network diagram that is used as the basis for the remaining three chapters.

Chapter 14: Troubleshooting the Physical Layer

This chapter focuses on troubleshooting the physical layer of the OSI model.

Chapter 15: Troubleshooting the Network Layer

This chapter will cover troubleshooting of the network layer of the OSI model.

Chapter 16: Troubleshooting Routing Protocols

This chapter completes the book by explaining the commands you need for retrieving information from the router IOS and providing suggestions on how to work with your hardware manufacturer to solve network problems.

I

Getting Started

1

Networking and TCP/IP

FOR THE MAJORITY OF THE AUDIENCE, this chapter will be used for three things:

- A foundation to set the standards of the remaining chapters.
- A review to refresh your understanding of the material that will be the basis for the book.
- For those already versed in the basics of networking, this chapter serves as a simple reference to thumb back through whenever needed.

I encourage you to have a strong understanding of the networking principles set forth in this chapter before attempting to understand the in-depth material we will discuss in the subsequent chapters of this book. If you feel that you have a firm understanding of networking, you should feel free to skip this chapter and proceed directly to Chapter 2, "Cisco Routers: An Overview."

When you complete this chapter, you should be able to comfortably springboard into the remaining material of the book and gain a thorough understanding of what is being discussed.

The OSI Reference Model

Let us begin with the foundation that all networking is built upon, the Open Systems Interconnection (OSI) model. For most readers, the OSI model should be more of a reference model than a new word on the block. If not, do not be alarmed. The following text will give you enough of an understanding to get started. The OSI model is a seven layer architectural model developed by the International Organization for Standardization (ISO) and the International Telecommunications Union-Telecommunications (ITU-T). The main use of the model is to help developers understand the functionality involved with the creation and flow of networking software. Within this book we will discuss the networking properties of how OSI Reference Model fundamentals are integrated within applications that are used in device to device communication.

The OSI model is divided into seven layers, each with its own characteristics and tasks. Each layer of the model specifies certain characteristics that software must be able to implement. Each layer is independent of the others. Communication between the layers is handled by a defined set of actions. This provides a very flexible palette for programmers to implement features in each layer without having to worry about interaction with software that has been (or will be) written for other layers of the OSI model. The model works as a family tree flow chart where each layer partakes in some manner of the next layer through a set of services and protocols. The seven layers of the OSI are (see Figure 1.1).

Application	7
Presentation	6
Session	5
Transport	4
Network	3
Datalink	2
Physical	1

Figure 1.1 The OSI model layers.

What Is Telnet?

For those that are new to networking, telnet is an application as well as a protocol that is used to communicate with a network device from a remote station. The operating systems of most network devices support the telnet protocol. However, you should never take for granted that it is available. Luckily, all Cisco devices that operate the Internetworking Operating System (IOS) support telnet.

The layers are listed in reverse order for ease of explanation. We will briefly review each layer starting with the application layer because that is what most of us see on a daily basis. To make things a little more realistic, we will see the steps taken when telnetting into a router.

Most software written for use on a network has sections that provide the functions outlined in the OSI model. For instance, a WWW browser does not simply display data; it is also responsible for collecting data from WWW servers at your request. The action of actually going out on the Internet and retrieving data uses all seven of the layers in the OSI model. The WWW browser software might implement layers 4 through 7 or it might simply implement layers 6 and 7 and rely upon the operating system of your computer to provide the other layers.

The Application Layer

The application layer is the window or interface with which the end user will interact. Some common examples of application layer communication are a telnet session logging into a remote router, downloading email (very common one right?), and downloading a file via a Web browser. These are just some of the application layer examples out there. These applications are unaware of the remaining six layers of the OSI Reference Model, which are working to produce the necessary communication.

The Presentation Layer

The presentation layer deals with the type of data that is being transferred between two communicating applications. The applications might reside on the same machine or they might be on servers separated by the distance of the globe. The point is that either situation requires the OSI model to be implemented the same way.

As the name implies, "presentation" means display. It is the responsibility of the presentation layer to make sure that the data sent from the application layer of one system is usable by the application layer of another system. The presentation layer acts as a translator to the data supplied by the application layer. The data is converted if needed and sent off to the next layer.

One common example of the presentation layer is *Abstract Syntax Representation #1* (ASN.1), in which a popular protocol called Simple Network Management Protocol (SNMP) comes into mind. Data compression and decompression, as well as encryption and decryption, are also tasks associated with this layer.

The Session Layer

The "Blind Dates" have finally met and a dialogue is opened between the two. The session layer deals strictly with communication between two applications that reside on networked devices. It serves to organize their communication by offering three different modes:

- Simplex
- Half-duplex
- Full-duplex

Each mode has its own way of communicating. Simplex mode is basically a one way conversation. One end is transmitting while the other is receiving. To get an accurate picture of this, think of the famous telegraph machine back in the good old days. Half-duplex mode takes turns in communicating. Think of the proper conversation etiquette when conversing through a speakerphone; you cannot have two people speaking at the same time. Full-duplex mode is based upon what is called *flow control*. This is only used due to the difference in the operating speed of the two nodes, where one might transmit faster than the other can receive.

The Transport Layer

The transport layer works as a "preparation for shipping" layer. The main tasks of the transport layer are to provide error correction, multiplexing, and flow control. By providing error correction in one of the OSI layers, application programmers do not have to worry about implementing it in software at other layers of the OSI model. Error detection is a big responsibility of the transport layer. *Error detection* is the process of determining if the data that is sent through the OSI layers has been changed from its original state. This is usually done via a checksum mechanism. *Multiplexing* enables data from several applications to share the same physical link. *Flow control* ensures that the device sending the data does not transmit faster than the device receiving the data can handle.

Reliable and unreliable delivery are the two transmissions the transport layer handles. Reliable delivery is kind of like *certified mail*. It doesn't guarantee a perfect delivery, but it does imply the material is important. In unreliable delivery, the transport layer doesn't check for errors. This does not mean that this method is useless. This mode of transport can be useful in a network that's known to be highly reliable, or when an individual packet contains a complete message. In the case of an individual packet, this would be known as a *datagram*.

The Network Layer

The network layer provides routing and related functionality so that multiple individual network segments can be combined into an internetwork. This is the layer where software, or logical, addressing occurs. Logical addressing at the network layer can be likened to the city, state, and zip code address format used by the United States Postal Service. Software addresses will get you as far as the *right city*, whereas the hardware address designates the *full home address*. The network layer deals with the *right city address*. When messages reach this layer, a directive is attached to them with the source and destination of the message. Next, the directive looks for the best route for the packet to take across the network. This is known as *routing*, and is handled by routers. Routing is only needed when data is sent from a device on one network segment to a device on a different network segment.

The Data Link Layer

The data link layer deals with finding the *full home address* of the packet. The data link layer is responsible for providing reliable communication across the physical layer of the network segments. The specifications of this layer define the characteristics of error notification, physical layer addressing, flow control, network topology, and datagram frame sequencing. Error notification alerts layers high in the OSI model that a transmission error has occurred. Physical layer addressing defines how network devices are addressed at the data link layer. Flow control moderates the transmission of data so that the receiver is not overwhelmed. Network topology defines how devices are attached to the physical layer, such as in a bus or ring configuration. Frame sequencing makes sure frames that might have been transmitted out of order are placed back in the correct order.

The data link layer formats the message into data frames and adds physical layer addresses. The data frame contains six sections:

- The start indicator.
- The source address.
- The destination address.
- The control portion, which handles special handling instructions.
- The actual data.
- The error control segment. This segment deals with Cyclical Redundancy Checksum (CRC).

The Institute of Electrical and Electronic Engineers (IEEE) further divides the data link layer into two sub-layers:

- Logical Link Control (LLC) layer
- Media Access Control (MAC) layer

The LLC layer manages communications between devices over a single link of a network. LLC is defined in the IEEE 802.2 specification and supports both connection-less and connection-oriented services used by higher-layer protocols. IEEE 802.2 defines a number of fields in data link layer frames that enable multiple higher-layer protocols to share a single physical data link.

The MAC layer manages protocol access to the physical network medium. The IEEE MAC specification defines MAC addresses, which enable multiple devices to uniquely identify one another at the data link layer.

The Physical Layer

The physical layer of the OSI Reference Model defines the electrical and mechanical specifications for the physical connection between two network devices. Physical layer specifications define characteristics such as voltage levels, timing of voltage changes, physical data rates, maximum transmission distances, and physical connectors.

The physical layer is responsible for the transmission and reception of bits. Bits come in values of 1's or 0's. This is the only layer of the OSI model that communicates directly with the various types of communication media.

Voltage Levels

The changing of voltage levels on the physical layer is what actually creates the 1's and 0's of a binary or digital system. A voltage level of +5DC can be defined as a binary one, whereas a voltage level of 0DC can be defined as a binary zero.

Hubs, Bridges, Switches

I will not spend too much time on the first three terms of this section because there's a good chance you are familiar with them anyway. Hubs are basically denoted as an Ethernet data link layer device that connects point-to-point physical layer links, such as twisted pair or fiber optic cabling into a single shared media network. Bridges and switches both operate under the data link layer. A bridge is a network device which helps connect multiple data link layer network segments into a single logical network segment. There are different types of bridges:

- Transparent or learning
- Encapsulation
- Translational
- Source-route
- Source-route translational

Even though the Cisco IOS implements each of the types of bridging above, the first three are the most common. Source-route and source-route translational are both commonly used in a token ring environment. The primary purpose of bridging is to enable physical and logical separation of traffic when necessary to reduce traffic loads on a network segment. Bridging ensures network reliability, availability, scalability, and manageability. The simplest form of a bridge is a transparent or learning bridge, which can handle only data link layer protocols. Encapsulation and translational bridges can be considered transparent bridges with the additional functionality of enabling different data link layer protocols to interoperate.

Now that we've covered what a bridge is, we can relate it to a switch. A Cisco switch is essentially a multiport bridge that runs the IOS. A switch functions at the data link layers performing the same basic functions as a bridge. The only difference between the switch and bridge is not technical, but packaging. A switch usually has more ports than a bridge, and possesses embedded management functions that a bridge does not have. Most of the ports support single data link layer protocol, such as Ethernet, and a smaller number of high-speed data link layer ports connect to faster medium, such as ATM or Fast Ethernet. If a switch has two or more different interfaces, it can be considered a translational bridge. Figure 1.2 shows an example of a small switched internetwork.

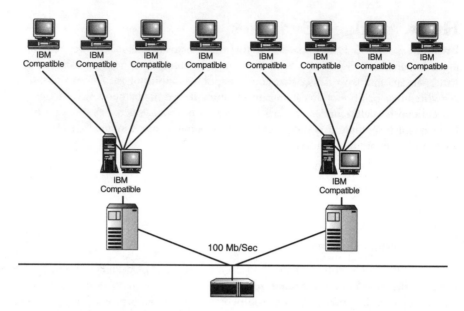

Figure 1.2 A small switched internetwork.

Hubs, bridges, and switches are only concerned with forwarding packets. They all operate at the second layer of the OSI model, the data link layer. They are not concerned with the routing of packets from the source (sender) to the destination. That is where routers come in.

Switches that Route?

Although switches do not make layer 3 routing decisions, they do handle a form of routing. Because their main job is to forward packets from one port to another based on the destination address in the packet, you could consider this a form of routing. There is a very fine line that many people make the mistake of blurring between routing and switching, especially with the newer switching technology that incorporates some of the layer 3 routing decisions into the layer 2 forwarding of packets.

Routers

Because a router is a network device that directs packets through the network, communication is based solely on the network layer of the OSI model. A router understands the network layer addressing in a packet. The algorithms used, called *routing protocols*, build tables to determine the route a packet should take to reach its final destination. For a multiprotocol router, the routers will keep a separate routing table for each network layer protocol that will be routed. For instance, a router can route TCP/IP traffic at the same time it routes AppleTalk traffic.

Comparing the bridge and switch to a router is simple. A bridge or switch connects two or more networks into a single logical network, whereas a router connects two or more logical networks and routes between them using the routing tables that are built by the routing protocols. Figure 1.3 shows of data that travels from a source host, through a Cisco switch, through a Cisco router, and arrives at a destination host.

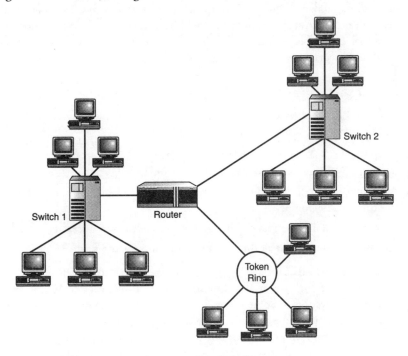

Figure 1.3   Data traveling from a source host to a destination host.

The Anatomy of the Corporate LAN

This chapter begins our discussion of the issues surrounding the network design structure. Some of the things discussed here and in later chapters include network goals, network design, media selection, and physical topology. In many cases, network engineers come into a company with an existing network to be managed.

The goal of this chapter is to familiarize you with designing your network; to help you figure out what you really want to do without worrying about the headaches that come with an existing network. Once you have your ideal network design in hand, you can apply the existing legacy system and other such constraints. When finished, you should have two designs, one for the ideal network and the other for the existing network.

The difference between your two designs is also important. It will help determine the decisions and compromises you will make. For example, if you have an existing network with network topology of FDDI, and your ideal network design consists of Ethernet within the LAN department, it would become clear that you do not want to add another FDDI topology when the time comes. Instead, you would work to eliminate FDDI and incorporate Ethernet.

Network Goals

In a corporate LAN, network goals should be a first part of any network design. Setting network goals consists of a number of things:

- Functionality—What is this network supposed to do?
- Reliability—How well will it perform this functionality?
- Availability—Where will the network be accessible from, and what percent of the time will it be up?
- Flexibility—Will it be easy to change the network when necessary?
- Cost—How much will all this cost presently and for the future?

All these are vital goals that the network engineer should set forth before designing an ideal network. Functionality relies on the importance of the network. Will it be vital to the company's revenue and employees? Reliability depends upon the type of network that will be used. In this case, there are different topologies that the network engineer can go with. Flexibility is for one purpose of future network design. Can it be upgraded to a larger and more technological network? Is it interchangeable? Finally, cost includes both initial and long-term investments as well as recurring investments. These costs can land under hardware, software, maintenance, or personnel costs.

Network Design

The goals have been determined and now you can consider the design of your network. Usually three major components come to mind.

- Core
- Distribution
- Access

The core part of the design lands under the backbone interconnect system. It usually involves high speed and high reliability and has no users attached to it. The core will be considered the mother source of the network. The core should be your high-speed routing system, and should have few demands placed on it. Any problems in this part of the network will affect the entire network tree.

The second component consists of the distribution system. The distribution tree connects multiple locations or sections of your network to your core. If you think of the core of your network as the trunk of a tree, then the branches are the distribution nodes. This is where you find aggregation of your lower speed network links into higher capacity links to the core. You might also find implementation of value added services and possibly differentiated services. Problems that occur at this part of the network affect only those access nodes serviced by the particular distribution node.

The third component consists of the access system. This is where your end users or customers connect to your network. This is where your lowest speed connections are aggregated into medium or high-speed connections into distribution nodes. Many access nodes can be serviced by one distribution node. Problems that occur at this level affect only a limited number of users or customers.

The Anatomy of the Internet

What is known as the Internet today began as a project funded by the United States government. The project was born in 1962 when the United States Air Force (USAF) asked the RAND Corporation how it could maintain command and control of its weapons and bombers after a nuclear attack. The finished document, written by Paul Baran, listed several ways that the USAF could survive a nuclear attack. His final conclusion called for a distributed network that spanned the United States. The network would be decentralized so that if any node (city) were attacked, the network would still function. The distributed network would be packet switched. *Packet switching* is the breaking down of data into datagrams or packets that are labeled to indicate the origin and the destination of the information and the forwarding of these packets from one computer to another computer until the information arrives at its final destination computer.

In 1968, the Advanced Research Project Agency (ARPA) awarded a contract to BBN for the construction of a private network based upon the paper written by Paul Baran. BBN chose to use Honeywell minicomputers as the switching mechanism for each of the nodes in the computer network.

The original network consisted of four nodes.

- The University of California at Los Angeles
- SRI at Stanford
- The University of California in Santa Barbara
- The University of Utah

All these locations were connected via 50Kbps leased lines. This computer network was called *ARPANET*.

In 1983, TCP/IP became the core protocol on the ARPANET. Up until that point, the Network Control Protocol (NCP) was used. Using TCP/IP enabled dissimilar computer systems to communicate with one another. During the same year, the Domain Name System (DNS) was developed. DNS enables English names to be used instead of the previous numerical notations.

In 1984, ARPANET was split into two separate networks. One of the new daughter networks would be used solely for military purposes. This network was called MILNET. The other new daughter network retained the name of its parent, ARPANET. This network was to be used to continue advanced research. During this same time, the CSNET, created by the National Science Foundation (NSF) in 1981, was upgraded from 56Kbps to T1 speed. This new network based on high-speed (1.5Mbps) T1 lines was called the NSFNET. In 1990, the original ARPANET was abandoned and the NSFNET took over its functionality.

In 1995, the NSF announced that it would no longer allow direct connections to the NSFNET. It contracted with four companies to provide access to the NSFNET. These companies were:

- MCI
- Sprint
- BBN
- ANS

These four companies could now sell access to NSFNET via their own private networks. They were the original Internet service providers (ISPs). After the NSFNET reverted to an educational and research only network, the commercial Internet was born.

The Internet, as it stands today, is composed of a group of privately operated networks. Some of these networks span the entire globe, whereas others span only a few square miles. Each network is built to service one basic purpose, to provide TCP/IP connectivity to end users. The end user might be a fortune 500 company or your grandmother.

In order for users of one ISP network to communicate with users of another ISP network, the two networks must be interconnected at some point. In the early days of the Internet, public interconnection points were established by neutral third parties. Companies wishing to provide Internet access would connect to these public access points in order to exchange traffic freely with other networks that were connected there.

Because of the explosion of the Internet over the past several years, these public exchange points became overloaded with the amount of traffic that was being exchanged. With the rise in traffic volumes came performance problems. The public network access points were not designed to handle the large amounts of traffic that were being exchanged by the hundreds of networks that are connected. When the public exchange points became overloaded, companies sought out new and better ways to exchange traffic between themselves. This gave rise to the concept of private network interconnects. A *private interconnect* is a direct connection between two networks for the sole purpose of exchanging traffic between those two networks. This approach allows for much better control over the performance of the traffic exchange. Private interconnects also allow for better capacity and growth planning.

The Anatomy of an ISP Network

The topology of an ISP network can vary a great deal. ISP networks are built to provide specific services efficiently. Typically, there are a number of access points of presence (POPs) that are connected back to a network hub. The number of POPs and the hub size depend on the size of the ISP and the geographic region being serviced. All the hubs on an ISP network are linked together via high bandwidth data circuits. All these hubs and POPs make up the ISP network.

VLANs, VPNs and Converged Network Services

Virtual local area networks (Virtual LANs or VLANs) are a relatively new beast in the networking world. The idea is basically to have many individual networks connected to a single layer 2 or layer 3 enabled switch. Each port on this switch can be configured to be its own virtual network. This means that broadcast traffic on a single port is only propagated to other ports on the switch that are configured for the same VLAN identifier. The implementation of VLANs allows Network Operators to control the broadcast traffic on the switch and prevent it from impacting other users or customers on their switch that might not be interested in that traffic. VLANs are also helpful as a security measure. Without VLANs, any device connected to the switch can sniff or intercept data packets on that switch. This can be a huge security problem. With VLANs enabled, devices can see traffic only meant for their VLAN identifier.

Virtual Private Networks (VPNs) are networks that connect via a shared internetworking medium with secured communications between the VPN segments. VPNs can be implemented in a variety of fashions. The more common methods of establishing VPNs are through the use of encrypted communication sessions, network address translation devices (NATs), network firewalls, or a combination of the three. VPNs are very useful for companies that wish to give their employees access to the corporate office that is connected to the Internet. Employees can then use regular ISP access accounts rather than the employer having to maintain its own dedicated network access devices. Because the employees would be accessing potentially sensitive corporate systems via a public network, a VPN service would be needed. VPNs can also enable two or more corporate satellite offices that are connected individually to the Internet to communicate.

More and more network operators are building networks that support the growing trend of service convergence. *Service convergence* refers to the combination of different functions or services onto a single platform. The most common convergence occurring today is the transmission of voice, video, and traditional IP data on the same IP based network. Convergence has the benefit of lowering network costs as well as support costs. It is far easier and cost effective to build and maintain one IP network than three separate networks, which is what has traditionally been required to support voice, video, and data services.

TCP/IP Addressing

TCP/IP is actually a suite of protocols. The one that we are concerned with is the Internet Protocol (IP). Every device connected to the Internet must have an IP address. An IP address is made up of four individual decimal numbers separated by a period. Each of the decimal numbers can range from 0 to 255. The numerical range is determined by the fact that each number is actually a binary octet. An octet is an eight-bit number. Each bit in the octet can be either a 0 or a 1. Each position in the octet is assigned a decimal value. The decimal value for each position can be determined by raising the numeral 2 to the power of the position. Positions are numbered from right to left starting with the number 0 (see Figure 1.4).

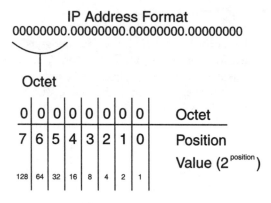

Figure 1.4 Octet calculations.

Having a bit value of one in position 7 indicates that the octet has a decimal value of 128. Having a bit value of one in positions 7 and 5 indicates that the octet has a decimal value of 160 (128 + 32 = 160). If all eight of the bit positions have a binary value of one, the decimal value of that octet is 255.

The format of an IP address is:

`xxx.xxx.xxx.xxx`

Each x above represents a numerical place holder for the decimal value of the binary octet of the IP address. A typical IP address looks like this:

`192.168.10.100`

Classless Inter-Domain Routing (CIDR)

There is a maximum number of networks and hosts that can be assigned unique addresses using the Internet's 32-bit long addresses. Traditionally, the Internet assigned "classes" of addresses: Class A, Class B and Class C were the most common. Each address had two parts:

- One part to identify a unique network

- A second part to identify a unique host in that network

Another way the old Class A, B, and C addresses were identified was by looking at the first eight bits of the address and converting it to its decimal equivalent (see Table 1.1).

Table 1.1   **IP Address Classes**

Address Class	Number of Network Bits	Number of Host Bits	Decimal Address Range of First Octet
Class A	8	24	1-126
Class B	16	16	128-191
Class C	24	8	192-223

Using the old Class A, B, and C addressing scheme, the Internet could support the following:

- 126 Class A networks that could include up to 16,777,214 hosts each

- Plus 65,000 Class B networks that could include up to 65,534 hosts each

- Plus over 2 million Class C networks that could include up to 254 hosts each

Some addresses were reserved for broadcast messages, and so on. Because Internet addresses were generally only assigned in these three sizes, there were a lot of wasted addresses. For example, if you needed 100 addresses you would be assigned the smallest address (Class C), but that still meant 154 unused addresses. The overall result was that while the Internet was running out of unassigned addresses, only 3% of the assigned addresses were actually being used. CIDR was developed to be a much more efficient method of assigning addresses.

Another problem was the size of the Internet global routing table. As the number of networks on the Internet increased, so did the number of routes. A few years back it was forecasted that the global backbone Internet routers were fast approaching their limit on the number of routes they could support.

Even using the latest router technology, the maximum theoretical routing table size is approximately 60,000 routing table entries. If nothing was done, the global routing tables would have reached capacity by mid-1994 and all Internet growth would have been halted.

Two solutions were developed and adopted by the global Internet community:

- Restructuring IP address assignments to increase efficiency
- Hierarchical routing aggregation to minimize route table entries

Impact On IP Address Assignment

Classless Inter-Domain Routing (CIDR) is a replacement for the old process of assigning Class A, B, and C addresses with a generalized network "prefix". Instead of being limited to network identifiers (or "prefixes") of 8, 16, or 24 bits, CIDR currently uses prefixes anywhere from 13 to 27 bits. Thus, blocks of addresses can be assigned to networks as small as 32 hosts or to those with over 500,000 hosts. This allows for address assignments that much more closely fit an organization's specific needs.

A CIDR address includes the standard 32-bit IP address and also information on how many bits are used for the network prefix. For example, in the CIDR address 192.168.1.48/25, the "/25" indicates the first 25 bits are used to identify the unique network, leaving the remaining bits to identify the specific host.

Table 1.2 **CIDR Block Equivalents**

CIDR Block Prefix	# Equivalent Class C	# of Host Addresses
/27	1/8th of a Class C	32 hosts
/26	1/4th of a Class C	64 hosts
/25	1/2 of a Class C	128 hosts
/24	1 Class C	256 hosts
/23	2 Class C	512 hosts
/22	4 Class C	1,024 hosts

CIDR Block Prefix	# Equivalent Class C	# of Host Addresses
/21	8 Class C	2,048 hosts
/20	16 Class C	4,096 hosts
/19	32 Class C	8,192 hosts
/18	64 Class C	16,384 hosts
/17	128 Class C	32,768 hosts
/16	256 Class C (=1 Class B)	65,536 hosts
/15	512 Class C	131,072 hosts
/14	1,024 Class C	262,144 hosts
/13	2,048 Class C	524,288 hosts

Impact on Routing Tables

ISPs must maintain a list of paths to each individual network connected to the Internet. These paths are stored in memory on network devices. Because the number of networks on the Internet is growing so dramatically, the number of entries in ISP routing tables is growing, too. Many service providers' routers are nearing the limits of their available memory.

CIDR is based on "route aggregation", the process of creating a single piece of routing information that specifies how to handle traffic for many destinations. In some ways, the result of this process is similar to that of IP subnetting. With subnetting, what appears to the outside world as a single IP network is actually broken up into a number of smaller subnets, each of which typically corresponds to a serial link or a LAN segment. With CIDR, several IP networks are combined, from the point of view of networks outside the group, into a single, larger entity.

Under CIDR, any entry in the routing table of a network device describes the path to a class of IP destinations whose addresses share a given initial bit string. Such an entry is called a "prefix route"; the shared initial bit string is a prefix of the address of every destination that the route covers. An ordinary IP network route is a prefix route; a route to the Class C network 192.168.35.0 includes all IP addresses whose first three octets are 192, 168, and 35. CIDR is different in that prefixes can be of any length; it would be valid for a route to include, for example, all IP addresses that started with 192 and 168, even though that route would cover 256 entire Class C networks.

Variable Length Subnet Mask (VLSM)

In order for CIDR to work, there must be a way to convey the appropriate host bit information along with the network address. In the old classful IP assignment system, there were fixed length subnet masks (see Table 1.3).

Table 1.3 **Fixed Length Subnet Masks**

Address Class	Subnet Mask
Class A	255.0.0.0
Class B	255.255.0.0
Class C	255.255.255.0

With CIDR, the subnet mask for each IP network can vary depending on the number of host addresses that are required. If you needed only 32 hosts, you could use 192.186.32.0/27. The subnet mask for that network would be 255.255.255.224. The numeral 224 in the last octet of the subnet mask signifies that the first three bits of that octet are binary ones. In the case of a subnet mask, the binary ones mark the bits within the IP network that should be considered the network portion of the IP address. Those bit positions left are the host portion of the IP address. A list of the possible VLSMs and their corresponding IP network CIDR notations are shown in Table 1.4.

Table 1.4 **CIDR Subnet Masks**

CIDR Notation	# Of Hosts	Subnet Mask
/8	16,777,216	255.0.0.0
/9	8,388,608	255.128.0.0
/10	4,194,304	255.192.0.0
/11	2,097,152	255.224.0.0
/12	1,048,576	255.240.0.0
/13	524,288	255.248.0.0
/14	262,144	255.252.0.0
/15	131,072	255.254.0.0
/16	65,536	255.255.0.0
/17	32,768	255.255.128.0
/18	16,384	255.255.192.0
/19	8,192	255.255.224.0
/20	4,096	255.255.240.0
/21	2,048	255.255.248.0
/22	1,024	255.255.252.0

CIDR Notation	# Of Hosts	Subnet Mask
/23	512	255.255.254.0
/24	256	255.255.255.0
/25	128	255.255.255.128
/26	64	255.255.255.192
/27	32	255.255.255.224
/28	16	255.255.255.240
/29	4	255.255.255.248
/30	2	255.255.255.252
/31	1	255.255.255.254
/32	0	255.255.255.255

Conclusion

Now that you have a firm understanding of IP networking basics, we can delve directly into the specifics of the many Cisco products available. This chapter should be used as a reference for the OSI model as well as IP subnetting and network architecture. I encourage you to make use of the material provided here as you move forward in the text. The stronger your understanding of the principles discussed in this chapter, the easier your absorption of the rest of the book will be.

Cisco Routers: An Overview

CISCO SYSTEMS IS A LARGE COMPANY THAT HAS DEVELOPED many devices related to the networking of systems and groups of systems. *Networking* is a term used to describe the connection of two or more computing devices for the purpose of sharing information between the devices or combining the functionality of the devices. Cisco coined the term *Internetworking* when they began producing intermediate devices that enabled separate networks to connect to one another and communicate. Cisco has also purchased a number of companies and has integrated technologies obtained through those purchases into its existing product lines—in fact, Cisco has bought entire groups of products from smaller companies.

Whether the products were developed in-house or purchased elsewhere, however, the one constant among many of Cisco's products is the look and feel of the user interface. Cisco goes to extreme lengths to make sure that users of Cisco products can easily add products from other Cisco product lines without having to worry about learning a new command interface or *graphical user interface* (GUI). This is especially true of the routing products. Some of the other Cisco product lines have similar command-line interfaces to the router product line, but have different commands and command structures.

Product Line

Cisco products span the spectrum of networking technology. No matter what your needs, Cisco has a product to do the job. Such products include high-end routers, WAN switches, remote access products, LAN switches, hubs, firewalls, network address translation devices, and network management software. The high-end routers and remote access routers are covered in detail in this chapter.

High-End Routers

Basically, five series of routers exist in the Cisco high-end router product line. The original high-end router offered was the 7000 series, meant for the corporate enterprise market. The 7500 series routers represented the next evolution, with routers meant for the high-bandwidth Internet service provider (ISP) market.

An intermediate product line called the 7200 series was developed to bridge the gap between the 7000 series routers and the 7500 series routers. These 7200 series routers are intended for applications in which the processing power of the 7500 series routers is needed but the high port density is not. These routers are often used when hardware cost is an important factor in the decision-making process.

In addition, 7100 series routers are meant for networks that require high security surrounding the data being carried on the network. Most recently, Cisco released the 12000 series routers as the flagship of the company's high-end router product line. These routers are meant for the high-speed backbones that large ISPs operate.

7000 Series Routers

Two routers are available in the 7000 series of high-end routers:

- Cisco 7000
- Cisco 7010

Who Needs Hot-Swapping?

In a global business market it is very important for companies to be operational 24 hours a day 7 days per week 365 days per year. In order to attain this level of operational uptime, networking devices must be able to be serviced while they are online. Having power supplies and modular components that can be removed and inserted while the router is running is key to reaching the goal of 100% uptime. The act of removing and inserting a component while a device is online is called *hot-swapping*. Not all Cisco products have hot-swapable components.

The Cisco 7000 has seven slots that accommodate a combination of interface line cards and routing/switching cards. Interface line cards enable the router to connect to various networking technologies, such as Ethernet, Token Ring, and Asynchronous Transfer Mode (ATM). Each of the cards interfaces directly with the Cisco Extended Bus (CxBus), often referred to as the backplane of the router. Of the seven available slots, only five (Slots 0 to 4) can be used by interface line cards. Slot 5 is reserved for either a switch processor (SP) or the newer and faster silicon switch processor (SSP). Slot 6 is reserved for the route processor (RP).

A newer route processor, the RSP7000, offers higher performance and more features than the original RP/SP combination. To use the RSP7000, you must install an additional card, the RSP7000CI (the CI stands for *chassis interface*), into Slot 6; the RSP7000 would be installed into Slot 5. The Cisco 7000 has two power supply bays for redundancy. These power supplies can be either AC or DC, but not a combination of the two.

The Cisco 7010 is a five-slot version of the 7000. Of the five slots, only three can be used by interface line cards (Slots 0 to 2). Slot 3 is reserved for the SP, and Slot 4 is reserved for the RP. The 7010 also can use the RSP7000 and RSP7000CI combination available for the 7000. The Cisco 7010 has only one power supply bay, which can accommodate either an AC or DC power supply. The power supply on the Cisco 7010 is not hot-swappable, however, so you must remove the case of the chassis to replace a faulty power supply.

The Cisco 7000 and 7010 model routers are no longer available for purchase from Cisco. They were removed from the active product line in 1997. Many networks still use them and the line cards are still available. Cisco recommends that they be replaced with 7500 series equivalents.

AC or DC Power?

The decision to use AC power or DC power for your routers will depend greatly on the environment in which the routers will be deployed. DC power is most often found in environments similar to a phone company central office (CO) environment. If your routers will be installed in a type of CO, you should use DC power supplies simply because a power rectifier must be installed to change DC to AC when supplying AC power in this type of environment. Whenever electrical power is changed from one form to the other, a little power is lost. This loss of power is the main reason why a single power type is used in most sites.

If you will be installing your routers in an environment in which other AC machines will be housed, it is better to use AC power supplies simply for consistency; all devices should use the same power type. Of course, some people are afraid of DC power because there is no receptacle and because the power feed is wired directly to the power supply. This means that you cannot simply unplug the router and move it. If you do decide to use DC power, it is a good idea to install a DC breaker switch between your router and the power source. This allows for quick and easy power interruption for maintenance.

The interface line cards available for the 7000 series routers enable the router to route or bridge packets on a variety of protocols. Some of the interfaces available include ATM, Ethernet, Fast Ethernet, Token Ring, Fiber Distributed Data Interface (FDDI), serial, and High Speed Serial Interface (HSSI).

Another interface card available for 7000 series routers that use the RSP7000 is the Versatile Interface Processor (VIP). The VIP has two bays for port adapters (PA). A number of PAs are available, each with a different interface type, such as Ethernet, FDDI, or HSSI. In fact, almost every one of the normal interface line cards has a PA equivalent. The VIP card gives the router more processing power because a separate CPU and memory on the VIP card can offload the routing functions from the RSP to the VIP card. Many of the interface cards available for the 7000 series routers can be used in 7500 series routers as well.

7500 Series Routers

Four routers are available in the 7500 series of Cisco high-end routers:

- Cisco 7505
- Cisco 7507
- Cisco 7513
- Cisco 7576

These Cisco routers use a Route Switching Processor (RSP) rather than the RP/SP combination used in the 7000 series. The RSP has a faster CPU and can accommodate more memory than the RP.

Three versions of the RSP exist. The original, now called the RSP1, can be used only in the Cisco 7505. The currently available RSPs are the RSP2 and RSP4. Each iteration of the RSP has a faster CPU and more memory capacity. RSP4 has a MIPS reduced instruction set (RISC) CPU with an internal clock speed of 200MHz and an external clock speed of 100MHz. In addition, it can accommodate up to 256MB of DRAM.

The Cisco 7505 is the 7500 series version of the Cisco 7010. This router has five slots, four of which can be used by interface line cards (Slots 0 to 3). Slot 5 is reserved for the RSP.

7010 Versus 7505

Because the Cisco 7505 router uses an RSP rather than the RP/SP combination, the additional free slot can be used for an interface line card.

The Cisco 7507 is an intermediate router that offers more slots for interface line cards. This router has a higher port capacity than the Cisco 7505, but is smaller than the Cisco 7513. The Cisco 7507 has seven slots, of which five are usable for interface line cards; the remaining two slots (Slots 2 and 3) are used for the primary and backup RSPs. The Cisco 7507 also has a second slot for a redundant RSP.

The Cisco 7507 can accommodate two power supplies, for redundancy. As with the 7000 series routers, the power supplies can be either AC or DC, but not both.

The Cisco 7507 has two CyBuses (the second generation of the Cisco Extended Bus that was introduced in the 7000 series routers) on the backplane, whereas the Cisco 7505 has only one. The CyBus has an aggregate bandwidth capacity of 1.2 billion bps. Of course, billions of bits per second are commonly referred to as gigabits per second (Gbps). This means that at a single point in time, no more that 1.2Gbps of data can be on the CyBus. Interface line card Slots 0 to 5 are on CyBus0, and interface line card Slots 8 to 12 are on CyBus1. To route packets between interface line cards on different CyBuses, the packet must travel across the RSP. Thus, the RSP is used to bridge the two CyBuses.

The Cisco 7513 is the powerhouse of the Cisco 7500 series routers. This router has 13 slots, 11 of which are usable for interface line cards. Slots 6 and 7 are reserved for the primary and redundant RSPs. As with the Cisco 7507, the Cisco 7513 has two CyBuses on the backplane. The Cisco 7513 also has two power supply bays that can accommodate AC or DC power supplies.

The Cisco 7576 is the newest model in the 7500 series product line. This basically involves two routers in one box, referred to as Router A and Router B. The physical size of the 7576 is the same as the 7513, but the Cisco 7576 has two distinct sets of interface line card slots, for a total of 13. Router A has seven card slots, and Router B has six card slots. One slot in each router is reserved for the RSP—that leaves six slots in Router A and five slots in Router B that can be used for interface line cards.

You might think that the Cisco 7576 offers no benefits beyond the Cisco 7513 router, but its key feature is that it has four CyBuses instead of the two in the Cisco 7513. In Router A, there are four interface line card slots on CyBus0 and two interface line card slots on CyBus1. In Router B, there are three interface line card slots on CyBus2 and two interface line cards on CyBus 3. Because fewer interface line card slots per CyBus are present on the Cisco 7576, you can install a greater density of high-speed interface ports without running the risk of oversubscribing the 1.2Gbps capacity of the CyBus.

Buses Impact Design

It is important to realize the impact that two separate buses in your router can have. Many engineers plan the layout of the cards in their routers to optimize every bit of CPU power available. Placing an inbound interface PA on the same VIP card as the outbound interface PA, keeps packets from even touching the backplane. Requiring all packets that cross from one CyBus to the other CyBus to be processed by the RSP diminishes potential optimization. It is best to plan your VIP card and port adapter layout within your router with this fact in mind. Of course, this is not an issue with the non-VIP interface line cards because they do not support the distributed switching features of the recent IOS versions.

For example, a Cisco 7513 has six interface line card slots on CyBus0. If you divide the aggregate bandwidth available on the CyBus (1.2Gbps) evenly among the six card slots, you are left with 200 million bits per second (Mbps) of capacity per card slot. Now if you want to put two OC3 port adapters on a VIP card and install that card configuration into all six card slots on CyBus0, you would not be able to run all the OC3 ports at the full-line rate. *Line rate* is a term used to describe the maximum transmission capacity of a particular interface type. Because each OC3 port has a line rate of 155Mbps, the total bandwidth per slot needed would be 310Mbps. Clearly, not enough bandwidth exists on CyBus0 of the Cisco 7513 to accommodate this configuration.

Now, take the same scenario on the Cisco 7576 CyBus0. Four interface line card slots are present on the Cisco 7576 CyBus0. Splitting the available bandwidth evenly among all the line card slots leaves 300Mbps of capacity per slot. Filling all the card slots of a Cisco 7576 with high-speed interfaces is a much more realistic idea if high performance is an issue for you.

7200 Series Routers

The Cisco 7200 is actually a member of the 7000 series product family. This series was not developed until after the 7500 series routers were released. Three models make up the 7200 series:

- Cisco 7202
- Cisco 7204
- Cisco 7206

The only difference among the three routers is the number of available interface slots. The 7202 has two usable interface slots, the 7204 has four usable interface slots, and the 7206 has six usable interface slots. All the 7200 series routers can accommodate two AC or DC power supplies.

The 7200 series routers use the same port adapters that are used on the VIP cards for the 7000 and 7500 series routers. However, the 7200 series routers do not require VIP cards. Instead, the port adapters install directly into the 7200 chassis. These routers were developed primarily for those customers who wanted the faster processing of the 7500 series routers, but did not necessarily need or want the larger chassis or the higher costs.

7100 Series Routers

The Cisco 7100 series routers were created to fill the need for a secure high-speed networking product. Two models are included in this product line:

- Cisco 7120
- Cisco7140

The only difference between the two routers in this series is the number of interfaces available. The Cisco 7120 offers singular port interfaces, whereas the 7140 offers dual port interfaces. The 7100 series routers act as a secure bridge between the local network segment and the wide area network segment. The major features of the 7100 series routers include IPSec encryption, various tunneling protocols, built–in firewall functionality, network address translation, and the capability to add hardware-based performance enhancements to software-based data encryption. The wide area network interfaces can range in type from DS1 to OC3 ATM.

12000 Series Routers

Two routers are available in the 12000 series:

- Cisco 12008
- Cisco 12012

Cisco intended this series of routers to be used in the backbones of large data networks. The smallest interface available for the 12000 series router is DS3; the largest interface is OC48 (2.4Gbps). Each of these routers is fully distributed, which means that all the packet processing is done on the line cards themselves. The only functions that the gigabit route processor (GRP) handles are dynamic routing protocol updates and administrative duties, such as responding to ping and SNMP requests directed at the router. The GRP is responsible for maintaining the main routing table as well. Every time a change is made to the main routing table, it is pushed out to the interface line cards. Each interface line card keeps a copy of the forwarding table locally. If the GRP were to fail, the interface cards would continue to forward packets until the route entries in the local copy of the main routing table were aged out.

Three cards are required for normal operation in the 12000 series routers:

- The GRP.
- The clock and scheduler card (CSC). A second CSC can be installed for redundancy.
- The switch fabric card (SFC).

Adding more SFCs to the chassis increases the amount of switch fabric available on the router.

GSR Architecture

The Cisco 12000 series routers use a dual buffered cross-bar switch fabric. This means that packets are buffered both at the input interface and at the output interface. The term *cross-bar switch* means that every port can talk to every other port directly via dedicated channels; there is no shared bandwidth on the backplane.

Another type of switch fabric is *bus*. With a bus fabric, all ports talk to each other via a shared pipe on the backplane.

Having buffering on both the input ports and the output ports enables the router to avoid blocking. *Blocking* occurs when multiple input ports try to send data to the same output port, but the output port cannot keep up with the amount of traffic being sent to it. This happens a lot on FDDI switches when multiple 100Mbps interfaces try to send data to one 100Mbps interface; the buffers fill up, and data is lost. The GSR software combats this by checking the output port's buffers before sending the data to it. If the output port buffer is full, the data is queued on the input port until room is available on the output port.

Each of the three routers can be equipped with dual load-sharing power supplies. You have a choice of either AC or DC power supplies.

Several line cards are available for the 12000 series routers, including OC3 ATM, OC3 Packet-over-SONET (PoS), OC12 ATM, channelized OC12, OC12 PoS, and Gigabit Ethernet cards. Cisco will also soon be releasing OC48 ATM cards.

Table 2.1 shows a comparison of the different high-end routers and the interface types that can be used in each.

Table 2.1 **Cisco High-End Routers and Their Interface Cards**

	7000	7100	7200	7500	12000
56K/64K	X		X	X	
ISDN BRI	X		X	X	
ISDN PRI	X		X	X	
Channelized DS1	X		X	X	
DS1 Serial	X	X	X	X	
E1 Serial	X	X	X	X	
Ethernet	X	X	X	X	
Channelized DS3	X		X	X	
DS3 Serial	X	X	X	X	X
E3 Serial	X	X	X	X	
Fast Ethernet	X	X	X	X	X
OC3 Packet over SONET		X	X	X	X
OC3 ATM		X	X	X	X
OC12 Packet over SONET				X	X
OC12 DPT				X	X
OC12 ATM					X
Channelized OC12					X
OC48 Packet over SONET					X
OC48 DPT					X
OC48 ATM					X
Gigabit Ethernet				X	X

The Cisco 12008 is an eight-slot version. It supports an IP switching capacity between 10Gbps and 40Gbps, depending on how many SFC cards are installed. Of the eight slots, seven are usable for interface line cards.

The Cisco 12012 is a 12-slot version. It supports an IP switching capacity of between 15Gbps and 60Gbps, depending on how many SFC cards are installed. Of the 12 slots available, 11 are usable for interface line cards. The Cisco 12008 can be equipped with up to four AC power supplies or two double-wide DC power supplies.

Remote Access Routers

Of the many products in the Cisco Access family, the two most often used are the 4000 series and the AS5000 series routers. The 4000 series of routers is used mainly to aggregate multiple LAN segments into a few WAN links. The AS5000 series of routers is used mainly for remote dial-in capabilities, either via analog modems or ISDN.

AS5000 Series Routers

Four routers are available in this family of Cisco products:

- AS5100
- AS5200
- AS5300
- AS5800

These four products vary in size and port density. Their main function is to provide analog and ISDN dial-in ports. The larger boxes (5300 and 5800) support quality of service (QoS) features, virtual private networking (VPN), and voice-over IP. The AS5800 is modeled after the 7200 series routers and supports the RIP, OSPF, and BGP routing protocols. The AS5100 and AS5200 are no longer available for purchase from Cisco.

As the model numbers get higher, the target market increases. The AS5200 is marketed toward small to medium-size corporate customers. The AS5800 is marketed toward the telephone carriers and large-scale ISPs.

Cisco access servers are popular because they support multiple services on one box. They also support *multilink PPP*, which is the capability to bond two dial-in calls between the same two devices into one pipe. This is often done with dual channel ISDN BRIs. Each B channel of the BRI is connected as a separate call, but the two channels are treated as one pipe between the devices.

Another nice feature of Cisco access servers is their capability to support multilink PPP across devices. This means that even if two calls from the same remote user are not answered by the same access server, the two calls can still be bonded.

4000 Series Routers

Two routers are left in this family that Cisco still sells:

- Cisco 4500M
- Cisco 4700M

The main difference between these two routers is the speed of the CPU and the amount of memory that can be installed. The 4500 has a 100MHz RISC processor that can handle up to 32MB of RAM. The 4700 has a 133MHz RISC processor that can handle up to 64MB of RAM.

Both routers can support three interface modules, each of which has a different network connection. The current available modules are Ethernet, Token Ring, FDDI, HSSI, ISDN BRI, ISDN PRI, DS3 ATM, OC3 ATM, and E3 ATM.

Both routers support redundant AC or DC power supplies.

Internetworking Operating System (IOS)

All the routers mentioned in this book run a version of the Cisco Internetworking Operating System (IOS). The current mainstream version of the IOS is Release 11. Release 12, which was just recently made available, has not yet made its way into widespread use. However, as time goes on and Network Operators become more comfortable with the stability of Release 12, it will undoubtedly become the IOS of choice for high-end users.

Each release of the Cisco IOS is classified by its intended audience. Three main classifications exist:

- The first classification is General Deployment. This code is intended for use by all Cisco customers. It is believed to be very stable and free of any significant bugs.

- The next classification is Early Deployment. This code offers new hardware or feature support, but it has not been deployed long enough to be sure that it is bug-free. Most people use IOS versions in this class to keep up with new technology.

- The third classification is Maintenance Release. This code is intended to replace the original General Release version in the same strain. It will contain many bug fixes and be tested rigorously. For instance, a General Deployment version would be 11.0, and a Maintenance Release would be 11.1 or 11.2.

Several sub-versions of the 11.0 IOS strain exist. Currently, three active sub-versions are used on the different Cisco products: 11.1, 11.2, and 11.3. Each sub-version offers different feature sets; it would take a complete book to discuss these and to cover which products use which version. Cisco has combined the features and hardware support of all three sub-versions into Release 12.0 of the IOS.

IOS Resource on the WWW

A detailed description of all the IOS features available in each version is available at Cisco's Web site. Point your Web browser to http://www.cisco.com/univercd/cc/td/doc/product/software/index.htm.

Within each sub-version are several versions of code. Each version is designated by a number. For instance, the first patch release of the 11.1 strain is numbered 11.1.1 or 11.1(1).

The Cisco IOS also includes all the specific hardware drivers that might be needed for certain interface line cards. It is very important that you review the documentation included with your hardware purchase to be sure that the IOS you plan to run on your router is sufficient to support the hardware you plan to install in your router. After a router has been installed for a while and you want to deploy a new Cisco line card, you will probably have to upgrade your IOS to the newest version if you are not running it already.

The Cisco IOS is also offered with different feature support. For example, you can download several versions of the 11.1 software. One version might include APPN support, whereas another might have support for the VIP card; still another might support neither of these Cisco offerings. Obtaining the correct IOS can save on memory requirements and loading time for your routers. After all, if your routers don't require VIP support, why bother making the router load all the instructions into memory?

Conclusion

In addition to the many router families, Cisco offers other networking equipment. For instance, Cisco makes LAN switches, such as the Catalyst 5000 family or the Lightstream 1010 family, and WAN switches, such as the BPX family. A network that offers a wide range of products or services will most likely need more than just routers.

The following list details a few of the product lines that Cisco offers:

- High-end routers—12000, 7500, 7200, 7100, and 7000 series
- WAN switches—IGX, MGX, TGX, and BPX series
- LAN switches—1200, 1900, 2900, 3000, 5000, 5500, 8500, and Workgroup series
- Hubs —1500 series as well as the FastHub 100, 200, and 300 series
- Access routers—AS5800, AS5300, AS5200, 6000, 4000, 3800, 3600, 2600, 2500, various ATM and xDSL models, and the 1000 series
- Intranet/Internet appliances—Distributed Director, Web Cache, and Local Director
- Security—CiscoSecure, PIX, various firewall products, Cisco Security Consulting Services, NetRanger, and NetSonar
- Network management software—CiscoWorks, CiscoView, Netsys, StrataView, Traffic Director, VLAN Director, and Cisco Access Manager

The list of Cisco products might seem endless, but establishing a good relationship with your Cisco account representative can make wading through all the choices easier. Cisco makes a great deal of information available to its customers, and it is certainly in your best interest to use whatever resources you can get your hands on. You could fill your day trying to keep up with Cisco's new products, but it is easier and faster to use the staff at Cisco to get the information you need. Experts in each department can give you any piece of information you might want—the trick is knowing who to ask.

II

Router Configuration

3

Initial Router Setup

Cisco routers come with no default configuration. Before you can use a Cisco router on a network, you must program it with the configuration you need to accomplish your predefined tasks. This chapter discusses the various programming options available to you. In addition, various different command-line programming modes are discussed.

Initial Start-up

When a Cisco router is first powered on and the bootstrap ROM has loaded the basic Internetworking Operating System (IOS) image into RAM, the non-volatile RAM (NVRAM) is checked for a pre-existing configuration. If no configuration file is found, the bootstrap program executes the setup script from the base IOS that has been loaded. This setup script asks a series of questions that are used to generate an initial router configuration. Each question asked has a default answer associated with it. The default choice is displayed in brackets at the end of the prompt.

Running the Setup Program

The setup script can be run from the privileged command mode at any time. The privileged EXEC mode (most often referred to as *Enable Mode*) is discussed later in this chapter. Running the setup script on an already configured router will wipeout any configuration parameters that are currently in place.

Listing 3.1 shows an example of some of the questions asked during an initial router power on. The setup program determines which questions to ask based upon responses that you give to the first few questions. For instance, if you answer "yes" to the question "Configure IGRP Routing?", the setup program will ask questions during the interface configuration dialogs that will allow the program to generate a basic IGRP configuration for those interfaces.

Listing 3.1 **Setup Script Example**

```
—· System Configuration Dialog —·
At any point you may enter a question mark '?' for help.
Refer to the 'Getting Started' Guide for additional help.
Default settings are in square brackets '[]'.
Would you like to enter the initial configuration dialog? [yes]:
Configuring global parameters:
 Enter host name [Router]: test-r1
 Enter enable password: cisco
 Enter virtual terminal password: termpwd
 Configure SNMP Network Management? [yes]: no
 Configure IP? [yes]:
 Configure IGRP routing? [yes]: no
Configure DECnet? [no]:
 Configure XNS? [no]:
 Configure Novell? [no]:
 Configure AppleTalk? [no]:
 Configure Vines? [no]:
 Configure bridging? [no]:
 Configure MOP? [no]:
Configuring interface parameters:
Configuring interface Ethernet0:
 Is this interface in use? [yes]:
  Configure IP on this interface? [yes]:
   IP address for this interface: 192.168.17.2
   Number of bits in subnet field [8]:
   Class B network is 192.168.0.0, 8 subnet bits; mask is 255.255.255.0
Configuring interface Serial0:
 Is this interface in use? [yes]: n
Configuring interface Ethernet1:
 Is this interface in use? [yes]:
 Configure IP on this interface? [yes]:
  IP address for this interface: 192.168.80.2
  Number of bits in subnet field [8]:
  Class B network is 192.168.0.0, 8 subnet bits; mask is 255.255.255.0
Configuring interface Serial0:
 Is this interface in use? [yes]: n
```

After answering all questions, the setup program generates the configuration file that matches the answers you provided. This new configuration is displayed on your terminal screen. You are then prompted as to whether this configuration should be used to program the router. The responses available will depend on which IOS version you are using. Listing 3.2 shows the sample configuration that is generated by the setup program answers shown in listing 3.1.

Listing 3.2 **Sample Configuration Generated from Setup Program**

```
hostname test-r1
enable  password cisco
line vty 0 4
 password termpwd
!
ip routing
!
interface Ethernet0
 ip address 192.168.17.2 255.255.255.0
!
interface Serial0
 shutdown
 no ip address
!
interface Ethernet1
 ip address 192.168.80.2 255.255.255.0
!
interface Serial1
 shutdown
 no ip address
!
end
```

Once the configuration has been loaded, the router displays the user EXEC mode prompt test-r1>.

You'll notice that the setup program does not prompt whether you would like to configure Open Shortest Path First (OSPF) or Border Gateway Protocol (BGP) or many other features that are available in the IOS. These other features must be configured manually either through the privileged EXEC mode command-line interface, or from a pre-built configuration file on a Trivial File Transfer Protocol (TFTP) server or flash card.

Subnet Bits Explanation

When prompted for the number of bits in the subnet field during Internet Protocol (IP) configuration of an interface, the IOS determines the default option based upon the class of the IP address that you enter in the preceding question. The correct response is not very intuitive. The actual response should be the number of bits to use to distinguish the subnet portion of the classful network you have input. If the interface is being configured with an IP address from a Class C network subnetted to a /30, the number of bits in the subnet field is 2. If the interface is being configured with an IP address from a Class B network that you are subnetting to a /24, the number of bits in the subnet field is 8. The newer Cisco IOS versions allow you to input the standard subnet mask that you would like to use. This negates the confusion caused by the original configuration format.

The setup program is an excellent tool for users that are new to the Cisco command-line interface (CLI). Most network operators that are comfortable with the Cisco CLI tend to skip the setup process when they are configuring routers initially.

Configuring from a TFTP Server

Another option available is to have a pre-existing configuration file built on a TFTP server. In order to copy the configuration file from the TFTP server to the flash RAM on the router, some basic programming must be done. It is not possible to access a file on a TFTP server if network connectivity is not yet enabled on the router. Therefore, one interface on the router connected to a network containing the TFTP server must be programmed and operating properly. (Chapter 4, "Local Area Networking," and Chapter 5, "Wide Area Networking," discuss the various interface configurations.)

Once this task has been accomplished, the following command can be used to copy the configuration file from the TFTP server to internal flash memory on the router:

```
copy tftp flash [file_id]
```

file_id is required on 7000 and 7500 series routers because those series routers offer the use of Personal Computer Memory Card Interface Adapter (PCMCIA) flash cards. The configuration file must be given a name in this case. There are two PCMCIA flash card slots on the RP, RSP7000, and RSP series route processor cards. The PCMCIA cards can be used to store IOS and router configuration files as well as router crash information for fault debugging. Recall from Chapter 2, "Cisco Routers: An Overview," that the route processor cards handle all the administrative functions of the router. These functions include responding to SNMP queries, receiving and processing routing updates, and in cases where VIP cards are not used, forwarding packets. The file_id is a combination of the PCMCIA flash card slot number and the actual file name given to the configuration file separated by a colon. For example, the following command would copy the configuration file from a TFTP server to a file named config-router1 on the flash card in slot0:

```
copy tftp flash slot0:config-router1
```

After this command is entered in the IOS command-line enable mode (which is discussed later in this chapter), a series of prompts allows you to define the IP address of the TFTP server as well as the file name on the TFTP server.

After the configuration file has been copied to the flash card, it must be moved into memory. The following command copies the configuration stored on the flash card into RAM:

```
copy slot0:config-router1 running-config
```

Now that the configuration file has been loaded into RAM, it must be stored into NVRAM so that it will not be lost should the router ever need to be reloaded. The following command copies the configuration from RAM to NVRAM:

```
copy running-config startup-config
```

Another option using a TFTP server is to copy the configuration file from the TFTP server directly to RAM or NVRAM. The following example copies a configuration file from a TFTP server into NVRAM. This procedure would be used to load a completely new configuration for your router that will be made active after the next reload of the router.

```
copy tftp startup-config
```

This next example copies a configuration file from a TFTP server to RAM. This procedure would be used to enable or modify options in the configuration currently running in the router. For example, this procedure might be used to add lines to an existing access-list or to enable Simple Network Management Protocol (SNMP) on a router that does not currently have it active.

```
copy tftp running-config
```

TFTP Configuration Pitfalls

Be aware that execution of this command probably does not do exactly what you think. What actually happens is the configuration file that is read from the TFTP server is merged with the current running configuration. Anytime a configuration is copied from an external source, be it a TFTP server, the local PCMCIA flash card, or RCP server to the running configuration, the file is combined with the current configuration in the router's flash memory. For this reason, if your intent is to replace a portion of the existing running configuration, you are better off storing the new full configuration with your modifications in the NVRAM (startup-config) and then reloading the router.

Configuring Using Cisco ConfigMaker

Cisco bundles the ConfigMaker software application with the 800, 1000, 1600, 1700, 2600, 3600, and 4000 series routers. It can be used to generate configurations for routers that connect LANs to WANs or the Internet using a graphical user interface by dragging and dropping devices onto a network diagram and entering pertinent information when prompted. ConfigMaker is capable of generating relatively complex IOS configurations for each router defined in a network diagram and requires some form of network connection to the device in order to configure it.

If you are setting up a multi-router network from scratch, ConfigMaker might be worth investigating, to save you time and reduce errors when generating an initial working configuration or developing part of the configuration which you are not as familiar with. ConfigMaker is geared toward organizations with more common network connections, such as, Ethernet, ISDN, and Frame Relay, and includes the more recent voice and virtual private networking (VPN) configuration options.

Manual Configuration

Manual configuration of a Cisco router encompasses building the router configuration piece by piece. This means that all options that you want enabled need to be programmed without the use of an interactive setup program.

This section will outline the Cisco IOS command modes that are mentioned in this book. A complete list of the command modes available in the Cisco IOS is as follows:

- User EXEC mode
- User Privileged EXEC mode (enable mode)
- Global Configuration mode
- Interface Configuration mode
- Subinterface Configuration mode
- Controller Configuration mode
- Hub Configuration mode
- Map-list Configuration mode
- Map-class Configuration mode
- Line Configuration mode
- Router Configuration mode
- IPX-router Configuration mode
- Route-map Configuration mode
- Key Chain Configuration mode
- Key Chain Key Configuration mode
- ROM Monitor mode
- APPN Command mode
- LANE Database Configuration mode
- IBM Channel Attach Command mode

Access to the interactive command mode on a Cisco router can be achieved in a number of different ways. The most common method used to connect to a Cisco router that has not been configured is through the console port. The *console port* is a serial connection on the router chassis or the processor board if the router is a model in one of the modular router families. The console port interface is usually an RJ-45 type connector but can also be a male DB-25 serial connector depending on the model of the router. Any VT100 terminal or PC with a serial port and communications software can be used to connect to the console port.

Access to a Cisco router can also be achieved via telnet from a remote host once the router is placed into a network and the appropriate configuration for the network interfaces and VTY lines is made on the router.

The auxiliary port (labeled AUX on the router itself) can also be used to configure most commands on a router. Furthermore, it can be configured as an asynchronous serial line and support SLIP and PPP. Once the AUX port has been configured as an asynchronous serial port, you can attach a modem and use it to access your router from a remote location over a dedicated phone line.

The basic prompt that is given when first connecting to a Cisco router is the user EXEC prompt. This prompt consists of the router name followed by a greater than symbol (>). If the router name has not been configured, the prompt is simply router>. In the basic user EXEC mode, a subset of the Cisco IOS commands area available. In order to gain access to the full set of IOS commands, you must enter the user privileged EXEC mode. The following command is used to change from the user EXEC mode to the privileged EXEC mode:

```
enable
```

If there is an enable password or a secret password configured on the router, the user is prompted for the password before the privileged EXEC mode prompt is returned. The commands available in the basic user EXEC mode do not offer the capability to alter the system parameters. All system-affecting commands are accessed through the privileged EXEC mode. For this reason it is a good idea to password protect access to the privileged EXEC mode.

The router prompt changes once you have entered into the privileged EXEC mode. It becomes the router hostname followed by the pound symbol (#). If no hostname is configured, the prompt is simply router#. To leave the privileged EXEC mode and return to the basic user EXEC mode, use either of the following commands:

```
disable
exit
```

Remote Access Configuration Pitfalls

A common mistake is to enable remote access on the router for the TTY and VTY lines, require that a password be given, and then not set a password. I have many times installed a router in a network and then tried to access it via telnet and been denied access because a password is required but not set.

The Power of the *exit* Command

The exit command not only takes you from the privileged EXEC mode to the user EXEC mode, it also exits you from the user EXEC mode. If you are connected to a router by a telnet session the exit command will end that telnet session and disconnect you from the router.

Global Configuration Mode

Access to the other configuration modes is possible from the privileged EXEC mode. This section will discuss the global configuration, interface configuration, line configuration, and router configuration modes.

Global configuration commands set parameters that affect the operation of the router as a whole. Use the following privileged EXEC command to enter global configuration mode:

```
configure
```

After entering this command, you will receive the following prompt:

```
Configuring from terminal, memory, or network [terminal]?
```

The three configuration options come from the directly attached terminal or session, NVRAM, or a network server. The default option [terminal] is displayed at the end of the command prompt. Any of the three global configuration options can be given along with the configure command to bypass the prompt. For example, to configure the router from NVRAM, the following command could be used:

```
configure memory
```

Once the system is in global configuration mode, the command prompt on the router changes to the hostname with the word config in parentheses followed by the pound symbol (#). If the hostname has not been configured, the prompt would simply be router(config)#. Using the configuration that was entered in the startup script from listing 3.1, the prompt is, test-r1(config)#. After the router has been placed into global configuration mode, all other configuration modes are accessible.

The rest of the configuration mode can be accessed from global configuration mode. To leave global configuration mode and return to the privileged EXEC mode, use one of the following commands:

```
exit
end
Ctrl-Z
```

Interface Configuration Mode

Many of the Cisco IOS features are configured on a per interface basis. Interface configuration commands are entered after the router has been placed in interface configuration mode. The following command is used to change from global configuration mode to interface configuration mode:

```
interface interface-type interface-number
```

Keep Track of Where You Are

It is a common mistake for users to attempt to enter sub-level configuration commands, such as interface configuration commands, directly after entering enable mode. Be sure that you are in the correct configuration mode before entering commands to the IOS.

interface-type can be any of the interfaces currently installed in the router. The *interface-number* is the corresponding port on the interface card to which you wish to apply the interface configuration commands. For example, if you wanted to assign IP address 192.168.300.10 with a 24bit subnet mask to interface Ethernet 4/0, the following series of commands would be used:

```
router> enable
password:
router# configure terminal
router(config)# interface ethernet 4/0
router(config-if)# ip address 192.168.300.10 255.255.255.0
router(config-if)#
```

The router prompt changes once the command mode is changed from global to interface. The router prompt becomes the hostname followed by (config-if) followed by the pound symbol (#). The router prompt will now read:

```
test-r1(config-if)#
```

What's In a Name?

The interface notation used here is from a modular router in the Cisco product family. The notation 4/0 means Slot 4, interface 0. To someone actually looking at the router, it is the first port on the interface card in Slot 4. Interface cards that have multiple ports on them are numbered sequentially starting with zero. Also remember from Chapter 2 that the slots on the modular routers are numbered from 0 as well. So Slot 4 is actually the fifth slot in the chassis.

IOS Can Read Your Mind

The commands used in the preceding example to configure the IP address for the Ethernet interface could have been entered in abbreviated notation as well. The Cisco IOS allows commands to be entered with only the first few letters of the actual command name. For instance, the IP address command could have been entered as ip add rather than ip address. The number of letters required before the command is recognized depends on the various other commands that are available at that command level. For instance, the interface configuration command ip a could mean *ip address*, *ip accounting* or *ip access-group*. The interface configuration command ip ac could be either *ip accounting* or *ip access-group*. Once you have reached a point in the spelling of the command that allows only one possible interpretation by the IOS, the IOS will accept the abbreviated command. You can determine the possible command variations available at anytime by either entering a question mark or pressing the Tab key when typing commands in the CLI.

Road Signs Tell You Where You Are

If you are beginning to see a recurring theme with the router prompts, you are correct. Every Cisco IOS command mode has a different prompt. This helps you keep track of where you are within the IOS command structure.

To leave interface configuration mode and return to global configuration mode, use the exit command. To leave interface configuration mode and return to the enable mode, use either the end command or type Ctrl-Z.

Line Configuration Mode

Line configuration mode is used to set parameters on the TTY and VTY ports of a Cisco router, as well as the console and auxiliary ports. To enter line configuration mode from global configuration mode, enter the following command:

```
line {aux ¦ con ¦ tty ¦ vty } line-number ending-line-number
```

The `line-number` is the port number to which you want the following commands applied. You can apply the line configuration commands to a series of line numbers by specifying an ending line number. For example, to have vty port 0 through 12 auto-disconnect after 15 minutes of idle time, execute the following series of commands:

```
test-r1> enable
password:
test-r1# configure terminal
test-r1(config)# line vty 0 12
test-r1(config-line)# exec-timeout 15 0
test-r1(config-line)# exit
test-r1(config)# exit
test-r1#
```

The router prompt changes once you have entered line configuration mode. The prompt becomes the hostname followed by (config-line) followed by the pound symbol (#). The router prompt is now:

```
test-r1(config-line)#
```

To exit line configuration mode and return to global configuration mode, use the exit command. To leave line configuration mode and return to the privileged EXEC mode, use the end command or type Ctrl-Z.

Router Configuration Mode

Router configuration mode is used to configure IP routing protocols. To enter router configuration mode from global configuration mode, use the following command:

```
router keyword
```

The keyword used can be any of the options listed in Table 3.1.

Table 3.1 **Router Configuration Mode Keywords**

Keyword	Description
bgp	Border Gateway Protocol
egp	Exterior Gateway Protocol
igrp	Interior Gateway Protocol

Keyword	Description
isis	ISO IS-IS
iso-igrp	IGRP for OSI networks
ospf	Open Shortest Path First
rip	Routing Information Protocol
static	Static CLNS Routing

The command prompt in the IOS changes once you have entered router configuration mode. The command prompt becomes the hostname followed by (config-router) followed by the pound symbol (#).

For example, to configure redistribution of static routes into OSPF process 1000, use the following series \of commands:

```
test-r1> enable
password:
test-r1# configure terminal
test-r1(config)# router ospf 1000
test-r1(config-router)# redistribute static subnets
test-r1(config-router)# ^Z
test-r1#
```

To exit the router configuration mode and return to global configuration mode, use the exit command. To leave the router configuration mode and return to the privileged EXEC mode, use the end command or type Ctrl-Z.

Each of the configuration modes can be accessed directly from another configuration mode. For instance, if you are in line configuration mode and want to program an Ethernet interface, it is not required that you exit line configuration mode and then enter interface configuration mode from global configuration mode. You can simply enter interface configuration mode from line configuration mode.

Conclusion

The configuration modes discussed here are only a few of those available in the Cisco IOS. All the configuration modes operate in the same fashion. You can enter them and exit them all the same way and with a similar syntax. Use of the ? operator in any of the EXEC or command modes will list the available command options. This help operator is an invaluable tool because no one wants to memorize the command syntax to every feature in the Cisco IOS and rarely do Network Professionals carry the complete IOS command set publications with them.

Table 3.2 recaps the most used command modes, their corresponding router prompts, what the command mode is used for, and the command used to enter that mode.

Table 3.2 **Common Cisco IOS Command Modes**

Command Mode	Router Prompt	Command Used to Enter Mode	Command Mode Use
Basic User Mode	`router>`	`none`	Display basic information on router funtionality.
Enable Mode	`router#`	`enable`	Display basic information on router functionality.
Global Configuration Mode	`router(config)#`	`configure`	Add/modify global configuration parameters, enter sub-level configuration modes.
Router Configuration Mode	`router (config-router)#`	`router <mode>`	Configure routing processes.
Interface Configuration	`router (config-if)#`	`interface <interface designation>`	Configure options on a Mode per interface basis.
Line Configuration	`router (config-line)#`	`line {con¦aux¦ tty¦vty} <line number>`	Configure options for Mode access lines and ports.

4

Local Area Networking

A LOCAL AREA NETWORK (LAN) IS ANY COMBINATION of networking segments that does not require the use of connections provided by a telecommunications company. There are a number of different protocols that can be used to connect multiple computers. In this chapter we will discuss a few of the most common protocols in use today. These are Ethernet, Fiber Distributed Data Interface (FDDI), and Token Ring. The protocol(s) you choose for your network will depend on your networking needs and the demands of the systems you want to network.

Ethernet is used mostly by end user stations or low to medium use servers. The most commonly used cable plant (physical layer wiring) for Ethernet is 10BaseT. Most companies use Category 5 twisted-pair wiring in their initial Ethernet networks because it offers a low cost upgrade option for future bandwidth needs. Because Category 5 cabling supports transmission speeds of 100Mbps and is relatively inexpensive, all that is required to upgrade the bandwidth of your LAN from 10Mbps to 100Mbps is higher speed network interface cards, 100BaseT hubs, and/or Fast Ethernet switching equipment.

FDDI is often found at the heart of a LAN. It is used to connect several routers or high bandwidth servers together. FDDI is so widely used because for a while it was the only protocol that offered transmission speeds of 100Mbps. Now that Fast Ethernet and Gigabit Ethernet are available, FDDI is quickly being replaced by switch Ethernet networks. Because the same cabling plant (fiber optic cabling) can be used for both Ethernet standards, it is easy to justify the cost of replacing your FDDI networks with switched Fast Ethernet. It is then simply a matter of upgrading interface hardware to support Gigabit speeds.

Token Ring is found in the end user station arena. It is also widely used to network point of sale (POS) machines and cash registers in retail marketplaces. Because IBM is a leader in the cash register market place, it is no wonder that Token Ring is prevalent there.

Ethernet

The Ethernet protocol was developed at the Xerox Palo Alto Research Center (PARC) laboratory in 1972. The Ethernet specification, as adopted by the Institute of Electrical and Electronics Engineers (IEEE), covers only the first 1 1/2 layers of the OSI model. These layers are the physical layer and the MAC portion of the Data Link layer. Although the Ethernet specification defines only the lowest portion of the model, it can have multiple protocol modules riding above it. Some of these protocols are TCP/IP, Novell IPX, AppleTalk, NetBIOS, SNA, and XNS.

The IEEE adopted the original Ethernet version with minor modification and labeled it 802.3. Ethernet protocol is based on the Carrier Sense Multiple Access with Collision Detect (CSMA/CD) access protocol.

Media Options

Ethernet supports a wide variety of bandwidths from 1 to 1000Mbps and on differing media types. These media types are as follows:

- Thick coaxial cable (baseband, thicknet or 10Base5).
- Thin coaxial cable (thinnet or 10Base2).
- Category 3 shielded or unshielded twisted-pair cable (10BaseT).
- Category 5 shielded or unshielded twisted-pair cable (100BaseT or Fast Ethernet).
- Fiber optic cable (1000BaseT or Gigabit Ethernet).

Fiber optic cable can also be used for 10BaseT and 100BaseT. Table 4.1 shows the different cabling types and the transmission speeds they support.

Collision Defined

A *collision* is defined as two or more stations attempting to transmit data to the shared media at the same time.

Table 4.1   **Cabling Types and Their Supported Transmission Speeds**

Cabling Type	Transmission Speeds
Thicknet	500MHz
Thinnet	50MHz
Unshielded twisted-pair (Category 3)	16MHz
Shielded twisted-pair (Category 3)	16MHz
Unshielded twisted-pair (Category 4)	20MHz
Shielded twisted-pair (Category 4)	20MHz
Unshielded twisted-pair (Category 5)	100MHz
Shielded twisted-pair (Category 5)	100MHz
Fiber Optic	Virtually unlimited

The advantage to using coaxial cable over twisted-pair cable is coaxial cable can be run for longer distances than twisted-pair cable can. Fiber optic cable can be run for much longer distances than coaxial cable or twisted-pair cable.

Interface Types

Cisco offers a number of Ethernet-based interfaces on the different routers and switches in their product lines. This discussion is meant as a general guideline for programming any of the interfaces for basic functionality. Some of the different flavors of Ethernet Cisco offers are

- Half-duplex Ethernet
- Full-duplex Ethernet
- Half-duplex Fast Ethernet
- Full-duplex Fast Ethernet
- Gigabit Ethernet

Category 4 Twisted-Pair Cabling

Category 4 twisted-pair cabling was created mainly for use in 16Mbps Token Ring networks. Beyond that application it has no real use that Category 3 cabling cannot provide for.

All these different Ethernet types are IEEE standards based and can be purchased with numerous media connection types. Any special considerations that might be required during configuration of any of these interfaces will be noted. As a general rule, if your network interface cards (NIC) support full-duplex operation then use it. Keep in mind that to operate your NIC in full-duplex mode it needs to be connected to a switch or router. Ethernet hubs cannot operate in full-duplex mode. Basic end user stations should use regular Ethernet interfaces whereas servers should use Fast Ethernet. Most mid to high-end servers come standard with auto-sensing 10/100Mbps Ethernet interfaces. Gigabit Ethernet should be used in the core of your LAN to link all your Fast Ethernet hubs or switches to your routing equipment. See Figure 4.1 for an example.

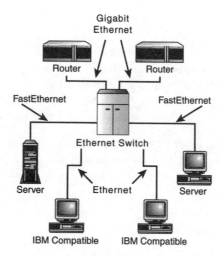

Figure 4.1   Sample Ethernet usage.

Configuring an Ethernet Interface

The procedure for configuring an Ethernet interface on a Cisco router is basically the same. Any network layer protocol you choose to run on the Ethernet interface will require the same basic interface configuration. The first task in configuring an Ethernet interface is to specify which encapsulation type is required. The following command is used to configure the encapsulation type on an Ethernet interface:

```
encapsulation type
```

The encapsulation type can be ARPA, SAP, or SNAP. ARPA is the standard for Ethernet version 2.0 encapsulation and the default choice if no encapsulation type is specified during the interface configuration. Specifying SAP signifies you want to use IEEE 802.3 encapsulation. Specifying SNAP signifies you want to use IEEE 802.2 encapsulation. For 99 percent of your Ethernet applications you will use the default encapsulation type of ARPA. An example of when you would use the SAP or SNAP encapsulation would be in a native Novell NetWare IPX network. Newer IOS versions do not enable the Ethernet encapsulation type to be changed. You should always check the release notes for the IOS version you plan to run if you need a specific feature.

The next task is to specify whether to run the interface in half or full-duplex. The default state for all the Ethernet interfaces offered by Cisco is half-duplex. To switch to full-duplex operation, issue the following command in interface configuration mode:

```
full-duplex
```

To change back from full-duplex operation to half-duplex operation, use the no form of the command:

```
no full-duplex
```

The next step is to enable the network layer protocols you want to run on the Ethernet segment to which this particular interface is attached. If you have Apple Macintosh computers on an Ethernet segment that are running AppleTalk, then you might want to enable the AppleTalk protocol on the interface. There are two interface configuration commands that need to be entered to accomplish this task. The first command defines the AppleTalk cable range and the AppleTalk address of the interface. The cable range values are used to define the number of logical networks that exist on the Ethernet segment. The two values need to be either the same number or a contiguous set of numbers and are entered in the form of *start-finish*. The second command defines the AppleTalk zone names that exist on the Ethernet segment the interface is attached to.

Ethernet Duplex Etiquette

It is important the Ethernet interface is configured for the correct operation mode. Full-duplex is only available when a port on a switch is directly connected to the Ethernet port on the router. In addition, both ends must be configured the same way. If an Ethernet interface is set to full-duplex and the Ethernet switch it connects to is set for half-duplex, the interface will operate but there will be a great many errors on the connections. This problem can be hard to troubleshoot if you have not encountered it in the field before. It is always a good idea to double-check all your interface configurations if you notice a high number of errors with low utilization of the interface.

The following interface configuration commands are used to initiate AppleTalk on an interface:

```
appletalk cable-range <cable-range> [network.node]
appletalk zone <zone-name>
```

The following example of AppleTalk commands defines the logical networks 30, 31, and 32 with a zone name of Engineering. The interface is given the AppleTalk address of network 30 node 100:

```
test-r1#conf t
test-r1(config)#interface ethernet1/0
test-r1(config-if)#appletalk cable-range 30-32 30.100
test-r1(config-if)#appletalk zone Engineering
test-r1(config-if)#exit
test-r1(config)#exit
test-r1#
```

You might want to also run IP on the same interface. All that needs to be done to enable IP on the interface is to assign an IP address to the interface. The following interface configuration command is used to specify an IP address:

```
ip address <address> <subnet mask>
```

The following example assigns the IP address 192.168.200.1 with a 24bit subnet mask to interface Ethernet 1/0:

```
test-r1#conf t
test-r1(config)#interface ethernet1/0
test-r1(config-if)#ip address 192.168.200.1 255.255.255.0
test-r1(config-if)#exit
test-r1(config)#exit
test-r1#
```

Finally, to put the interface into an operational mode, execute the following command in interface configuration mode:

```
no shutdown
```

Putting an interface into an operational mode without a network layer protocol defined is not useful except in a testing environment. No routable network traffic will be passed on the interface. However, this type of operation is useful when using the Cisco Discovery Protocol (CDP). CDP is discussed in Chapter 11, "Troubleshooting."

FDDI

The FDDI standard is actually a set of standards that was established by the American National Standards Institute (ANSI). FDDI uses a ring architecture that is token based. FDDI design consists of two counter-rotating rings. One is an active ring on which data is transmitted. The other is a fail-over ring. A station attached to both the primary and secondary ring is called a *dual-attached station (DAS)*. A station that is connected to the primary ring and not the secondary ring is called a *single-attached station (SAS)*.

In the event of a station failure or cable break, the primary and secondary rings are connected together to form one ring. This is called *wrapping*. This enables the FDDI ring to continue to operate even after a physical failure. If two physical failures occur to the same FDDI ring, the ring becomes split and two separate rings are formed. FDDI allows stations to access the ring at a rate of 100Mbps. FDDI can connect up to 500 dual-attached stations to a maximum network length of 100km.

FDDI differs from other ring architectures in that it is a timed token protocol. Each station is guaranteed access to the ring for a period of time. The period of time is negotiated among all stations on the ring at ring initialization (or when a new station is added to the ring).

FDDI networks are still useful in situations where zero downtime is needed. Because of the dual ring architecture the fault tolerance for FDDI is very high.

The FDDI interface processor for the various Cisco products has two ports. It supports operation as either a SAS or DAS. If you plan to use the FDDI port as a SAS, then you will need a FDDI concentrator, which will be dual-attached to both rings. See Figure 4.2 for an example of a SAS and DAS.

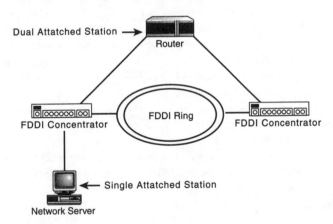

Figure 4.2   Single-attached station versus dual-attached station.

Use of a FDDI interface on a Cisco router requires no programming at all, except for defining the protocol address of the networking protocol you are using on your FDDI network. Simply wire the FDDI card to either a FDDI concentrator or another FDDI host and enable the FDDI port. To enable the FDDI port, enter the following command in the FDDI interface configuration mode:

```
no shutdown
```

Defining network protocol addresses on a FDDI interface is the same as described previously in the Ethernet interface section.

The Cisco FDDI card supports both transparent and translational bridging. *Transparent bridging* is used to bridge two like interfaces together, such as two FDDI interfaces. *Translational bridging* is used to bridge two dissimilar interface types together, such as a FDDI interface and an Ethernet interface. To enable bridging on a FDDI interface, enter the following command in interface configuration mode:

```
fddi encapsulate
```

Token Ring

Token Ring was first developed by IBM. It was later adopted by IEEE and labeled as 802.5 in 1985. Token Ring avoids collisions by requiring a station wanting to transmit data to the shared media to have the permission token. This permission token is passed from one station to the next according to a set of rules. There are two versions of Token Ring. The first version enables transmission of data on the ring at a rate of 4Mbps. The second version ups the transmission rate to 16Mbps. Token Ring can operate on several different media types, such as coaxial cable and twisted-pair cable.

Token Ring has a logical ring topology but is physically wired in a star formation. This means each individual station on the Token Ring is wired directly to a concentrator that links all the individual stations together. This concentrator provides the ring functions specified in the standards documentation. Having a ring architecture implemented on a star infrastructure enables the addition and removal of stations without serious interrupts to ring functionality.

The Cisco Token Ring cards support both the 4Mbps and 16Mbps versions of Token Ring. The Token Ring interface uses SNAP encapsulation as defined in RFC 1042. For this reason, it is not necessary to define an encapsulation type for the Token Ring interface. The first task to complete when configuring a Token Ring interface is to set the ring operating speed. Use the following interface configuration command to set the Token Ring speed to either 4Mbps or 16Mbps:

```
ring-speed <speed>
```

Cabling Problems

If the Cisco Token Ring interface detects a cabling problem, it puts the interface into a reset state. Once in the reset state, the IOS might not restart the interface after the cabling problem has been fixed. You might need to manually restart the interface by issuing the `clear interface tokenring` `<number>` at the enabled user command prompt. *number* is the Token Ring interface number to restart.

Set the Token Ring Interface to the Correct Speed

Be careful to set the Token Ring interface to the correct speed. If the Token Ring interface is set to a speed other than what the ring is transmitting at, the ring will shut down completely.

The default nature of Token Ring requires the frame data is transmitted in be returned to the transmitting station before the permission token is placed back on the Token Ring. A feature of Token Ring protocol is to enable a station to place the permission token back on the ring before it receives the frame back it used to transmit data. This is called *early token release*. The Cisco Token Ring interface supports early token release. Use the following interface configuration command to configure the Token Ring interface for early token release:

```
early-token-release
```

Early token release might be of use to you if there are a large number of stations on one token ring and you are concerned with efficient bandwidth utilization.

Token ring is not the best choice for a new LAN. It is limited in transmission speed compared with the current Ethernet standards. Token ring is most often found in large corporate networks that have IBM mainframes.

Spatial Reuse Protocol/Dynamic Packet Transport (SRP/DPT)

The newest networking technology to be developed by Cisco is *Dynamic Packet Transport (DPT)*. This technology is also referred to as the *Spatial Reuse Protocol (SRP)*. SRP is in fact the media–independent MAC layer protocol that provides the capability for addressing, packet stripping, managing bandwidth, and controlling messages on a DPT ring. A good analogy to use is SRP is to DPT as HDLC is to V.35. SRP is supported on the OC–12 line cards for the 12000 routers and the 7200/7500 port adapters. DPT is very similar to FDDI in that it is a ring-based architecture. SRP is actually the protocol used to transmit data and control messages inside a DPT ring. Because DPT uses a counter-rotating ring topology it provides the capability to transmit and/or receive data in both directions on the ring at the same time. DPT also uses destination striping (the destination station on the ring removes the packets from the ring) instead of forcing the entire ring to be used. Because of this functionality, multiple pairs of adjacent stations are capable of communicating between each other without interference from other transmissions on the ring. This enables the available bandwidth to be used more efficiently.

DPT can be run on several types of media. It can be used on traditional SONET services that are purchased from a telecommunications carrier. It can be used on dark fiber. *Dark fiber* is a term used to describe fiber optic cable that connects to buildings or locations. Fiber optic cable needs to have a light source connected to it to transmit data. This light source is usually a laser for long distance transmission. If the fiber optic cable is purchased without the light source, it is called dark because it is up to you to provide the laser light that will be used to transmit the data on it. All the optical line cards offered by Cisco come in two variations. One is for intermediate reach applications and the other is for long reach applications. If you are using dark fiber you most likely want to use the long reach cards because they can transmit for distances up to several miles without the use of repeaters. They can also be used on a single wavelength of a fiber system that has been terminated with wave division multiplexing equipment.

DPT is an exciting new technology that might find a great deal of use in metropolitan area networks (MANs).

Conclusion

Of the three LAN protocols discussed here, Ethernet is the most widely used. FDDI has a very large installed base because, until recently, it was the only option available to transmit data at high rates. As time goes on, FDDI installations will slowly switch to Fast Ethernet or more likely Gigabit Ethernet. Ethernet has many strong points that make it the protocol of choice for local area networking. It is cheap, easy to implement, and every networking hardware vendor in the world supports it. It will run on almost any physical media and it also supports many of the layer three protocols in use today.

FDDI still has uses today because of its fault tolerance and collision avoidance. Token Ring is still usable for LANs with high station counts that do not require high bandwidth and are concerned with collisions. The only application left for token ring in my opinion is in the world of retail sales.

5

Wide Area Networking

AWIDE AREA NETWORK (WAN) IS GENERALLY considered to be any network that incorporates links which are supplied by a telecommunications company (telco) of some sort. A telco might be a long distance carrier or Regional Bell Operating Company (RBOC). RBOCs are the result of the AT&T split by the United States government (such as Bell South and Bell Atlantic) and are only found in the United States.

There are basically two types of circuits that can be ordered from a telecommunications provider.

- Leased line—where the circuit path from point A to point Z is sold and dedicated solely to one company for the duration of the service contract.

- Switched line—where the circuit path from point A to point Z is neither permanent nor reserved for the purchasing party.

Switched circuits are generally cheaper because the telcos can sell more circuits on their network than there is physical bandwidth to support. The telcos do this in the hopes that all circuits on the physical path won't require the bandwidth at the same time. This is called *over-subscribing*. Over-subscribing can be implemented effectively because the telcos know that not all users of the sold bandwidth will require the full bandwidth available at the same moment in time.

To accommodate the instances when more bandwidth is required than is physically available, the telcos only guarantee a minimum amount of bandwidth to the subscriber. Any bandwidth over and above the guaranteed amount is available on a first come first serve basis. The telcos usually reserve the right to drop packets in times of congestion. If your business does not require the full bandwidth of a leased line all the time, it is much more cost effective to install a switched service line.

In this chapter you will learn the differences between all the major WAN technologies in use today. Everything will be covered from the physical installation of each technology to the configuration of Cisco equipment to utilize each type of service.

Circuit Termination

The termination of the physical line from the telco is usually done by an external device called a *Channel Service Unit Digital Service Unit (CSU/DSU).* On one end of a WAN connection, the CSU/DSU converts data frames from a LAN into frames that can traverse WAN connections. On the other end of the WAN connection, the CSU/DSU converts WAN frames back to frames on another local area network (LAN). The CSU part of the device manages communications with the WAN side of the connection, and the DSU manages communications with the LAN side of the connection. Cisco has recently released a number of interface cards that have CSU/DSUs built into them. The POET port adapter for the Versatile Interface Processor (VIP) cards is one example of an interface with a built-in CSU/DSU.

The Upside to Integrated CSU/DSUs

Having a built-in CSU/DSU reduces potential single points of failure, enables the use of redundant power supplies that are common in Cisco's enterprise routers, reduces the need for an out of band management system to administer the device, and it is also generally more cost-effective than using an external DSU/CSU.

To upgrade the UPS power in a Data Center during a project, one feed off of the UPS was shorted and consequently the circuit breaker tripped. The routers were not affected by this because the dual power supplies were fed by different UPS feeds. However, many of the external DSUs were left without power because they happened to be fed from the UPS leg that was shut off. Had those DSUs been built into the line cards on the routers, the circuits would never have gone down.

Physical Transports

Depending on the type of service you buy and the speed of the circuit, the local telco will deliver the circuit to your company on either copper or fiber optic cable. Circuits delivered on a copper based cable are referred to as *electrical terminations*. Circuits delivered on fiber optic based cable are referred to as *optical terminations*. The distinction becomes important at the DS3 and OC-3 level because both have specifications for electrical or optical interfaces. The termination type you request from your telecommunications provider will depend on the interface type you have elected to install in your router.

A T1 circuit is actually made up of 24 DS0 channels. Each of these DS0 channels is usually 64Kbps, which gives an overall capacity of 1.536Mbps for a full T1. An actual clear channel T1 has an available bandwidth of 1.544Mbps because of the lack of signaling overhead that is found in the channelized version. Clear channel means that the circuit operates on one large pipe rather than a group of smaller pipes. In a similar fashion, T3 circuits are made up of 28 DS1 channels. Each channel is 1.544Mbps giving an overall capacity of 43.232Mbps. Table 5.1 shows some of the common transport types and their equivalent speeds.

Table 5.1 **Physical Transport Types and Their Speeds**

Type	Speed
DS0	56Kbps or 64Kbps
DS1/T1	1.544Mbps
E1	2.048Mbps
E3	34Mbps
DS3/T3	45Mbps

How Do the Numbers Add Up?

You many wonder why a T3 or DS3 is often referred to as a *45Mbps circuit*. The fact is that a clear channel DS3 circuit is actually capable of speeds close to 50Mbps. Most hardware vendors support transmission rates of 45Mbps on their DS3 interfaces. If the DS3 service leased from the telco is channelized, the actual throughput of the circuit is a little less than 45Mbps because of the signaling overhead of maintaining the 28 individual DS1 channels with the DS3. If the DS3 is not channelized, the full 45Mbps can be utilized by the transmitting and receiving interfaces. The European equivalents to the T1 and T3 are the E1 and E3. An E1 is essentially a bundle of 32 channels and has a bandwidth capacity of 2.048Mbps. An E3 consists of 16 E1 channels and has an available bandwidth of 34.368Mbps (including overhead).

It All Comes Together

The letter "c" trailing the circuit designation for the optical circuits stands for *concatenated*. Most carriers will offer OC-3 and above circuits as bundles of DS3 channels. Hence the need for the "concatenated" designation. An OC-3c enables the full use of the 155Mbps, whereas an OC-3 loses some available bandwidth to signaling for the separate DS3 channels.

It is important to understand the transmission speeds that are available from telecommunications providers, especially if you are the architect for an international network. Every country in the world besides the United States uses synchronous digital hierarchy (SDH) based framing systems for their data services. It is based on multiples of 155.52Mbits/s and is referred to in synchronous transport module (STM) increments. The United States uses SONET based framing systems for their data services. For example, in SDH terms, STM-1 is 155.52Mbits/s and is equivalent to OC-3 in the SONET based hierarchy in the United States. Table 5.2 shows SONET types and the SDH equivalents.

Table 5.2 **SONET and SDH Equivalents**

SONET Type	SDH Type	Speed
OC-1	N/A	51.84Mbps
OC-3	STM-1	155.52Mbps
OC-9	STM-3	466.56Mbps
OC-12	STM-4	622.08Mbps
OC-18	STM-6	933.12Mbps
OC-24	STM-8	1244.16Mbps
OC-36	STM-12	1866.24Mbps
OC-48	STM-16	2488.32Mbps
OC-192	STM-64	9953.23Mbps

This dissimilarity can be compared to the United States' use of the Standard weights system while the rest of the world uses the Metric system. Special arrangements might be needed when connecting locations in the United States with locations in other parts of the world. For instance, suppose that you wish to connect New York to London with 155Mbps of capacity. United States-based providers offer OC-3c and European based providers offer STM-1. OC-3c uses SONET framing at Layer 2 of the OSI model, whereas STM-1 uses SDH framing at Layer 2. A conversion needs to take place at some point along the circuit path in order for the two systems to interoperate. In today's market of global communications carriers, the need for conversions is reduced because United States based telcos offer SDH based services.

Another common problem is found in the lower level transmission circuits such as DS3 and DS1. Because the 2Mbps of an E1 does not match directly to the 1.5Mbps of a DS1, you will encounter a slightly more complex problem than simple Layer 2 framing formats. The actual transmission speeds of the circuits do not match. It is sometimes easier to side step this problem with the use of a switched service, such as *Asynchronous Transfer Mode* (ATM).

Copper Hand Off

Most circuits of 45Mbps and lower are delivered on some type of copper cabling. Circuits between 56Kpbs and 1.544Mbps (DS1/T1) are delivered on twisted-pair cabling. Two pairs of cables are used for the circuit. One pair handles transmit data and the other pair handles receive data. Because the transmit and receive data are carried over separate physical wires, the circuit is full-duplex by nature. *Full-duplex* refers to the capability of the router to transmit and receive data at the same time. This in effect doubles the actual throughput of any given circuit. This means that a DS1, which is 1.544Mbps, can actually transmit and receive 1.544Mbps simultaneously (see Figure 5.1). This makes the circuit 3.088Mbps full-duplex.

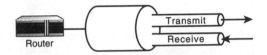

Figure 5.1   Full-duplex operation of a circuit.

If your company has many DS1 circuits terminated into a site, the telco might install a 25-pair cable and terminate it on a 66 or 110 block. See Figure 5.2 for examples of the two types of twisted-pair hand-off blocks. A 25-pair cable is a single cable jacket that houses 25 individual pairs of insulated copper wire.

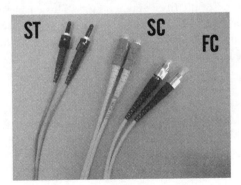

Figure 5.2   High density hand-off blocks.

Telco terminology can be confusing for newcomers. It is very important for network professionals to learn and understand this terminology to be successful. There is an increasing trend toward the convergence of voice, data, and video onto the same network. Rather, there will most likely be one or more high density interconnection blocks that will be used to hand off your circuits. The termination block provides cross-connect capabilities for the individual DS1s delivered on the 25-pair cable. Pairs 1–12 are the receive pairs for the individual 12 DS1s that the 25-pair cable will accommodate. Pair 13 is left unused. Pairs 14–25 are the transmit pairs for the 12 DS1s that the 25-pair cable will accommodate. So, if the telco has terminated five of your DS1s on a 25-pair cable as described, the two pairs for transmit and receive of DS1 number 1 would be pairs 14 and 1 respectively. DS1 number 2 would be pairs 15 and 2, and so on.

For circuits greater than DS1 but lower than OC-3 (155Mbps), the delivery cable plant is coaxial cable. One pair of cable is installed for every E3 or DS3 ordered. Each wire in the pair serves the same function as a single pair in the DS1. That is, one cable is used for transmission while the other cable is used for (?) reception.

If your company leases many high bandwidth circuits (DS3 and higher) from the same telco, it is possible the telco will install a fiber optic entrance into your building. *Entrance* refers to the physical cable which is installed into your building by the telco. This fiber optic entrance can be an OC12 SONET ring or even an OC48 SONET ring. The amount of capacity available on the fiber optic system depends on the type of equipment that your telco uses to "light" the fiber optic cable. The individual circuits are then broken off of the fiber optic entrance. This enables the telco to install the initial cabling once and then deliver circuits of varying bandwidth via software and hardware configuration on the fiber optic SONET multiplexer rather than installing individual copper cabling for each circuit you order.

Why Fiber Optics Instead of Copper?

OC-3 circuits can be delivered on coaxial cable, but most telcos use fiber. The reason for this is that internally to the telco, all inter-office trunks are fiber optic. It is easier and cheaper to deliver the circuit on fiber than coax because no demultiplexors are required. With a DS3 or lower circuit, a demultiplexor is required to break out the individual channel anyway, so the telcos use the cheaper copper wire rather than the fiber optic cable.

Fiber Optic Hand Off

Circuits at OC-3 level or higher are delivered on fiber optic cable. It is important to determine what type of fiber optic cable your local telco uses. There are two types:

- Single-mode (SM) cable
- Multi-mode (MM) cable

You will need to match the type of cable to the type of card you buy for your Cisco router. It is very important that you do not plug a single-mode circuit into a multi-mode card. This can easily damage the router line card. Conversely, it is also very important that you do not use a SM line card with an MM circuit. The laser on the line card can damage the telco's hardware. Using mismatched cables for patching will work but is not recommended. SM cable has a smaller diameter glass core (the part of the cable that carries the laser light) than MM cable. Using a SM cable on an MM circuit will cause a portion of the laser light to not be transmitted because the MM transmitter is expecting a larger diameter glass core than the SM cable provides. Using a MM cable on a SM circuit will cause some of the laser light to be lost due to refraction within the glass core. Neither of these instances will cause the circuit to not operate, but you will see Cyclical Redundancy Checksum (CRC) errors and other seemingly unexplainable errors on the circuit. The longer mismatched cables exist in your network, the greater the chances become that permanent damage will be done to your hardware.

Also, find out what type of connectors your telco uses on its hand-off patch panel so that you can have the correct type of patch cables made. The most commonly used fiber optic connector types are ST, SC, and FC. ST connectors resemble BNC connectors that are used on coaxial cable and test set leads in laboratory environments. ST connectors are found most often on hubs and patch panels within the cable distribution plant. SC connectors are keyed plug-in connectors. Being *keyed* means that the plug will only enter the receptacle in one position. SC connectors are the most common type used on interface cards. FC connectors are similar to ST but are threaded rather than a simple twist on like the BNC. This enables the fiber optic jumpers to be screwed onto the patch panel receptacle for a more secure connection. Telcos like FC connectors.

Leased Lines

Leased lines can be purchased as small as 56Kbps and as large as 2.4Gbps or higher. Usually leased lines are purchased at T1 rate or higher because of their cost. It is much cheaper to have a switched 56Kbps circuit than a dedicated 56Kbps leased line. Cisco supports a number of encapsulation types for their available WAN interfaces. The two most commonly used are the Point-to-Point Protocol (PPP) and High-level Data Link Control (HDLC) protocol.

Cisco also supports the use of the following encapsulation types on its synchronous serial interfaces:

- Frame Relay
- SMDS
- X.25
- Synchronous Datalink Control (SDLC)
- ATM Data Exchange Interface (ATM-DXI)
- Cisco's Serial Tunneling (STUN)

PPP

To enable PPP encapsulation on an interface, enter the following command in interface configuration mode:

```
encapsulation ppp
```

Some available benefits when using PPP encapsulation are Link Quality Monitoring (LQM) and a greater availability of debugging commands. LQM enables the definition of a quality percentage. When the quality of the line drops below the configured percentage, the link is deemed unusable and is shut down. When LQM is enabled on an interface, Link Quality Reports (LQR) are used instead of keepalives. Keepalives, as well as LQRs, are basically small messages that are sent in the device on the remote end of the circuit. The messages are acknowledged by a response message that lets the originating router know that the line is still up and the remote device is still active.

To enable LQM on an interface running PPP, enter the following command in interface configuration mode:

```
ppp quality <percentage>
```

In this example, *percentage* is a number from 1 to 100.

In Chapter 14, "Troubleshooting the Physical Layer," we will discuss the debugging commands available. PPP is a good encapsulation choice when interconnecting a Cisco router to hardware from another vendor. PPP is standards-based, and all network devices that have synchronous serial interfaces support PPP.

Cisco also supports data compression when PPP is used as the encapsulation type for synchronous interfaces. Two different compression algorithms are supported. The first is called the *predictor algorithm*. This uses a random number and compression dictionary to predict what the next character in the packet will be. The other type is the *proprietary algorithm* developed by Stacker corporation.

There are two forms of the `interface configuration` command used to enable data compression on a PPP interface. The two forms of the command are

compress [*predictor*¦*stac*]

or

ppp compress [*predictor*¦*stac*]

Compression is all done in software by the main CPU. You should not use compression on a router that normally runs at a high CPU load. A high CPU load is considered sustained utilization above 65 percent.

Cisco also provides a separate hardware card that can be installed in the modular series routers to handle the compression of data. This frees the main CPU to perform normal administrative functions.

HDLC

The default encapsulation type on a synchronous interface is HDLC. The Cisco HDLC is more efficient than PPP, but lacks some of the troubleshooting features of PPP. This is an important distinction when you are concerned with getting every bit you can out of your WAN circuits. One nice feature of HDLC is that it enables you to see when there is a loop in the circuit connected to an interface. A loop is when the transmit portion of the circuit is wired directly to the receive portion. Using PPP will sometimes show loopbacks in circuits but HDLC is guaranteed to always show loopbacks. Changing a synchronous interface from another encapsulation type to HDLC can be done in one of two ways. The first is to simply enable HDLC encapsulation on the interface with the following command:

    encapsulation hdlc

Or, you can disable the current encapsulation on the interface which will revert the interface encapsulation to the IOS default, HDLC. For instance, to change a serial interface from PPP encapsulation to HDLC, enter the following command in the interface configuration mode:

    no encapsulation ppp

Changing from PPP to HDLC would be recommended if you were replacing another vendor's box with a Cisco box. Cisco's proprietary version of HDLC uses larger packet size to reduce fragmentation and is generally the preferred encapsulation type for point-to-point links.

The *show process cpu* **Enable Mode Command**
Use the show process cpu enable mode command to display the current status of the CPU load and the processes that are currently running.

Switched Lines

Switched lines are similar to leased lines in that the telco will deliver a dedicated service line to your company. This dedicated line terminates on a piece of switching equipment in the telco's central office rather than at an end point of your choosing as with a leased line.

The type of switched service you purchased determines which type of switch your circuit is terminated on. If you are buying Frame Relay service, your local dedicated circuit will be connected to a Frame Relay switch in the telco's central office.

ATM

ATM is a common switched service used in WANs. ATM is a packet switched protocol that uses small fixed-length cells. Each cell is 53 bytes long (48 byte payload and 5 byte header). Because ATM cells are a fixed length, ATM can be run at very high speeds. The small fixed length cells also make ATM a good candidate to carry multiple traffic types, such as voice, video, and data. The fixed length cells makes switching the traffic in a predictable manner easier. ATM is widely used because it will run on DS1 and higher transports. Also, ATM enables traffic to be shaped and limited to predefined limits. Another strong point for ATM is if the quality of service (QoS) features are inherent in the protocol.

Although ATM can be configured on a standard serial interface (with the use of an external ATM DSU), Cisco offers an ATM interface processor (AIP) card. An ATM Data Service Unit (ADSU) takes ATM cells from the remote sender and strips off the ATM protocol encapsulation information before sending the packet to the router. It also adds the ATM encapsulation information to packets as they are leaving the router to be sent to a remote end station. Configuration of an AIP card is described in this section.

PVCs

Permanent virtual circuits (PVCs) are statically assigned paths from one end point to another through an ATM network. These static paths are available all the time, although their physical path inside the ATM network might not always be the same.

PVCs are the most common type of service used with ATM. PVCs must be defined in three places:

- The originating router
- The intermediate ATM switches
- The terminating router (see Figure 5.3)

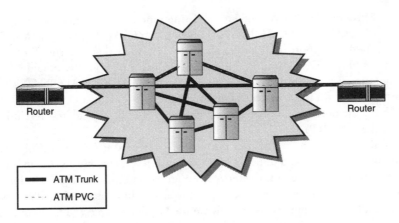

Figure 5.3   PVC path though ATM cloud.

The ATM switch determines the virtual path identifier (VPI) and the virtual circuit identifier (VCI). The VPI can be any number from 0 to 255. The VCI can be any number from 0 to 65535. Every PVC configured on an ATM switch has a unique VPI/VCI pair. The VPI/VCI assignments are locally significant to the ATM switch. The VPI/VCI configured on the router must match the VPI/VCI assign at the ATM switch.

The VPI is used in switch to switch communications. The VCI is used to identify the exact end point once the cell reaches the final ATM switch in the path. This communications scheme is analogous to a local phone call. The telephone switch looks at the first three digits that you dialed (the prefix code). It needs no other information to route your call to the next phone switch in the path to the party whom you are calling. The prefix code specifies which area of the city the call should be routed to. Once the call reaches a phone switch that handles calls for the prefix that you dialed, it looks at the last four digits that you dialed to determine which line it should apply ringing voltage to. The prefix code is like the VPI and the last four digits are like the VCI. PVCs are configured at the AIP interface level. The command to define a PVC is

```
atm pvc <vcd> <vpi> <vci> <encapsulation type>
```

The virtual circuit descriptor (VCD) is an AIP specific mechanism. The VCD enables the AIP to reference a VPI/VCI pair. Encapsulation type defines which ATM adaptation layer (AAL) encapsulation to use for the PVC. AAL is what makes ATM so versatile. It enables ATM cells to carry differing types of traffic. There are several versions of AAL defined. We will be using AAL version 5 for IP traffic. AAL5 enables lightweight variable bit rate traffic. The AAL5 encapsulation is combined with one of either

MUX, NLPID, or LLC/SNAP sub encapsulation types. The configurable encapsulation types for AAL5 are AAL5MUX, AAL5NLPID, and AAL5SNAP. AAL4MUX would be used to support other protocols over ATM other than Internet Protocol (IP), such as Novell IPX, Banyan VINES, and DECnet. AAL5NLPID would be used to communicate over a HSSI port that is using an external ADSU. AAL5SNAP is used to support the Logical Link Control/Subnetwork Access Protocol (LLC/SNAP) version of IP. This is the only encapsulation that will support the inverse address resolution protocol (inverse ARP).

Next, in order to send traffic over our newly configured PVC, a protocol must be mapped to the PVC. This is done on a per interface level. This means that in the PVC, protocol mapping is done in the interface configuration mode for the ATM interface. Cisco provides a mechanism called a map-list to make these protocol to PVC associations. The following group of commands are used to define an ATM map-list and then assign it to an AIP interface:

```
map-list <name>
 <protocol> <protocol address> atm-vc <vcd> [broadcast]
 !
interface a2/0
  map-group <name>
```

The `map-list` name is a user selected descriptive name. The VCD defined here should match the VCD configured on the ATM interface for the VPI/VCI pair that connects to the end node with the specified protocol address. The optional broadcast keyword defines whether this PVC should have regular protocol broadcasts (such as routing updates) sent on it.

SVCs

Another option available besides the use of PVCs is switched virtual circuits (SVCs). SVCs act much like X.25 and are good for applications that require bandwidth on demand. With SVCs, the virtual circuits are created and destroyed on demand. This requires a signaling protocol between the router and the ATM switch. In order for this signaling to take place, one PVC must be configured so there is an open communication path between the router and the ATM switch at all times. SVCs are difficult to implement and not used very often. More often than not, PVCs are created for each destination end point that needs to be reached. Each PVC will be configured for the bandwidth that is needed even though the sum of the bandwidth of all PVCs on an ATM circuit might be greater than the physical limit of the ATM circuit. This is called over-subscribing. The intention is that all the PVC will not require the bandwidth at the same time.

Unlike X.25, ATM SVCs handle all call setup, maintenance, and cleanup on a separate connection rather than in the data path. The configuration of the out-of-band signaling PVC is the same as a standard PVC except for the encapsulation type. The encapsulation type for the out-of-band signaling PVC is `qsaal`.

```
atm pvc <vcd> <vpi> <vci> qsaal
```

After the signaling PVC is created, the ATM interface must be configured for a network service access point (NSAP) address. The NSAP address is unique to every ATM interface in the ATM network. The NSAP address is configured at the ATM interface level. The command to assign a NSAP address to an ATM interface is

atm nsap-address <*address*>

The NSAP address is a dotted hexadecimal number with the following format:

XX.XXXX.XX.XXXXXX.XXXX.XXXX.XXXX.XXXX.XXXX.XXXX.XX

In this format, each X represents a hexadecimal digit.

Frame Relay

Frame Relay is a packet switching protocol that statistically multiplexes data on a circuit to provide better bandwidth usage. Packet switching is only slightly different than cell switching. The main difference is that cells are fixed lengths, and packet lengths can vary. The nature of data communications on a LAN is very bursty. By *bursty* I mean that there are periods of time when there is no traffic being transmitted, and there are other times when a great deal of traffic is being transmitted. There is a great contrast to the peaks and valleys if you were to plot the traffic over a period of time. Frame Relay takes advantage of this fact to use the "silent" periods between data transmissions for transmission of data that might be queued or on another permanent virtual circuit (PVC). This is good for the consumer because it enables the telcos to offer Frame Relay service at a cheaper rate than a dedicated leased line. The telcos do not need as much bandwidth between their central office sites to carry your traffic. With a leased line, the telco must allocate the bandwidth you purchased on every link between central offices that your circuit path follows whether you are transmitting data on it or not. With Frame Relay, the telcos can use one trunk for all Frame Relay traffic and use the quiet periods from one Frame Relay customer to transmit data for another Frame Relay customer.

Frame Relay PVCs are similar to ATM PVCs in that they are statically mapped paths from one end point to another end point through one or more Frame Relay switches. Configuration of Frame Relay PVCs are considerably less complicated than ATM PVCs. Instead of a VCI/VPI pair as in ATM, Frame Relay uses a data link control identifier (DLCI) to distinguish between multiple PVCs on the same physical switch. Every switch maintains its own DLCI table. For this reason, the DLCI number is significant only to connections on that single Frame Relay switch. Two separate switches can have PVCs configured with DLCIs of 16, whereas there can only be one PVC on a switch with a DLCI of 16. Frame Relay encapsulation can be run on physical transports of DS1 to DS3 speeds. Frame Relay on OC-3 will most likely be available in the very near future. See Table 5.2 for a list of interfaces and which protocols are supported on each. Frame Relay also uses out of band signaling to maintain the PVCs, error detection, and congestion management. The out-of-band signaling is called the *Link Management Interface* (LMI).

Table 5.2 **Cisco Interfaces and Their Supported Data Link Protocols**

Interface	PPP	HDLC	Frame Relay	ATM	SMDS	X.25
DS1 Serial	X	X	X	X	X	X
E1 Serial	X	X	X	X	X	X
DS3 Serial	X	X	X	X	X	X
E3 Serial	X	X	X	X	X	X
OC-3 ATM				X		
OC-12 ATM				X		
OC-48 ATM				X		
OC-3 POS	X	X				
OC-12 POS	X	X				
OC-48 POS	X	X				

Configuring Frame Relay

The first step in configuring Frame Relay on a router is to enable the Frame Relay encapsulation on the appropriate interface(s). This is done with the following interface configuration command:

```
encapsulation frame-relay
```

If the router on the other end of the Frame Relay cloud is made by a vendor other than Cisco, use the following command instead:

```
encapsulation frame-relay ietf
```

The next step is to define the LMI type for the interface. The default LMI type is Cisco. Use the following command to specify the LMI type for a particular interface:

```
frame-relay lmi-type [ansi ¦ cisco ¦ q933a]
```

The newer versions of the Cisco IOS support a Frame Relay feature called LMI autosense. This feature automatically detects what LMI type the telco switch is using. The interface is then set to that LMI type automatically. This makes Frame Relay configuration a little more *plug n play*.

The final step in configuring Frame Relay on an interface is to map a specific data protocol to a PVC. This is done with the following interface configuration command:

```
frame-relay map protocol procotol-address dlci [broadcast ¦ ietf ¦ cisco]
```

Protocol can be one of the following: IP, DECnet, AppleTalk, XNS, IPX, VINES, or
CLNS. Usually, you would use the IP protocol for WAN services and encapsulate
other protocols like IPX and AppleTalk within IP packets for WAN transmission. Use
the broadcast keyword to run routing protocols, such as OSPF, over a Frame Relay
PVC. If the terminating end point of the PVC is not a Cisco router, use the
ietf keyword.

Sub-Interfaces

In order to more easily support protocols that require split horizons or assume a fully
meshed network, the use of sub-interfaces is supported. Using sub-interfaces, each PVC
on a Frame Relay circuit can be treated as a separate logical interface on the router.

Split horizons prevents the transmission of a routing update out the same interface
that it was received on. Assume that station A has a PVC to station B on a Frame
Relay interface. Assume that station A also has a PVC to station C on the same Frame
Relay interface. If station A receives a routing update from station B that needs to be
sent to station C, split horizons will prevent that same routing update from being
transmitted. To combat this problem, Cisco enables each PVC to be defined on a separate sub-interface. Because the router treats each of these sub-interfaces as a separate
and distinct logical port, transmission of a routing update from station B to station C
is enabled.

To use sub-interfaces for each DLCI, configure the physical interface for Frame
Relay encapsulation as described earlier in this section. Next, create a sub-interface for
the PVC using the following command in interface configuration mode:

```
interface serial interface number.sub-interface number [multipoint |
point-to-point]
```

Interface number is the physical interface number of the Frame Relay circuit. The
sub-interface number is any decimal number between 0 and 4294967295. Use either
the multipoint or point-to-point keywords to specify which type of circuit the sub-
interface should be treated as. The following example creates the point-to-point
sub-interface number 3 on physical interface serial8/0:

```
Router(config)#interface serial8/0.3 point-to-point
```

Once the sub-interface has been created, use the Frame Relay map command that was
introduced earlier to map protocols to DLCIs, if the sub-interface type is multipoint.
Otherwise, use the following command to assign DLCI to a point-to-point Frame
Relay sub-interface:

```
frame-relay interface-dlci dlci
```

SMDS

Switched multi-megabit data services (SMDS) is a wide area packet switched protocol offered by many of the RBOCs. SMDS is a high-speed WAN protocol that can be run on either a serial or HSSI interface. SMDS does require an external SMDS data service unit. Until Frame Relay was supported on DS3 interfaces and ATM was standardized, SMDS was the only option for high-speed WAN service from a telco. If you needed more than DS1 bandwidth in your WAN, then you most likely deployed SMDS. SMDS is not used much in the United States now that ATM, Frame Relay, and PPP can be run on high-speed circuits.

SMDS uses addresses assigned by the service provider to identify every end point on an SMDS cloud. A nice feature within SMDS is the capability to define groups of destination addresses. Each SMDS address begins with a C if it is a single end station or an E if it is a group address.

The first step in configuring SMDS service on an interface is to enable SMDS encapsulation on that interface. This is done with the following interface configuration command:

```
encapsulation smds
```

Next, assign your RBOC provided SMDS address to the interface using the following command in interface configuration mode:

smds address *smds-address*

A Router and a Switch?

Cisco routers can also be configured to act as a Frame Relay switch. This is very rarely used in a production network. However, this feature is very useful in a lab environment. There are several steps to configuring your router to be a Frame Relay switch. First, enable Frame Relay switching entering the following command in global configuration mode:

```
frame-relay switching
```

Next, use the frame-relay route command on each of the interfaces that will be used to switch Frame Relay packets. The frame-relay route command maps one DLCI on an interface to another DLCI on another interface. The following configuration example maps DLCI 500 on Serial1/0 to DLCI 600 on interface Serial2/0 and vice versa.

```
interface Serial1/0
 no ip address
 encapsulation frame-relay
 keepalive 15
 frame-relay lmi-type ansi
 frame-relay intf-type dce
 frame-relay route 500 interface Serial2 600
!
interface Serial2/0
 encapsulation frame-relay
 keepalive 15
 frame-relay intf-type dce
 frame-relay route 600 interface Serial1 500
```

An SMDS-address takes the form of CXXX.XXXX.XXXX or EXXX.XXXX.XXXX. For example, C141.5555.1212 is an end station address and E180.0555.1212 is a group address.

The final step is to map a data protocol to an SMDS end point station or group address. This is done using the following interface configuration command:

```
smds static-map protocol protocol-address smds-address [broadcast]
```

Protocol can be any of the following: AppleTalk, VINES, DECnet, IP, IPX, XNS, or CLNS. Use the broadcast keyword to enable broadcast packets to be sent to this end station or group.

ISDN

Integrated Services Digital Network (ISDN) is a digital circuit offered by RBOCs that offers a wide range of features for both voice and data transmission. ISDN circuits consist of two types of channels. The first channel, called the *D channel*, handles all the circuit signaling and call setup, maintenance, and termination. The second channel, called the *B channel*, handles all the data transmission whether it be voice or data information.

ISDN was originally thought to be the solution for telecommuters and homes with multiple phone lines. The idea was to have one ISDN line serve as your home phone, fax, and modem line. The high price of ISDN and difficulty in getting service from the telcos hindered the growth of the ISDN service. It is easier to get multiple phone lines than deal with the high hardware and service costs of ISDN. Also, many telcos implemented ISDN in different ways so there were initial communications problems between carriers.

ISDN circuits are offered in basically two forms.

- Basic Rate Interface (BRI) circuit
- Primary Rate Interface (PRI) circuit

The main differences between these two type of circuits is that a BRI consists of one 16Kbps D channel for signaling and two 64Kbps B channels for voice or data. BRI circuits are delivered on a standard single telephone twisted-pair cable. A PRI circuit consists of 24 64Kbps channels, one of which is used as a D channel. The remaining 23 channels are B channels. PRIs are delivered on the same wiring as DS1 circuit (usually twisted pair).

ISDN lines are mostly used for backup dial on demand bandwidth or to support multiple high bandwidth remote users on one interface. One PRI can support 23 BRI remote callers if only one B channel is used per call.

Configuring a BRI Interface

Some Cisco routers have the option of having a BRI interface. To configure a BRI interface on a Cisco router, two pieces of information must be obtained from the ISDN service provider. The first piece of information needed is the ISDN switch type that the ISDN service provider is using. The next piece of information needed is the service profile identifier (SPID) of each B channel in the BRI. It is also helpful to know whether your telco uses seven digit or ten digit dialing for its ISDN service.

The first task in configuring a BRI interface on a Cisco router is to define the switch type. This is done with the following interface configuration command:

```
isdn switch-type switch-type
```

switch-type is one of the options listed in Table 5.3, which lists the ISDN switch types available.

Table 5.3 **ISDN Switch Types Available**

Switch	Description
Basic-ts013	Australian TS013 switches
Basic-ltr6	German 1TR6 ISDN switches
Basic-nwnet3	Norway NET3 switches (phase 1)
Basic-net3	NET3 ISDN switches (UK and others)
Primary-net5	European ISDN PRI switches (UK and others)
Vn2	French VN2 switches
Vn3	French VN3 switches
Ntt	Japanese NTT ISDN switches
Primary-ntt	Japanese ISDN PRI switches
Basic–5ess	AT&T basic rate switches
Basic-dms100	Northern Telecom basic rate switches
Basic-nil	National ISDN-1 switches
Primary-4ess	AT&T ISDN switches (PRI only)
Primary-5ess	AT&T ISDN switches (PRI only)
Primary-dms100	Northern Telecom switches (PRI only)
Basic-nznet3	New Zealand Net3 switches

Next, configure the SPID for each B channel on the BRI. The following interface configuration commands are used to configure the SPIDs:

```
isdn spid1 spid-number
isdn spid2 spid-number
```

SPID-number is the number assigned by your ISDN service provider for each B channel on the BRI. They are usually in the form of a ten digit phone number, but might include extra identifying digits.

Configuring a PRI Interface

A channelized T1 controller is required to use a PRI circuit on a Cisco router. The first step in configuring a PRI on a Cisco router is to specify the ISDN switch type. The following global configuration command accomplishes this task:

    isdn switch-type *switch-type*

switch-type is one of the choices listed previously in the BRI configuration section.

    The next step is to configure the actual T1 controller interface. There are three items that need to be configured on a PRI interface before it will become operational:

- Framing type
- Line coding type
- Define which channels of the PRI will be used

Use the following interface configuration command to set the framing type:

    framing esf

Use the following interface configuration command to set the line coding type:

    linecode b8zs

Use the following interface configuration command to set the T1 controller for PRI use:

    pri-group

Listing 5.1 shows a sample configuration of a PRI interface that is used to support remote dial-in users.

Check for Buffers

It is very important to make sure that there are enough buffers available for the BRI interface. If there aren't, the BRI interface will not operate properly.

Listing 5.1   **Sample Configuration for PRI Used for Remote ISDN Callers**

```
isdn switch-type primary-5ess
!
controller T1 4/0
 framing esf
 linecode b8zs
 pri-group timeslots 1-24
!
interface Serial4/0:23
 description PRI for Remote ISDN users
 ip address 192.168.199.1 255.255.255.0
 no ip mroute-cache
 encapsulation ppp
 dialer idle-timeout 1800
 dialer map ip 192.168.199.65 name mtripod speed 56
 dialer hold-queue 100
 dialer load-threshold 100
 dialer-group 1
 no fair-queue
 ppp multilink
 ppp authentication pap chap
```

Dial on Demand

ISDN BRI lines can be used as backup interfaces if the primary interface(s) go down or reach a specified traffic threshold. Several tasks need to be completed in order for an ISDN BRI to be used as backup bandwidth. First, define at what load point the BRI should initiate a call to increase the bandwidth available. The following BRI interface configuration command is used to define the load threshold:

```
dialer load-threshold load [inbound ¦ outbound ¦ either]
```

Load is a number between 0 and 255 representing a percentage of traffic to interface capacity. To determine which number to use, apply your desired percentage to the following formula:

$$\frac{Percentage}{100} = \frac{X}{255}$$

Multiply your desired percentage by 255 and then divide the result of that by 100. For instance, to calculate the value to use for 75% utilization you would do the following math:

$75 \times 255 = 19{,}125$

$19{,}125 / 100 = 191.25$

Round to the nearest whole number and you are left with 191.

A common mistake is to enter the actual percentage value into the load-threshold command. If you were to enter your actual percentage (75%) into the load-threshold command the IOS would interpret it as 29% of link utilization.

Use the `inbound`, `outbound`, or `either` keywords to specify which direction of traffic to use for the threshold calculation. If you specify `inbound` then the backup line will be activated when the inbound traffic on the primary interface reaches the defined threshold. If you specify `outbound` then the backup line will be activated when the outbound traffic on the primary interface reaches the defined threshold. If you specify `either` then the backup line will be activated when the traffic either entering or leaving the primary interface reaches the defined threshold.

The next step is to define the idle time limit before the BRI call is disconnected. The following BRI interface configuration command is used to set the idle time:

dialer idle-timeout *seconds*

Seconds denote any positive nonzero number. The default setting is 120 seconds (two minutes).

Next, the number to dial to establish an ISDN call must be configured. The following BRI interface configuration command is used to map a protocol to a dialer number:

dialer map *protocol protocol-address* **name** *hostname dial-string*

Protocol can be any of the choices listed earlier in the Frame Relay or ATM section. The name/hostname pair is optional. It is used to define a descriptive name to the dialer map. The dial-string is the number to dial in order to connect to the device that is assigned the protocol address defined.

It might be desirable to have an ISDN call initiated only for certain types of data packets. This can be configured through the use of access-lists, dialer-lists and dialer-groups. First, define an access-list to match the type of data you want to initiate an ISDN call. The following example states that neither OSPF nor non-IP packets should initiate a call, but IP packets should.

```
access-list 101 deny ospf 0.0.0.0 255.255.255.255 255.255.255.255 0.0.0.0
access-list 101 perimt ip 0.0.0.0 255.255.255.255 255.255.255.255 0.0.0.0
```

Don't Forget the Catch All

Remember that there is an implicit deny any any at the end of all access-lists defined in the Cisco IOS.

Now that the access–list has been defined, it can be applied to a dialer–list. The following command states that any interfaces in dialer group 1 will initiate calls when packets matching access–list 101 are encountered.

```
dialer-list 1 list 101
```

Now dialer–group 1 must be assigned to the BRI interface. This is done using the following BRI interface configuration command:

```
dialer-group group-number
```

Following our example, the correct command would be

```
dialer-group 1
```

If the ISDN backup call is going to be expensive this feature becomes very handy. Some other options you might want to configure on an ISDN BRI interface are multilink PPP or PPP authentication. These are both enabled via BRI interface configuration commands, such as:

```
ppp multilink
ppp authentication pap
```

DSL

Digital Subscriber Line (DSL) technology is the newest in the list of high-speed data transmission options. DSL uses standard telephone (POTS) wiring to carry data at much higher rates than a traditional modem would be able to on the same wire. This is done by removing the traditional digital to analog conversions that modems do. Instead, DSL modems place data on the wires in their native digital format. This removes the voice transmission limit of 3400Hz that the voice telephone network was built around.

Transmission speeds can vary greatly depending on the service offering from your telco. There are many variations of DSL technology. Each has certain benefits and drawbacks. One thing that all DSL offers have in common is the fact that the termination point for the service must be within 11,000 – 13,000 feet of the telco central office that is servicing your location. The term xDSL is used to describe the many forms that DSL service can take.

Why DSL Works

Because the average human can only hear sounds within the frequency range of 50Hz to 3000Hz, the original phone system was built around a transmission frequency range of 0Hz to 3400Hz. For this reason an analog modem has a maximum transmission speed of 3.4KHz. At this maximum rate compression modems can transmit data at speeds of approximately 50KBps. Because DSL removes the conversion of the data to analog, the full transmission potential of the telephone wire can be used. This enables much higher data transmission speeds.

HDSL

High bit-rate DSL service uses two pairs of telephone wire. HDSL offers the same amount of bandwidth upstream as well as downstream. *Upstream* refers to the transmission of data from the subscribers home/business location to the telco central office. *Downstream* refers to the transmission of data from the telco central office to the subscriber's home/business.

SDSL

Symmetrical DSL (SDSL) services uses one pair of telephone wire. SDSL offers the same amount of bandwidth upstream as well as downstream. SDSL usually offers transmission speeds up to 1.5Mbps. SDSL is basically a single pair version of HDSL.

ADSL/RADSL

Asymmetric DSL (ADSL) is the most popular form of DSL. As the name implies, ADSL offers different transmission speeds for the upstream and downstream channels. Typically, the downstream channel operates at a high transmission speed while the upstream operates at a lower transmission speed. For instance, you might have 1.5Mbps of bandwidth on your downstream channel, but only 128Kbps of bandwidth on your upstream channel. ADSL uses only one pair of telephone wire and can accommodate transmission speeds up to 1.5Mbps.

Rate Adaptive DSL is a twist on ADSL that enables varying transmission speeds. RADSL connects at a certain speed initially and then adjusts the upstream and downstream channels to the highest transmission speeds possible.

VDSL

Very high bit rate DSL offers the highest transmission speeds of all the DSL family. VDSL uses a single pair of telephone wire. The downstream channel has a maximum transmission speed of 52Mbps. The upstream channel has a maximum transmission speed of 2.3Mbps. The drawback to this technology is that you need to be very close to the telco central office, no more that 4500 feet.

IDSL

ISDN-based DSL is simply ISDN services over a traditional ISDN BRI. The two B channels of the BRI are bonded together with the D channel to provide a maximum of 144Kbps of transmission capacity. This version of DSL was developed by Ascend Communications.

DSL Configuration

The configuration of DSL service on Cisco products could be covered in a book by itself. For the purposes of this book we will walk through the configuration of a Cisco 6200 DSL concentrator for a typical subscriber line connection. A subscriber line connection is the service connecting an end user to a DSL router.

The first step is to enable the subscriber line card (SLC) in the DSL router. Using a Cisco 6200 DSL router as an example the command would be as follows:

```
c6200(config)# c6200 card <slot #> <card type>
```

The slot number is the DSL router slot number corresponding to the card that you are enabling in the router. There is only one card type available and that is scl1-8-cap. Here is the command as it would be entered at the command prompt:

```
c6200(config)# c6200 card 5 scl1-8-cap
```

Now that the card is enabled, you can configure the individual ports on that card. This is done as on all the other routers mentioned in this book so far, by entering the interface configuration mode. Select the subscriber line port that you wish to configure and enter interface configuration mode for that port.

```
c6200(config)# interface dsl 5/7
```

At this point, all you really need to do is set the bit rates for both the upstream and downstream connections. The bit rate values that you enter are in kilobits per second.

```
c6200(config-if)# bitrate downstream 1500 upstream 128
```

Once that is complete, you can enable the connection by activating the port.

```
c6200(config-if)# no shutdown
```

The subscriber line connection is now ready for use.

Conclusion

Most of the more widely used WAN protocols have been covered in this chapter. Each protocol was covered in enough depth to get a circuit connected to your router and routing traffic. There are other options available for each interface type. Some options are specific to the region of the world in which the service will be used or might be necessary only in unusual situations. It is always a good idea to review the release notes for the specific version of IOS that you are using to make sure there are no caveats for the technology that you have chosen to implement.

6

Configuring Dynamic Routing Protocols

THIS CHAPTER DISCUSSES SOME OF THE DIFFERENCES between static routing and dynamic routing. The main subject matter discussed here covers some of the different dynamic routing protocols and how they are usually implemented.

With a network that is larger than three routers, it becomes clear that the usefulness of static routes is limited. In order to operate a stable and flexible network, you need a dynamic routing protocol. A *protocol* is one that changes and adapts to changes in the *dynamic routing* network architecture. For instance, in a routing system composed solely of static routes, the routing table stored in the system memory (RAM) of each router does not change. Suppose that there are two links between two routers on a network. The paths to the networks of each individual router are statically configured to go over both links between the two routers. If one of those links should become unavailable, the route still exists in the routing table but the underlying path is gone. This results in the packets being dropped as they are sent to an interface that has no capability to forward packets to the other side of the link. A dynamic routing protocol is aware of the link failure and removes any routes that point to that interface from the route table. This is illustrated in Figure 6.1.

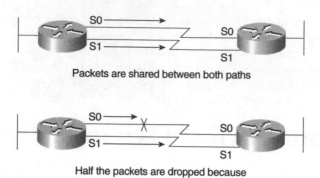

Packets are shared between both paths

Half the packets are dropped because
one link is unavailable

Figure 6.1   Why dynamic routing is needed.

There are several types of dynamic routing protocols that are in wide use today as Interior Gateway Protocols (IGPs). IGPs are used to route within an *autonomous system* (AS). The phrase "autonomous system" is used heavily in this chapter. Outside the context of the IGP routing protocol, an AS is defined as a group of routers that make up one entity. Each AS can be thought of as a separate company. Some of the earlier routing protocols don't conform to the AS model. Protocols such as Routing Information Protocol (RIP) have no way to limit the scope of their network updates except to disable RIP altogether on interfaces that connect to another AS.

The most basic form of dynamic routing employs distance vector protocols. The RIP is the most common distance vector protocol. It is based on "hop-count" which represents the number of routers that must be traversed in order to reach the destination network. Other types of IGPs are based on link states rather than hop count, such as OSPF and IS-IS. These protocols take into account the bandwidth, congestion, or other costs associated with a router to router link when deciding the best path. These other factors are user defined based upon your routing policy. There are also hybrids of these two types of protocols that were developed by Cisco, such as Interior Gateway Routing Protocol (IGRP) and Enchanced Interior Gateway Routing Protocol (EIGRP). A hybrid protocol is one that has characteristics of both distance vector and link state protocols.

Dynamic routing protocols can also be used to route between ASs. The de facto standard for exchanging routing information between ASs is the Border Gateway Protocol (BGP) version 4.

Distance Vector—RIP

RIP is an older but still commonly used distance vector routing protocol. RIP uses broadcast UDP packets to pass routing information. The updates are sent every 30 seconds. If a router does not receive an update for 180 seconds, it marks all routes learned from that neighbor as unusable. If no updates are received for 240 seconds, all route entries learned from that neighbor are removed from the routing table. If a router receives an update for a route from the router that originally reported the route, the route is placed in a hold-down state. The route can remain in a hold-down state for a maximum of four times the update interval.

The only metric that RIP uses to determine the best path to a network is hop count. The hop count for each reachable network in the routing table is limited to 15. A directly connected network has a hop count of 0 and an unreachable network has a hop count of 16. The single metric for RIP makes it almost unusable for large networks. One advantage to a protocol based solely on hop count is that it is very quick to converge. There is not a lot processing required for network updates. A disadvantage is that the shortest path to a destination network might not be the best. If one of the links along the short path is a 56Kbps leased line, and the longer path consists of all DS1 leased lines, then the limited bandwidth available on the best path makes it less desirable than the longer path.

Because RIP broadcasts all routing information on all RIP enabled interfaces, it is very likely that the router that originated the route to a network will receive the route announcement from another router in the network that had originally learned the route from the originating router. This in effect makes the originating router think that the route for the network that it originated is through another router. So instead of sending packets destined for the directly connected network to that interface, the originating router sends the packets to the other router in the network from which it thinks it learned the route. Because of this, routing loops are common in distance vector routing systems. There are several features available in RIP to prevent routing loops between two routers.

Split Horizon

Routing loops would be very common in a RIP network if not for the use of split horizons. *Split horizons* basically prevent the routing system from sending route updates to interfaces from which the original routing information was received. Split horizon's functionality is built into the RIP protocol.

Poison Reverse

Poison reverse can be used in addition to split horizons to prevent routing loops between two routers. The basic idea behind poison reverse is to send a route update back to the sender stating that the network is unreachable via this interface. Poison reverse sends a network update back to the interface it was received from with a metric of 16 (unreachable). This ensures that the originating router will never try to send traffic destined for a directly connected network to another router. This procedure makes for faster convergence but has a price. It also increases the network traffic and the size of the routing table.

Routing loops between three or more routers are still possible. This can only be combated by the hop count metric. This is often referred to as "count to infinity." Packets will loop for 15 hops and then die.

Configuring RIP

Configuring RIP on a Cisco router is very simple. The only tasks that are required are to enable the routing process and define which interfaces on the router will send and receive RIP updates.

The command to enable the RIP routing process on a Cisco router is

```
router rip
```

Next, enter network statements for each interface that will be included in the RIP routing system:

```
network <network address>
```

The *network address* is the network number for the IP address of the interface to be included in the RIP routing system. Because RIP is a classful routing protocol, no subnet mask can be defined. A classful protocol is one that stores routes in its routing table based on the original IP address class assignments. IP addresses with the first octet in the range of 1-126 are assigned to class A. IP addresses with the first octet in the range of 128-191 are assigned to class B. IP addresses with the first octet in the range of 192-223 are assigned to class C. All other addresses are either used for multicast or are reserved for special uses.

Because RIP relies on UDP broadcasts to exchange routing updates, specific neighbor addresses must be defined when RIP is run on a nonbroadcast multi-access (NBMA) network. Some examples of a NBMA network are frame relay, SMDS and X.25. The syntax for defining a neighbor is

```
neighbor <ip address>
```

RIP Version 2

RIP version 2 supports Classless Inter-Domain Routing (CIDR), route summarization, and Variable Length Subnet Masks (VLSM). By default, when RIP is enabled on a Cisco router, it will accept both version 1 and version 2 updates. In order for the router to send version 2 packets it must be explicitly enabled. This is done within the RIP process configuration. The command syntax to enable RIP version 2 is

```
router rip
        version 2
        network
        network
```

Link State—OSPF

The next evolution of the dynamic routing protocol was a protocol based on link states rather than hop count. Open Shortest Path First (OSPF) is an example of a link state protocol.

The OSPF routing protocol was developed specifically with IP networks in mind. Because OSPF is based on link states (the availability of links connecting routers together) rather than hop count, there is no count to infinity problem (as there are in distance vector routing protocols). OSPF transmits no update packets unless a link state change has occurred or 30 minutes have gone by since the last Link State Advertisement (LSA). OSPF uses LSAs to communicate the availability of directly connected interfaces from one router to another. There are five types of LSAs described in RFC2328. Table 6.1 gives a brief description of each type as well as the LSA extensions that have been added.

Table 6.1   **OSPF LSA Types**

LSA Type	Description
Type 1 (Router LSA)	Propagate information about the connected interfaces on a router.
Type 2 (Network LSA)	Propagate information about the routers connected to each network.
Type 3 (Summary LSA)	Propagate information about inter-area routes. These enable route summarization when originated from an area border router (ABR). Type 3 LSAs contain information about networks.
Type 4 (Summary LSA)	Propagate information about inter-area routes. These enable route summarization. Type 4 LSAs contain information about routes to area boundary routers.
Type 5 (External LSA)	Propagate information about routes external to the OSPF autonomous system. These are originated by the AS boundary routers. Redistributed static routes are carried at LSA Type 5.
Type 6 (MOSPF LSA)	Multicast extension. Used to enable OSPF to carry information about multicast networks. Cisco does not support this LSA type.
Type 7 (NSSA LSA)	Not So Stubby Area LSA is basically the same as the Type 5 LSA. There are two small differences, Type 7 LSAs can only be originated within NSSA and are not flooded into other areas.

OSPF supports CIDR, route summarization, and redistribution from and to other routing processes. It also provides the capability to segregate portions of the network into areas.

The Cisco implementation of OSPF assigns a metric to each interface type. This metric is based upon the bandwidth of the interface and is used in the best path calculation before a network entry is placed in the routing table. The metric is determined by dividing a reference bandwidth value by the actual bandwidth value of the interface. The reference bandwidth value defaults to the numeral represented by 10^8. Table 6.2 shows the OSPF metric values for each of the more commonly used interface types.

Table 6.2   **Default OSPF Interface Metrics**

Interface Type	Default OSPF Metric
OC48	1
Gigabit Ethernet	1
OC12	1
OC3	1
FDDI	1
Fast Ethernet	1
DS3	2
DS1	64
64K	1562

As you can see, the calculation worked well until the wide spread deployment of high-speed technologies. To make the automatic metric calculation feature of OSPF usable on a high-speed network, Cisco enables the modification of the reference bandwidth value. The following router configuration command is used to change the bandwidth reference value for OSPF metric calculation:

```
router(config-router)# opsf auto-cost reference-bandwidth <ref-bw>
```

If you were to increase the reference bandwidth to 10^{12}, then the OSPF metrics that the Cisco IOS would calculate would be much more useful. Table 6.3 shows the same interface types but with OSPF metrics updated to reflect the reference bandwidth change to 10^{12}.

Table 6.3   **Modified OSPF Interface Metrics**

Interface Type	Default OSPF Metric
OC48	402
Gigabit Ethernet	1,000
OC12	1,608
OC3	6,452
FDDI	10,000
Fast Ethernet	10,000

Interface Type	Default OSPF Metric
DS3	22,222
DS1	647,668
64K	15,625,000

This example works well for high-speed networks. If you have a combination of medium to low-speed links and high-speed links, you might wish to use a reference bandwidth value a little lower than 10^{12} but higher than 10^8.

Another way to control the OSPF metric calculation is to explicitly define the interface bandwidth value for individual interfaces on your router(s). This can be done with the following interface configuration command:

```
router(config-int)# bandwidth <bandwidth>
```

If you do not want to rely on the IOS to determine the OSPF interface metrics for you, there is a command that enables you to specifically set the link costs on a per interface basis. The interface configuration command is

```
router(config-int)# ip ospf cost <cost>
```

It is not a good idea to mix and match the two types of metric calculations. If you configure one interface with a specific cost, you should configure all the interfaces in your OSPF system with relative costs.

Process IDs

The Cisco IOS supports multiple OSPF processes on a single router. This is most often used when a router is on the edge of two different OSPF areas. It participates in one area using one process ID, and in the other area using a different ID. Normally, you would also tell it to summarize one area's routes for advertisement into the other area, but this is not a requirement. It can also be used to limit the number of routes that are propagated from one area into another or when special route summarization is required. Your company would want to use OSPF in this way to safeguard against mis-configurations at the edge of your network propagating invalid LSAs throughout your network. Another reason would be to advertise only aggregate summary netblocks into your backbone area rather than numerous individual subnets. The process ID on a Cisco router can be either a positive decimal number or a dotted decimal number similar to an IP address.

The command to enable an OSPF routing process on a Cisco router is

```
router ospf <process id>
```

For example, to create an OSPF routing process with an ID of 10 you could use

```
router(config)# router ospf 10
```

or

```
router(config)# router ospf 10.0.0.0
```

Areas

OSPF supports the segmenting of networks into *areas*. Each area can act as an autonomous system within the larger OSPF network. By separating a network into multiple areas, the propagation of link state advertisements can be controlled and localized to specific geographic regions or functional departments, such as engineering or marketing. All OSPF networks have a backbone area, area 0. Every other area configured must connect to the backbone area. The routers that connect the backbone area to another defined area are called *area border routers (ABRs)*. A router that connects an OSPF area to an external routing source is called an *autonomous system border router (ASBR)*. A sample basic OSPF network diagram is shown in Figure 6.2.

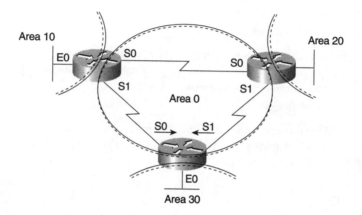

Figure 6.2   Basic OSPF network layout.

Areas are defined by placing individual interfaces on a router into that area using the IP network assigned to each individual interface. In order for an interface to be put into an OSPF area, it must have an IP address defined. The following example places the interface Serial0/0 into the backbone area, interface Ethernet0/0 into area 10, and interface Ethernet0/1 into area 20:

```
interface Serial0/0
description WAN link to Corporate
ip address 192.168.10.1 255.255.255.252
!
interface Ethernet0/0
description Marketing LAN Segment
ip address 192.168.20.1 255.255.255.0
!
interface Ethernet0/1
description R&D LAN Segment
ip address 192.168.21.1 255.255.255.0
!
router ospf 1000
network 192.168.10.0 0.0.0.3 area 0
network 192.168.20.0 0.0.0.255 area 10
network 192.168.21.0 0.0.0.255 area 20
```

Another OSPF configuration option that helps limit the need for future configuration changes is the use of the 0.0.0.0 network in area definition. If you know that all interfaces on a router are going to be in OSPF area 100, then you can use the following command in the OSPF configuration:

```
network 0.0.0.0 255.255.255.255 area 100
```

Use of this form of the configuration commands can be dangerous. It should be used in conjunction with the `passive-interface` command (if it is ever used at all). The `passive-interface` OSPF configuration command tells the Cisco IOS not to send OSPF updates on certain router interfaces even if the IP address of that interface is included in an OSPF network statement. The following command removes interface Serial5/1/0 from OSPF:

```
router(config)# router ospf 10.0.0.0
router(config-router)# passive-interface Serial5/1/0
```

The `passive-interface` command can also be used to remove a link from OSPF during debugging. This is particularly useful when a WAN link becomes unstable. Constant flapping of an interface between the up and down states can cause the generation of an enormous number for LSAs. The CPU load on routers can increase dramatically because of all the LSA processing. This can have a serious impact on your network stability if you are using routers with smaller CPUs and memory sizes.

Cisco has implemented several other features of the OSPF specification that enable you to control the behavior of the LSA communications. All the commands listed in Table 6.4 are interface configuration commands. This means you need to configure them for each interface in your OSPF system. It is very important that you configure the same time intervals on every OSPF interface if you decide that changing the default value is warranted.

Moving Interfaces Between Processes

During network growth it is sometimes necessary to move an interface on a router from one area to another. In earlier releases of the Cisco IOS, area and process changes were not allowed in order to maintain the integrity of the OSPF database in memory. Cisco has overcome this hurdle since the release of IOS 11.0. However, the router might still need to be reloaded for the change to take effect. I have run into situations, especially when moving an interface from one OSPF process to another, where this action was required. Another option is to remove the OSPF process completely and reconfigure it. This can be dangerous because if OSPF is your IGP, you might lose connectivity to the router if you are configuring from a VTY session.

Table 6.4   **OSPF Timer Modification Commands**

Cisco Interface Configuration Command	Description
command>>ip ospf retransmit-interval <seconds>	Set the number of seconds between LSA retransmissions.
command>>ip ospf hello-interval <seconds>	Set the number of seconds between OSPF hello packet transmissions.
command>>ip ospf dead-interval <seconds>	Set the number of seconds that must elapse between LSA hello packets before a router is declared dead.

The natural behavior of OSPF is to flood LSAs to all interfaces in the same area except the interface from which the LSA was learned. In a fully meshed network, this can cause destabilization of your network due to a massive number of duplicate LSAs being processed by your routers. One way to reduce the number of LSAs being processed is to limit the broadcast of LSAs to certain interfaces or neighbors. The Cisco IOS offers two commands to accomplish this task. Which one you use depends on the medium that your OSPF network is deployed on. On broadcast, non-broadcast, and point to point networks, you would use the following interface configuration command:

```
router(config-int)# ospf database-filter all out
```

On point to multipoint networks you would use the following OSPF router configuration command:

```
router(config-router)# neighbor <ip address> database-filter all out
```

If security is a concern, there are a couple OSPF communication authentication options available within the Cisco IOS. The first authentication type uses a simple password to verify that the OSPF updates a router receives come from an authorized host. The router configuration command used to enable this authentication scheme is

```
router(config-router)# area <area id> authentication
```

The second authentication type uses MD5 encryption of the password so that if an intruder were to intercept an OSPF hello packet, they would not be able to retrieve the password. The router configuration command used to enable MD5 authentication is

```
router(config-router)# area <area id> authentication message-digest
```

Virtual Links

A group of routers can be defined as an area without a physical connection to the backbone area. In this case, a virtual link must be created from an ABR in the area to an ABR in the backbone area. Both ABRs must have an area in common that will be used as the transit area. The virtual link must be configured on both ABRs. The following command must be entered in the OSPF process configuration to configure the virtual link:

```
router(config-router)# area area-id virtual-link router-id
```

In this command, `area-id` is the area number that will be used for transit between the two ABRs. The `router-id` is the ID of the ABR that the virtual link terminates on as shown in the `show ip ospf neighbor` command. This is usually the IP address of the interface that extends into the transit area or an IP address of a loopback interface if it is so configured on the router. Use the following command to display the current status of OSPF virtual links configured on your router:

```
router# show ip ospf virtual-links
```

Stub Areas

An area that has only one ABR can be defined as a *stub area*. This is to say that any area that has only one link to the backbone can be configured as a stub area. An ABR that connects a stub area to the backbone area does not advertise external routes into the stub area. Instead, it advertises a single default route. Because there are no individual destination advertisements, CPU, memory, and network bandwidth are saved. Figure 6.3 shows a basic stub area.

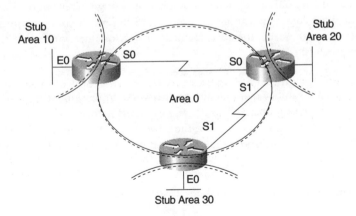

Figure 6.3 OSPF stub area.

All routers contained in a stub area must have the following command in the OSPF process configuration:

```
area <area id> stub [no summary]
```

Because stub areas do not enable their ABRs to advertise external route information, it is usually not possible to place an ASBR in a stub area. You can also reduce the number of LSAs sent into a stub area by adding the *no summary* option to the stub area configuration command. This prevents summary LSAs from being broadcast into stub areas. I say *usually* because with Cisco IOS 11.3 the definition of Not So Stubby Areas is possible.

Not So Stubby Areas

Not So Stubby Areas (NSSA) are similar to stub areas in that they do not enable the propagation of external LSAs. NSSAs do enable the ABRs to translate Type 7 Link State Advertisements (LSAs) into Type 5 LSAs. This in effect creates the capability to have AS external routes imported into the NSSA. Type 5 LSAs are flooded to the rest of the OSPF network by the NSSA ABRs. This enables the propagation of external AS routes from an ASBR within a stub area to the entire OSPF network.

The router configuration command that you would use to configure a NSSA is

```
router(config-router)# area <area id> nssa
```

Route Summarization

Summarization of network advertisements is essential for maintaining an efficient and stable routing system. OSPF enables the summarization of network advertisements between areas. If (and only if) there are a number of contiguous networks within an area, the following command can be used in the OSPF process configuration on the ABRs for that area to enable the advertisement of only one network rather that all its smaller components:

```
router(config-router)# area area-id range address mask
```

area-id is the area number that contains the networks to be summarized. *address* is the IP network of the summarized route. *mask* is the IP netmask of the summary advertisement. For example, to configure the advertisement of 192.168.10.0/24 for area 10, the following command would be placed in the ABR for area 10:

```
router(config-router)# area 10 range 192.168.10.0 255.255.255.0
```

OSPF LSA Types

Don't be concerned with the difference between the various LSA types. The main point of this section is to illustrate that there is a way to propagate external route information through a stub area.

External routes being distributed into OSPF can also be summarized. This command accomplishes the task of summarizing redistributed routes:

```
router(config-router)# summary-address address mask
```

For instance, the following example generates only one LSA for all four of the static routes being redistributed into the OSPF process:

```
Router ospf 1000
redistribute static subnets
summary-address 192.168.50.0 255.255.255.0
network 192.168.10.0 0.0.0.3 area 0
network 192.168.10.0 0.0.0.255 area 100
!
ip route 192.168.50.0 255.255.255.192 192.168.90.2
ip route 192.168.50.64 255.255.255.192 192.168.100.2
ip route 192.168.50.128 255.255.255.192 192.168.110.2
ip route 192.168.50.192 255.255.255.192 192.168.111.2
```

OSPF supports a maximum of four paths to a network by default. The limit can be increased to six by using the following command in OSPF process configuration:

```
Maximum-paths <1-6>
```

Hybrid—EIGRP

The Enhanced Interior Gateway Routing Protocol (EIGRP) was developed by Cisco as an extension of its IGRP protocol. IGRP is a distance vector protocol similar to RIP, but with more metrics and faster convergence along with CIDR support, VLSM, and automatic route summarization. EIGRP is called a hybrid protocol because is uses metrics from both distance vector protocols and link state protocols.

Configuration of EIGRP on a Cisco router is similar to enabling other routing processes. All that needs to be done to start EIGRP on a Cisco router is to define an EIGRP routing process.

Process IDs

The command to define an EIGRP routing process on a Cisco router is

```
router eigrp <autonomous system number>
```

Once the EIGRP process has been defined, network statements need to be added for the ports on the router that will send and receive EIGRP updates. The following command is used to add ports to the EIGRP process:

```
network <IP network number>
```

Variance

EIGRP enables the use of multiple unequal cost paths to reach a destination network. This type of load balancing makes for better use of available bandwidth. An alternate route to a destination network will be used only if its metrics are within a predefined variance. An alternate route is feasible if the next router in the path is closer to the destination (has a lower metric value) than the current router and if the metric for the entire alternate path is within the variance.

Variance is used as a multiplier to the local best route. If the alternate route to a destination network is equal to or lower than the metric of the local best path times the variance, it is a viable path to the network. To configure the variance multiplier, use the following command in EIGRP process configuration:

```
variance <multiplier>
```

Figure 6.4 shows a group of routers running EIGRP as the internal routing protocol. Router R1 has three possible paths to reach the network 192.168.235.0/24. The default EIGRP configuration parameters only allow all three paths into the routing table if the metric cost of each path are equal. By adjusting the variance, you can force unequal cost paths to be allowed into the routing table. The variance for this example has been set to 2 (rather than the default of 1). The lowest cost path is path B. With the variance set to 3, any path that has a metric of 2 × 100 (the metric for path B) or lower is allowed in the route table. Because the metric cost for path A is 275, it is not added to the route table as a possible path to 192.168.235.0/24 from router R1. However, because the metric for path C is 125, path C is entered into the route table as a valid path to the 192.168.235.0/24 network from router R1.

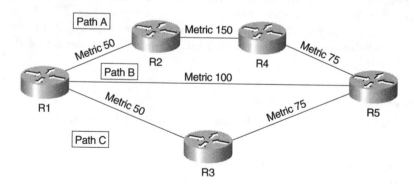

Figure 6.4 Variance use in EIGRP path selection.

EIGRP supports a maximum of four paths to a destination network. Because EIGRP is a Cisco proprietary protocol, it can be used only between Cisco routers.

External Routing—BGP

The Border Gateway Protocol (BGP) was developed to provide a way to exchange network reachability information between ASs. The main reason BGP is used today to pass network information between autonomous systems is because it enables Network Operators to implement a routing policy.

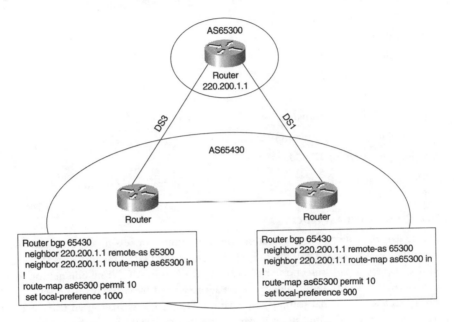

Figure 6.5   Implementing a simple BGP policy.

Who Determines Policies?

People define routing policies. You make certain choices about how you would like to route traffic between your network and other networks that you interconnect with. BGP enables you to program your routers to select paths to other networks based upon criteria that you establish before you begin BGP peering with other autonomous systems.

Suppose that you connect to the same AS at two separate locations in your network. One connection is a DS3 whereas the other is a DS1. You would naturally prefer to send the majority of your traffic to your peer via the DS3 connection rather than the DS1 connection. Because BGP has no knowledge of the bandwidth of the connections in your network, you must tell the routers that you would prefer to route traffic to the networks that you learn from that peer over the DS3 rather than the DS1.

This preference, or policy, can be applied to the routes you learn from the peer on the router that the BGP peering session is configured on. Using a route-map to set the local preference, you implement your policy in your autonomous system (see Figure 6.5). By setting the local preference higher on the routes that are learned from the peer on the router that the DS3 terminates on, rather than the routes learned from the peer on the router that the DS1 terminates on, you make the DS3 the preferred path to the peer.

Manual configuration of your routers enables you, the Network Operator, to decide how network information will be treated inside your autonomous system. Routing policies are implemented through the use of local preferences, Multi-Exit Discriminators (MEDs), and administrative weights, among other things. Cisco's implementation of BGP version 4 uses a somewhat standard checklist for BGP path determination. BGP path selection is based upon the following criteria:

- Administrative weight
- Local preference
- Locally originated route
- AS path length
- Origin code
- Multi-Exit Discriminator
- Closest BGP neighbor (IGP metric)
- Lowest neighbor IP address

Each of these steps is described in more detail in the following section.

Path Selection Criteria

Because it is possible to have several options for getting packets to a specific destination network, how does BGP choose which path is the best? The answer is it doesn't: you do. There is a path selection criteria built into Cisco's BGP implementation, but many of the steps rely upon values that are administered by you. This is why BGP is used to exchange external routing information. How packets are routed from your network to another is based in large part by the policies that you configure.

If there are multiple paths to a destination network, the path with the highest administrative weight is preferred. If the administrative weight for all paths is equal, then the path with the highest local preference is preferred. If all paths have the same local preference, then routes that are originated locally are preferred (it is assumed that you know how to get to a local network better than an external party does). If none of the paths were originated locally, then the path with the shortest AS list is preferred. (The AS list is a list of ASs that the packet must travel through before reaching the destination network.) If all AS path lengths are the same, then the path with the lowest origin code is preferred. The *origin code* is a stamp on the network specifying how the route was originated, either via an IGP, EPG, or incomplete if unknown. If all origin codes are the same, then the path with the lowest MED is preferred. The default behavior of BGP is to compare MEDs on routes learned from the same ASN only. Because different providers have different methodologies for setting their MED values, it is a fairly safe bet that the MEDs received for the same network from two different peers will not be comparable.

The Cisco IOS enables you to override this default behavior with the `always-compare-meds` BGP command. This option is set in the BGP router configuration mode. It is generally considered not a good practice to set this option. More often than not, the MEDs that you receive from different peers have no meaning. One provider might use his internal IGP metrics as his MED while another peer might use arbitrary values between 1000 and 50000 as his MEDs. If all paths have the same MED, then the closest neighbor is preferred. The closest neighbor is defined as the one with the lowest IGP metric. When all else fails, the path through the neighbor with the lowest ID is chosen. The neighbor ID is the IP address that the BGP session is established with.

For example, examine the output from the `show ip bgp <network>` command for network 4.0.0.0/8 taken from a router attached to the Global Internet (Listing 6.1).

Listing 6.1 **Output from *show ip bgp* Command**

```
test-r1#show ip bgp 4.0.0.0
BGP routing table entry for 4.0.0.0/8, version 803822
Paths: (2 available, best #1)
  1
    192.168.220.41 (metric 10) from 192.168.220.41
      Origin IGP, metric 0, localpref 1000, valid, internal, best
  1
    192.168.220.106 (metric 20) from 192.168.220.106
      Origin IGP, metric 5 (not lowest), localpref 1000, valid, internal
test-r1#
```

The first step in the BGP path selection criteria is to check the administrative weight. The output in listing 6.1 says nothing about the weight value of the network entries. The reason for this is the administrative weight was not set for routes learned from the peer with ASN1. If the administrative weight had been set it would be displayed directly after the local preference value. Because the administrative weight was not set, it defaults to the value of 0.

Because both entries for the network have an equal administrative weight, we move to the next step in the path selection criteria, local preference. The output in listing 6.1 shows that the local preference value for both network entries is 1000.

Because both entries have an equal local preference value, we move to the next step in the path selection criteria, local origination. Neither of the network entries were sourced locally. If they had been, that fact would be displayed in the output in place of the `internal` keyword. The output would say something like:

```
Local
  0.0.0.0
    Origin IGP, metric 0, localpref 100, weight 32768, valid, sourced, local
```

Because neither entry was sourced locally, we check the `AS_PATH` length. There is only one ASN in the `AS_PATH` so the length is equal for both entries.

Now we look to the route origin code to break the tie. Both entries were generated by an IGP. Both entries are still equal so we move on to the multi-exit discriminator. Because the first entry has a MED of 0, which is lower than the MED of 5 on the second entry, the first entry is tagged as the best route.

Very rarely does the BGP path selection get beyond this point. The only real instance when it would be necessary is if you have multiple links between ASs on the same router. Then you would want to use some other means to promote load balancing across the multiple links because the link with the lowest IP address would always be preferred. This would cause all traffic to flow over one link while the others sat idle.

EBGP

External BGP (EBGP) is the default form of the protocol. The original design intent for the protocol was to enable the exchange of network reachability information between ASs. The use of EBGP enables you to tell other peer networks how to reach IP netblocks that are in your networ.

A BGP session must be configured on both routers participating in the peering session. Because autonomous systems are generally thought to be equal peers (in theory at least), the exchange of routing information between two ASs is called a *peering session*. The configuration of a BGP routing process is similar to the other routing protocols available on a Cisco router. Each router may have only one BGP process defined at one time. The reason for this limitation is that the BGP process ID is the AS number for that router. It is not possible for a router to exist in two different ASs at the same time.

Loopback Peering

One method to load balance across multiple links is to peer with an IP address behind the next hop router, usually the IP address of a loopback interface. This way, the IGP takes care of load balancing across however many paths exist to reach that loopback IP address. In this configuration scenario, there is only one BGP peering session configured on the router.

Another option is to use the Cisco `maximum-paths` command in BGP configuration mode. This configuration requires that there be multiple BGP peering sessions to the same AS on the router, one peering session for each link to the peer router. This command enables the BGP routing process to take into account the fact that there are multiple paths to the destination networks learned from the multiple peering sessions.

Changing the Configured BGP AS

In order to change the AS configured on a Cisco router, the change must be made in the startup configuration and the router must be reloaded.

BGP enables many of the features that we have covered in the IGP sections, most importantly route summarization and aggregation.

Configuring BGP on a Cisco Router

To add a Cisco router into a BGP autonomous system, the BGP routing protocol must be enabled on the router. You do this by defining a process ID for BGP on the router. The process ID is the ASN for your particular company. The Internet Assigned Numbers Authority (IANA) assigns ASNs. The following command enables the BGP routing protocol for AS 65400:

```
router bgp 65400
```

The main purpose for using BGP is to exchange network reachability information with other ASs. In order for your AS to announce the reachability of your networks to your peer ASs, the networks must be configured in your BGP process. The following command defines a network for announcement via BGP:

```
network 192.168.0.0 255.255.0.0
```

In order for this network to be announced via BGP, there must be an underlying path for it in the routing table. This underlying path can be provided by your IGP or a static route. Usually a static route to the Cisco Null0 interface is used as an anchor route. The term *anchor* is used because the static route never changes; hence, it never leaves the routing table. The BGP announcement will always occur because the IGP route is "anchored" in the routing table. The following command is used to define an anchor route for the network used in the last example:

```
ip route 192.168.0.0 255.255.0.0 Null0 254
```

This is done to reduce the occurrence of route flapping due to IGP instability. The static route is tagged with an administrative weight of 254 so that it is the least preferred route in the routing table (because all packets forwarded according to this static route are dropped). The term *tag* is used a great deal in discussions that are centered on IP routing. Adding an attribute to a route before it is processed or entered into the routing table on a router is called *tagging*.

BGP has a dampening feature that ignores a network if it is flapped (announced and then withdrawn) a predetermined number of times. By default, each time a route is withdrawn it is increased by a penalty of 750. If the penalty for a route exceeds 2000 it is dampened. If a dampened route is stable for 15 minutes straight, the penalty for that route is reduced by half. Once the penalty for a route drops below 750, it is removed from the dampened list and entered back into the route table. The dampening behavior can be altered using the following router configuration command:

bgp dampening *<half-life> <reuse> <suppress> <max-suppress-time>*

- *Half-life*   Time in minutes after which the penalty for a dampened route is decreased; the default is 15 minutes. Possible values are 1-45.
- *Reuse*   Penalty value that a dampened route must drop below in order to be removed from the dampened list; the default is 750. Possible values are 1-20000.

- *Suppress*   Penalty value that a route must reach in order to be placed on the dampened list; the default is 2000. Possible values are 1–20000.

- *Max-suppress-time*   Maximum time in minutes that a dampened route is allowed to be suppressed; the default is four times the half-life. Possible values are 1–20000.

Neighbors (Peers)

To define another router as a BGP peer, you must specify the directly connected interface IP address as a neighbor. The following command does this:

```
neighbor 192.168.100.5 remote-as 65500
```

If the IP address of the neighbor is not a directly connected network, Cisco provides a feature called `ebgp-multihop` that enables the neighbor address to be any IP address as long as there is a path to it in the routing table. The format for the command is as follows:

```
neighbor 192.168.100.5 ebgp-multihop 255
```

The last number in the command is the maximum hop count to reach the specified neighbor. It can be a number between 1 and 255.

Distribute-Lists

Distribute-lists are used to filter the BGP network information coming in from a peer or going out to a peer. Distribute-lists use basic IP access-lists. (IP access-lists are discussed in Chapter 8, "Access and Traffic Management.")

The format for the command is as follows:

```
neighbor 192.168.100.5 distribute-list 5 in
```

This command tells the router to pass all network information received from the peer at the IP address of 192.168.100.5 through the standard access-list 5. This type of distribute-list is useful to safeguard your network from configuration errors in your peer networks. For example, access-list 5 could be

```
access-list 5 deny 10.0.0.0 0.255.255.255
access-list 5 deny 172.16.0.0 0.15.255.255
access-list 5 deny 192.168.0.0 0.0.255.255
access-list 5 permit any any
```

This access-list prohibits the propagation of the reserved IP networks.

Multi-hop and Loopback Peering

The `ebgp-multihop` command must be used if you are configuring peering to a loopback interface address.

Prefix-Lists

Prefix-lists act the same as distribute-lists. There are a couple of major benefits of using prefix-lists over distribute-lists.

One benefit is that prefix-lists are configured by name rather than number. This makes for a much more understandable configuration. An added enrichment to having prefix-lists use names rather than numbers is that more of them can be configured.

The second helpful feature of prefix-lists is the syntax of the command. It uses bit-mask lengths rather than actual subnet masks. The syntax for the `prefix-list` definition is

```
ip prefix-list <name> seq <sequence number> <permit¦deny> <ip prefix>
```

Here is a sample `prefix-list` definition:

```
ip prefix-list Sample seq 5 permit 192.168.62.64/26
ip prefix-list Sample seq 10 permit 192.168.62.16/28
```

The assignment of a prefix-list to a BGP neighbor is identical to that of a distribute-list:

```
neighbor <ip address> prefix-list <name> <in¦out>
```

Filter-Lists

Filter-lists work in the same way as distribute-lists except that they filter based on AS path rather than IP networks. AS path filters are discussed in Chapter 8, "Access and Traffic Management."

The following command enables AS path filtering for the BGP neighbor with IP address 192.168.100.5:

```
neighbor 192.168.100.5 filter-list 10 out
```

This can be useful to prevent the propagation of reserved autonomous system numbers (ASNs). For instance, as-path access-list 10 would take the following form to accomplish this task:

```
as-path access-list 10 permit _64511_
as-path access-list 10 deny _6[45]5[123456789][123456789]_
as-path access-list 10 permit .*
```

The regular expression syntax follows the same methodology as the UNIX regex handlers. The same wildcard characters can be used to represent groups of digits that you need to match.

- * matches 0 or more of the preceding character
- . matches any character
- ^ matches the beginning of the string
- $ mathes the end of a string
- _ matches whitespace

Brackets can be used to group a series of possible characters to match, as was shown in the preceding example. The local ASN is defined as `^$` in the regular expression notation.

Suppose you want to match the AS_PATH of 701 3967 11555; you can use either of the following commands:

```
permit ^701_3967_11555$
permit ^701 3967 11555$
```

The same regular expression rules that are used in defining AS_PATH access-lists are used in conjunction with the `show ip bgp regex` command. This command enables you to display information from the BGP route table based upon AS_PATH information that you specify. For instance, to display all networks being advertised by the ASN 7260 behind the ASN 701 you would use the `show ip bgp regex ^701_7260` command.

Route-maps

Route-maps are the key to implementing policy with BGP. Route-maps are used to define catches for BGP network announcements and then set certain conditions based on those catches. Route-maps can be defined with multiple steps so that multiple metrics can be set for multiple match conditions. The format for a `route-map` definition is as follows:

```
route-map <route-map name> {permit¦deny} <sequence number>
```

The `route-map` name is the user-defined name that the route-map will be referenced by at other places in the configuration. The `permit` or `deny` keywords are optional. If permit is specified, then any routes not matching the criteria defined within that route-map sequence are passed to the next sequence route-map with the same name. If the `deny` keyword is defined, no further checking of the defined route-map sequences occurs. The `sequence number` is a positive decimal. If neither `permit` nor deny is specified in the route-map definition, then `permit` is assumed.

Within the route-map sequence definition there are several metric types that can be matched upon to enable policy definition. Some of these are as-path, BGP community, propagation interface, ip address, as well as next hop address. Listing 6.2 shows the specific commands used to match these criteria.

Listing 6.2   **BGP Route-map *match* Criteria**

```
match as-path <as-path access-list number>
match community <community list number>
match interface <interface type interface number>
match ip address <ip access-list number>
match ip next-hop <ip access-list number>
```

After matching the defined criteria, there are several options available to set metrics on the route announcements. Some of these are as-path, community, interface, next hop, local preference, and metric. Listing 6.3 lists the specific commands used to set these policy implementation values.

Listing 6.3   **BGP Route-map** *set* **Commands**

```
set as-path prepend <as-path-string>
set community <community number>
set interface <interface type interface number>
set ip next-hop <ip address>
set local-preference <local preference>
set metric <metric>
```

For example, let's say that all BGP route announcements from the peer with IP address 192.168.200.10 should have the local preference set to 1000. Also, we do not want to allow a default route to enter or leave our network via this peer. Additionally, this peer should only receive BGP networks originating from AS65435. This could be accomplished with the following configuration:

```
Router bgp 65435
  neighbor 192.168.200.10 remote-as 65530
  neighbor 192.168.200.10 distribute-list 1 in
  neighbor 192.168.200.10 distribute-list 1 out
  neighbor 192.168.200.10 route-map lp1000 in
  neighbor 192.168.200.10 filter-list 1 out
!
access-list 1 deny 0.0.0.0
access-list 1 permit any
!
ip as-path access-list 1 permit ^$
!
route-map lp1000 permit 10
  set local-preference 1000
```

Peer Groups

Cisco provides the capability to apply a set of BGP neighbor configuration commands to multiple peers. BGP neighbors that share these common commands are called peer groups. The first step in configuring a peer group on a Cisco router is to define the group and establish which BGP neighbor commands each member of the group will inherit. The following configuration shows a sample peer group definition:

```
router bgp 65435
  neighbor mae-east-peers peer-group
  neighbor mae-east-peers distribute-list 1 in
  neighbor mae-east-peers distribute-list 1 out
  neighbor mae-east-peers filter-list 1 out
  neighbor mae-east-peers route-map mae-east out
  neighbor 192.41.177.9 remote-as 3320
  neighbor 192.41.177.9 peer-group mae-east-peers
!
```

Peer groups make configuration of new peers fast and simple. The only step required to enable a new peering session once a peer group has been defined is to define the peers neighbor address and ASN. You can override certain portions of a peer groups definition with specific neighbor commands. If a neighbor is part of a peer group and you decide that you want a special filter-list for that one peer, you can use the `neighbor <address> filter-list` command to supersede any filter-list that was defined for the peer group.

Peer groups are also special in that the processing of routing information is handled a little bit differently. Instead of the router having to process update information for each individual BGP peer, it can process the update once for the peer group and then propagate the information to each neighbor in the peer group. This can reduce the load on the route processor a great deal when you have a large number of peers configured.

Communities

One of the BGP attributes passed between peers when they exchange network reachability information is the *community attribute*. A *community* is a numeric value between 1 and 4294967200 inclusive. Recently, Cisco integrated support for a new community format into their IOS. This new format is a pair of decimal numbers separated by a colon. For instance, you could tag a BGP network with the community 10, or you could tag it with the community 0:10. Internally, the community attribute is stored the same way. The colon notation is converted to a decimal number within the aforementioned range. Support for the colon community notation must be enabled. The `bgp new-format` router configuration command is used to do this. The community attribute for a network is set via the `route-map` command discussed earlier. The discussions in this section will use the new BGP community format because it is more popular.

In order to match a community in a route-map, a community-list must be defined. A community-list is similar to an access-list. The syntax is

```
ip community-list <list number> [permit¦deny] <communities>
```

For example, if you want to match all routes with the community tags 0:50 and 0:90, your configuration would look something like:

```
ip community-list 1 permit 0:50 0:90
!
route-map match-comm permit 10
 match community-list 1
 set metric 500
```

If you wanted to match all routes except those with the community tags 0:20 and 0:40, your community-list configuration might look like:

```
ip community-list 10 deny 0:20 0:40
ip community-list 10 permit internet
```

Communities are often used to group routes for a geographic region together. This allows Internet service providers to set metrics for geographically dispersed routes differently, in effect specifying where they would like traffic routed to their network. This is very useful when there are many paths to a provider's network, some more optimal than others.

Community attributes can be set to disallow propagation to EBGP peers, using the no-export keyword on the set community command. This feature would be used on a network that uses IBGP heavily but does not want to share its internal routing policies with its EBGP peers. You can also prevent communities from being propagated beyond the local router, even to IBGP peers, using the no-advertise keyword on the set community command.

Because BGP routes can be tagged with multiple communities, many ISPs use them heavily in their routing policy implementations.

Confederations

Confederations enable a single AS to be broken into smaller ASs. To all EBGP peers there is only one AS, but internally there might be any number of ASs configured. This feature is most widely used to reduce the need for a fully meshed IBGP network. Rather than running IBGP between every router in a network, the Network Operator breaks the network into several groups of routers. Each of these groups is configured for fully meshed IBGP. Each group is configured with a different ASN. Then, each group is peered with each other. Each router group is configured with a confederation identifier, which is the ASN that will be seen by external BGP peers.

Listings 6.4 and 6.5 show a sample configuration of two routers within the same network but in different confederations. To external BGP speakers (devices that communicate via the BGP protocol), the network is identified by ASN 700. Internally, there are four ASNs: 64500, 64501, 64502, and 64503. Each of these internal ASNs are groups of routers that are fully meshed with IBGP.

Listing 6.4 **Router 1**

```
Router 1router bgp 64500
bgp confederation identifier 700
bgp confederation peers 64501 64502 64503
neighbor 192.168.200.1 remote-as 64501
neighbor 192.168.300.1 remote-as 64502
neighbor 192.168.400.10 remote-as 64503
neighbor 192.168.600.2 remote-as 64500
neighbor 192.168.600.3 remote-as 64500
```

Listing 6.5   **Router 2**

```
router bgp 64501
bgp confederation identifier 700
bgp confederation peers 64500 64502 64503
neighbor 192.168.300.1 remote-as 64502
neighbor 192.168.400.10 remote-as 64503
neighbor 192.168.200.2 remote-as 64501
neighbor 192.168.200.3 remote-as 64501
```

Confederations are not used very often because of their complexity. Communities are much easier to work with. The learning curve for new engineers with confederations is much steeper than communities.

IBGP

Because BGP enables you to implement complex routing policies, some Network Operators use it to exchange routing information within a single AS. The use of BGP in this way is called *Internal BGP*, or *IBGP*.

There are some special considerations to be aware of when using IBGP. A router that establishes a BGP session with another router in the same AS behaves a little differently than a router that peers via BGP with a router in another AS. First of all, the local preference values along with next hop information are passed between peers within the same ASN. Secondly, routers that peer via BGP within the same AS do not forward their entire BGP routing table. They only exchange routing information that is originated on each router along with the best path for routes learned from other ASs. There is a way to force your routers to exchange their full BGP routing table with other routers in the same AS.

In order for a router to exchange its full BGP routing table, it must be configured as a Route Reflector (RR). Any router in the same AS that peers with this router is called a Route Reflector Client (RRC). Use the following command in the BGP neighbor configuration to specify that the peer is a RRC:

neighbor *<neighbor IP address>* **route-reflector-client**

Conclusion

Determining which routing protocols, if any, to use in your network can be a daunting task. The best approach that I have found is to list all the requirements for my network. I find all the routing protocols that match my needs, and then pick the one that will be the easiest to configure and maintain. Then I go about learning everything I can about that protocol. The more familiar you become with a certain protocol, the more ways you will find to enhance your current routing system.

In some instances, the complexity of a network design or particularly unusual routing needs might require more than one routing protocol. A nice feature of the Cisco IOS is that several routing protocols can be enabled on a router at one time. Also, some routing protocols can have several instances running separately on a single router at one time. OSPF is one protocol that can have multiple process IDs running at one time on a single router.

7

Multicast

*M*ULTICAST IS THE ACT OF ONE SOURCE MACHINE SENDING packets to multiple destinations via a single data stream. In normal unicast communications, every data requester is sent an individual data stream from the data source. There are only two modes of communication, one-to-one or one-to-all. This can be a waste of resources if hundreds of requesters are asking for the same data source. Imagine how much bandwidth 500 home users wanting to download the same movie clip from a Web site use. One multicast data stream rather than hundreds of individual connections could service all those requests. Cisco supports multicast routing on all its series 1000 and higher routers.

How Multicast Works

Multicast sources send data packets to multicast groups. There can be any number of clients within a group. In fact, multicast group membership changes constantly. Multicast systems use Class D Internet Protocol (IP) address space. The four high order bits of the first octet of Class D IP address space are 1110. This gives the Class D IP address space a range of 224.0.0.0–239.255.255.255.

There are three modes of communication within any multicast system.

- Host to many receivers
- Many groups to one host
- Many sources to many multicast groups

The first two are the most common uses for multicast at this point in time. However, with the recent push for online meetings and virtual offices, the third communication type is becoming more and more prevalent. Table 7.1 shows some possible uses for each type of multicast communication.

Table 7.1   **Uses for Different Multicast Communication Types**

One to Many	Many to One	Many to Many
Caching	Data collection	Distance learning programs
Live concerts	Auctions	Multimedia conferences
Database updates		Chat rooms
Lectures		Multi-player games

Multicast Routing Protocols

There are several different protocols used in a multicast system to complete communication between a sender and a multicast group. The Internet Group Management Protocol (IGMP) handles the communication between multicast hosts and the router that connects them to other networks. The router uses the IGMP message to maintain a table of which hosts are joined to which multicast groups. Protocol Independent Multicast (PIM) is used to share information between multicast enabled routers. The Distance Vector Multicast Routing Protocol (DVMRP) is used on the original multicast backbone and is not supported by Cisco. Multicast Border Gateway Protocol (MBGP) is used to communicate multicast routing information between autonomous systems. Before any type of mutlicast communication can take place, multicast device addressing must be implemented.

Multicast Addressing

In order for a host to send and receive multicast data packets, it must have a multicast IP address. Any set of hosts that responds to an individual multicast address is called a group. Multicast groups can span multiple networks and can change in size rapidly.

The Internet Assigned Numbers Authority (IANA) has reserved several multicast IP addresses for special use. These well-known addresses are similar in nature to the well-known TCP and UDP ports reserved by IANA. Multicast group addresses in the range of 224.0.0.xxx are always sent with a time to live (TTL) of one. This makes communication using these group addresses usable only on directly connected subnets. Table 7.2 shows some of the reserved multicast addresses and their purposes.

Table 7.2 **Reserved Multicast Addresses**

Multicast Address	Purpose
224.0.0.1	All hosts on the connected subnet
224.0.0.2	All routers on the connected subnet
224.0.0.4	All DVMRP routers on the connected subnet
224.0.0.5	All multicast OSPF (MOSPF) routers on the connected subnet
224.0.0.9	RIPv2
224.0.1.1	Network Time Protocol (NTP)
224.0.1.2	Silicon Graphics (SGI) Dogfight Game
224.0.1.7	Audio News Broadcast
224.0.1.11	Internet Engineering Task Force (IETF) audio
224.0.1.12	IETF video
224.0.1.13	Protocol independent multicast

The IANA owns a block of Ethernet addresses that in hexadecimal is 00:00:5e. This is the high-order 24 bits of the Ethernet address, meaning that this block includes addresses in the range of 00:00:5e:00:00:00 to 00:00:5e:ff:ff:ff. The IANA allocates half of this block for multicast addresses. Given that the first byte of any Ethernet address must be 01 to specify a multicast address, the Ethernet addresses corresponding to IP multicasting are in the range 01:00:5e:00:00:00 through 01:00:5e:7f:ff:ff.

This allocation enables 23 bits in the Ethernet address to correspond to the IP multicast group ID. The mapping places the low-order 23 bits of the multicast group ID into these 23 bits of the Ethernet address, as shown in Figure 7.1. Because the upper five bits of the multicast address are ignored in this mapping, the resulting address is not unique. Thirty-two different multicast group IDs map to each Ethernet address.

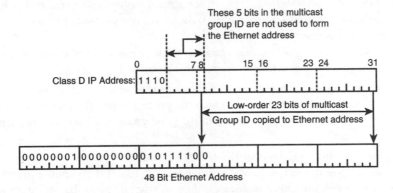

Figure 7.1   Multicast Ethernet address mapping.

Because the mapping of multicast addresses to Ethernet addresses is not unique, and because the interface card might receive multicast frames in which the host is really not interested, the IP software must perform some filtering in order to operate properly. You should consider this when choosing what multicast group to have your application send to. For instance, 225.0.0.1 is a valid IP multicast address, but its Media Access Control (MAC) layer address will be the same as 224.0.0.1. This is also true for 224.128.0.1. If you use these addresses for your multicast application, you might have problems in your network.

There is only one global configuration command that needs to be issued on your router to enable multicast routing.

```
router(config)# ip multicast-routing
```

Internet Group Management Protocol (IGMP)

The *Internet Group Management Protocol (IGMP)* is an integral part of IP multicast communication. All hosts wishing to receive IP multicast streams must implement it. IGMP is part of the IP layer and uses IP datagrams (consisting of a 20-byte IP header and an 8-byte IGRP message) to transmit information about multicast groups. IGMP messages are specified in the IP datagram with a protocol value of 2. Figure 7.2 shows the format of the 8-byte IGMP message.

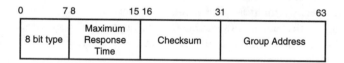

Figure 7.2   IGMP version 2 message format.

The value of the type field is 0x11 (hexadecimal) for a membership query sent by a router. The type value is 0x16 (hexadecimal) for a membership report sent by the host and 0X17 for a leave request sent by the host. Backward compatibility to IGMPv1 0x12 (hexadecimal) is reserved.

Multicast routers use IGMP messages to keep track of group membership on each of the networks physically attached to the router. The following rules apply:

- A host sends an IGMP report when the first process joins a group. The report is sent out on the same interface on which the process joined the group. Note that if other processes on the same host join the same group, the host does not send another report.

- In IGMPv2, a host will send an IGMP leave to the router if the host believes it was the last one to send an IGMP host report. The router then sends a group specific query to the group multicast address so that any hosts that still want to receive data for the group can prevent the router from pruning its interface.

- A multicast router sends an IGMP query at regular intervals to see whether any hosts still have processes belonging to any groups. The router sends a query out each interface. The group address in the query is 0 because the router expects one response from a host for every group that contains one or more members on a host.

- A host responds to an IGMP query by sending one IGMP report for each group that still contains at least one process. Because all hosts on the network listen to the IGMP reports being sent, if one host responds for a specific group, the others on the LAN will suppress sending the report.

Using queries and reports, a multicast router keeps a table of its interfaces that have at least one host in a multicast group. When the router receives a multicast datagram to forward, it forwards the datagram (using the corresponding multicast Open Systems Interconnection [OSI] Layer 2 address) on only those interfaces that still have hosts with processes belonging to that group. The multicast datagram is forwarded according to the multicast routing protocol running. IGMP does not determine how packets are forwarded.

The TTL field in the IP header of reports and queries is set to 1. By default, a multicast datagram with a TTL of 1 is restricted to the same subnet. Higher TTL field values can be forwarded by the router. By increasing the TTL, an application can perform an expanding ring search for a particular server. The first multicast datagram is sent with a TTL of 1. If no response is received, a TTL of 2 is tried, then 3, and so on. In this way, the application locates the server that is closest in terms of hops.

IGMP is supported by default in the Cisco Internetworking Operating System (IOS) and is enabled on any interface that is configured for multicast.

Protocol Independent Multicast (PIM)

Protocol Independent Multicast (PIM) is a routing protocol used to exchange multicast information between routers. It is the most widely used multicast routing protocol within autonomous systems. PIM can be enabled in one of three different modes.

- Dense mode
- Sparse mode
- A combination of the two, called sparse-dense mode

Dense Mode PIM

Dense mode PIM initially floods all interfaces with multicast information. It is assumed that all subnets connected to the router have multicast hosts on them. This mode of operation is continued until a prune message is received for a subnet that has no multicast hosts. The last router in the path to a possible multicast destination generates a prune message. *Prune messages* tell the originating multicast router that there are no multicast hosts along this path.

PIM dense mode is enabled on your Cisco router with the following interface configuration command:

```
router(config-int)# ip pim dense-mode
```

PIM must be configured on every interface that you wish to send and receive multicast traffic over.

Sparse Mode PIM

Sparse mode PIM sends multicast traffic only to those hosts that have requested it. The rendezvous point (RP) router handles the coordination of bringing senders and receivers together. A multicast sender directs traffic to the RP. The RP then sends the traffic out over the interfaces which have receivers registered in its tables to receive data for the multicast group specified in the senders data stream.

Sparse mode PIM is enabled on your Cisco router with the following interface configuration command:

```
router(config-int)# ip pim sparse-mode
```

PIM must be enabled on every interface that you wish to send and receive over.

If you configure PIM to operate in sparse mode, you might want to choose one or more routers to be RPs. An RP will automatically be chosen if you do not explicitly configure one. RPs are used by senders to a multicast group to announce their existence and by receivers of multicast packets to learn about new senders.

If you choose to manually define an RP, you need only configure the IP address of the RP in leaf routers. *Leaf routers* are those routers that are directly connect either to a multicast group member or to a sender of multicast messages. As the term *leaf* implies, they are typically found at the edge of your network (where all traffic either originates or terminates).

The RP address is used by first-hop routers to send PIM register messages on behalf of a host sending a packet to the group. The RP address is also used by last-hop routers to send PIM join/prune messages to the RP to inform it about group membership. The RP does not need to know it is an RP.

A PIM router can be an RP for more than one group and a group can have more than one RP. The conditions specified by the access-list in the following command syntax determine for which groups the router is an RP.

To configure the address of the RP, use the following command on a leaf router in global configuration mode:

```
router(config)# ip pim rp-address <ip address> [access-list number]
```

Auto Rendezvous Point Configuration

Auto-RP is a feature that automates the distribution of group-to-RP mappings in a sparse mode PIM network. This feature has the following benefits:

- It is easy to use multiple RPs within a network to serve different group ranges.
- It enables load splitting among different RPs and arrangement of RPs according to the location of group participants.
- It avoids inconsistent, manual RP configurations that can cause connectivity problems.

Multiple RPs can serve different group ranges or serve as hot backups of each other. To make Auto RP work, a router must be designated as an *RP-mapping agent*, which receives RP announcement messages from the RPs and arbitrates conflicts. The RP mapping agent then sends the consistent group-to-RP mappings to all other routers. Thus, all routers automatically discover which RP to use for the multicast groups they support.

One way to start is to place the default RP for all global groups at or near the border of your routing domain, while placing another RP in a more central location for all local groups.

A router is configured to announce itself as an RP using the following global configuration command:

```
ip pim send-rp-announce <interface> scope <ttl> group-list <access-list number>
```

For instance, to configure a router to use the IP address of its looback0 interface as the RP for multicast groups in the 236.xxx.xxx.xxx range, you would use the following configuration:

```
ip pim send-rp-announce loopback0 scope 16 group-list 1
access-list 1 permit 236.0.0.0 0.255.255.255
```

The TTL value determines how far the RP announcement will propagate into your multicast network.

The RP mapping agent is the router that sends the authoritative Discovery packets telling other routers which group-to-RP mapping to use. Such a role is necessary in the event of conflicts (such as overlapping group-to-RP ranges).

Find a router whose connectivity is not likely to be interrupted and assign it the role of RP mapping agent. All routers within *ttl* number of hops from the source router receive the Auto-RP Discovery messages. To assign the role of RP mapping agent in that router, use the following command in global configuration mode:

```
ip pim send-rp-discovery scope ttl
```

Sparse-Dense Mode PIM

Some environments might require PIM to run in sparse mode for some groups and in dense mode for other groups in a single region .

An alternative to enabling only dense mode or only sparse mode is to enable sparse-dense mode. In this case, the interface is treated as dense mode if the group is in dense mode and as sparse mode if the group is in sparse mode. You must have an RP if the interface is in sparse-dense mode, and you should treat the group as a sparse group.

A benefit of sparse-dense mode is that Auto-RP information can be distributed in a dense mode manner while multicast groups for user groups can be used in a sparse mode manner. Thus, there is no need to configure a default RP at the leaf routers.

Sparse-dense mode is configured on your Cisco router using the following interface configuration command:

```
router(config-int)# ip pim sparse-dense-mode
```

It should be noted that using sparse-dense mode PIM automatically configures your router for PIM version 2. All Cisco routers running version 11.3(2)T or later are automatically enabled for PIM version 2 as well.

Multicast Border Gateway Protocol (MBGP)

Multicast Border Gateway Protocol (MBGP) offers a method for providers to distinguish which prefixes they will use for performing multicast reverse path forwarding (RPF) checks. The RPF check is fundamental in establishing multicast forwarding trees and moving multicast content successfully from source to receiver(s). RPF is an algorithm used for forwarding multicast datagrams. The algorithm works as follows:

- The packet has arrived on the RPF interface if a router receives it on an interface that it uses to send unicast packets to the source.

- If the packet arrives on the RPF interface, the router forwards it out the interfaces that are present in the outgoing interface list of a multicast routing table entry.

- If the packet does not arrive on the RPF interface, the packet is silently discarded to avoid loop-backs.

Sparse mode PIM uses the RPF lookup function to determine where it needs to send joins and prunes. Shared-tree state joins are sent to the RP. Source-tree state joins are sent to the source.

Dense mode PIM groups use only source-rooted trees and make use of RPF forwarding as described above.

MBGP is based on RFC 2283, Multiprotocol Extensions for BGP-4. This brings along all the administrative functionality that providers and customers like in their inter-domain routing environment. Because MBGP is an extension of BGP, the policy controlling functions (route-maps, access-lists, filter-lists, communities, and so on) available in the Cisco IOS can also be applied to MBGP sessions. MBGP is a simple way to carry two sets of routes   one set for unicast routing and one set for multicast routing. The routes associated with multicast routing are used by the multicast routing protocols to build data distribution trees.

MBGP is configured basically the same as regular BGP. Everything is the same except for a small modification on the BGP neighbor command. You must add the multicast network layer reachability information tag to the end of the command. The syntax is

```
neighbor <ip address> nlri multicast
```

Networks are advertised into MBGP by the same mechanism as regular BGP with the same modification as the previous neighbor command. The syntax is

```
network <ip network> mask <subnet mask> nlri multicast
```

The same type of commands you use to verify regular BGP operation can be used to verify MBGP operation. Table 7.3 shows a few common commands you might find useful.

Table 7.3 **MBGP Show Commands**

Command	Use
show ip mbgp	Display the MBGP routing table
show ip mbgp summary	Display the status of MBGP peers
show ip mbgp neighbor <ip address>	Display information on a specific MBGP peer
show ip mbgp community <community-list>	Display MBGP routes matching the specified community-list

Multicast Backbone (Mbone)

The Multicast Backbone (Mbone) began as a tunnel between the original BBN backbone (now known as GTE Internetworking) and Stanford University in 1988. A tunnel was used as a temporary solution until routers learned how to deal with multicast traffic. The Mbone evolved as more and more networks interconnected with the purpose of exchanging multicast traffic. DVMRP was the original multicast routing protocol used on Mbone. In fact, it is still in use today. Cisco routers do not support DVMRP directly. However, Cisco multicast routers using PIM can interoperate with non-Cisco multicast routers that use DVMRP.

PIM routers dynamically discover DVMRP multicast routers on attached networks. Once a DVMRP neighbor has been discovered, the router periodically transmits DVMRP Report messages advertising the unicast sources reachable in the PIM domain. By default, directly connected subnets and networks are advertised. The router forwards multicast packets that have been forwarded by DVMRP routers and, in turn, forwards multicast packets to DVMRP routers.

Multicast Internet Exchange (MIX)

Multicast exchange points (MIX) are public interconnect points where multicast enabled networks can connect to one another for the purpose of exchanging multicast routing information and traffic. Multicast exchange points are typically implemented at locations where unicast exchange points already exists. A separate router interface is used to connect to the MIX for diagnostic purposes. When a robust multicast deployment is available on all networks, there is no technical reason why multicast traffic cannot be exchanged on the same interfaces and exchange points as the current unicast Internet.

Public Multicast Exchanges exist today at the NASA AMES Mae-West facility located in Moffett Field, California; the Palo Alto Internet Exchange (PAIX) located in Palo Alto, California; and the Sprint Network Access Point (NAP) in Pennsauken, New Jersey. The list of multicast enabled exchanges is growing rapidly and this is by no means an exhaustive list.

Diagnostic Tools

There are a great many tools available within the Cisco IOS that enable you to troubleshoot a multicast enabled router and its connections to other multicast enabled routers. Many of them are close cousins to some of the commands you have already encountered in this book. Some are new and specific to multicast troubleshooting. Table 7.4 shows a list of a few of these commands and their purpose.

Table 7.4 **Multicast Troubleshooting Commands**

IOS Command	Purpose
mrinfo	Display information about neighboring multicast routers
mstat <source IP>	Display statistics on multicast traffic forwarding and packet loss
mtrace <destination IP>	Multicast Traceroute. Display the path taken from the router to the given destination.
ping	Send ICMP echo request to multicast group address

IOS Command	Purpose
show ip dvmrp route	Display entries in the DVMRP routing table
show ip igmp groups	Display the multicast groups that directly connected hosts are members of
show ip igmp interface	Display multicast information about a specific router interface
show ip mcache	Display fast path forwarding statistics for multicast traffic
show ip mroute	Display routing table information for multicast networks
show ip pim interface	Display information for a PIM enabled interface
show ip pim neighbor	Display information for multicast enabled routers discovered by your router
show ip pim rp	Display the rendezvous points associated with multicast groups learned by your router
show ip sdr	Display cached groups learned via the Session Directory Protocol

Listing 7.1 shows a sample output from the show ip pim interface command. It is given here as an example of what you should expect to see and to show the similarity to output from the show ip interface brief command.

Listing 7.1 **Sample Output from show ip pim Interface Command**

```
mae-west-ames#sh ip pim int

Address            Interface    Version/Mode      Nbr   Query   DR
                                                  Count Intvl
198.9.201.113      Fddi2/0      v2/Sparse          13    30    198.9.201.254
209.1.220.11       Loopback0    v2/Sparse-Dense     0    30    209.1.220.11
209.1.220.11       Tunnel1      v2/Sparse-Dense     1    30    0.0.0.0
209.1.220.11       Tunnel2      v2/Sparse-Dense     1    30    0.0.0.0
192.148.252.237    Tunnel3      v2/Sparse-Dense     1    30    0.0.0.0
209.1.220.11       Tunnel4      v2/Sparse-Dense     1    30    0.0.0.0
205.166.254.254    Tunnel5      v2/Sparse-Dense     1    30    0.0.0.0
209.1.220.11       Tunnel6      v2/Sparse-Dense     0    30    0.0.0.0
209.1.220.11       Tunnel8      v2/Sparse-Dense     1    30    0.0.0.0
209.1.220.11       Tunnel9      v2/Sparse-Dense     1    30    0.0.0.0
```

Listing 7.2 shows the output from the show ip igmp group command. This command lists all active groups at the time of execution. Because membership in groups along with group creation and destruction are highly dynamic, the output from this command can vary widely between executions.

Listing 7.2   **Sample Output from the show** *ip igmp groups* **Command**

```
mae-west-ames#sh ip igmp groups
IGMP Connected Group Membership
Group Address       Interface        Uptime    Expires    Last Reporter
239.255.255.255     Fddi2/0          7w0d      never      198.9.201.113
239.255.255.255     Loopback0        7w0d      never      209.1.220.11
224.2.127.254       Fddi2/0          7w0d      never      198.9.201.253
224.2.127.254       Loopback0        7w0d      never      209.1.220.11
224.0.1.111         Fddi2/0          5w6d      00:02:54   198.9.201.254
224.0.1.39          Tunnel6          2w2d      never      0.0.0.0
224.0.1.39          Tunnel5          3w5d      never      0.0.0.0
224.0.1.39          Tunnel4          4w4d      never      0.0.0.0
224.0.1.39          Tunnel8          6w5d      never      0.0.0.0
224.0.1.39          Tunnel3          7w0d      never      0.0.0.0
224.0.1.39          Tunnel2          7w0d      never      0.0.0.0
224.0.1.39          Tunnel9          7w0d      never      0.0.0.0
224.0.1.39          Tunnel1          7w0d      never      0.0.0.0
224.0.1.39          Loopback0        7w0d      never      209.1.220.11
224.0.1.39          Fddi2/0          7w0d      never      198.9.201.113
224.0.1.40          Loopback0        7w0d      never      209.1.220.11
```

The show ip igmp interface command shows the multicast groups that have been joined on a per interface basis. It also gives IGMP specific information for each particular interface. Listing 7.3 shows an abbreviated output from this command.

Listing 7.3   **Sample Output from show** *ip igmp* **Interface Command**

```
mae-west-ames#sh ip igmp inter
Hssi0/0/0 is up, line protocol is up
  Internet address is 216.32.132.194/30
  IGMP is disabled on interface
  Multicast routing is disabled on interface
  Multicast TTL threshold is 0
  No multicast groups joined
ddi2/0 is up, line protocol is up
  Internet address is 198.9.201.113/24
  IGMP is enabled on interface
  Current IGMP version is 2
  CGMP is disabled on interface
  IGMP query interval is 60 seconds
  IGMP querier timeout is 120 seconds
  IGMP max query response time is 10 seconds
  Last member query response interval is 1000 ms
  Inbound IGMP access group is not set
  IGMP activity: 19 joins, 15 leaves
  Multicast routing is enabled on interface
  Multicast TTL threshold is 0
  Multicast designated router (DR) is 198.9.201.254
  IGMP querying router is 198.9.201.2
```

```
  Multicast groups joined (number of users):
      224.2.127.254(1)  239.255.255.255(1)  224.0.1.39(1)
POS3/0/0 is up, line protocol is up
  Internet address is 209.1.10.182/30
  IGMP is disabled on interface
  Multicast routing is disabled on interface
  Multicast TTL threshold is 0
  No multicast groups joined
Loopback0 is up, line protocol is up
  Internet address is 209.1.220.11/32
  IGMP is enabled on interface
  Current IGMP version is 2
  CGMP is disabled on interface
  IGMP query interval is 60 seconds
  IGMP querier timeout is 120 seconds
  IGMP max query response time is 10 seconds
  Last member query response interval is 1000 ms
  Inbound IGMP access group is not set
  IGMP activity: 4 joins, 0 leaves
  Multicast routing is enabled on interface
  Multicast TTL threshold is 0
  Multicast designated router (DR) is 209.1.220.11 (this system)
  IGMP querying router is 209.1.220.11 (this system)
  Multicast groups joined (number of users):
      224.0.1.40(1)  224.2.127.254(1)  239.255.255.255(1)
      224.0.1.39(1)
```

Conclusion

This chapter has given you a solid foundation on the uses and implementation of multicast. Multicast is an ever-changing canvas and will most likely evolve a great deal before it is used on an everyday basis. For this reason, you are not likely to find much wide scale use for it yet. However, the need for multicast is growing rapidly. This need is fueling rapid development and deployment of the existing technologies, which will probably find limited use in the very near future.

8

Access and Traffic Management

WHEN ROUTERS ARE FIRST BEING INSTALLED INTO A NETWORK, the last configuration task is usually security. This is the case for a number of reasons. You certainly don't want to lock yourself out of your router before you have a chance to log into it remotely. Nor is it advisable to restrict packets flowing through your routers until you are sure that the basic routing functionality is working properly. Throughout this chapter, several methods of how to limit access to, and manage the traffic flowing through, the routers in your network will be discussed.

Covering Your Bases

I usually make sure that console access to the routers I am installing is available before adding filters to a router configuration, especially filters that impact the remote availability of the router being installed. This can be accomplished using a modem, terminal server, or remote pair of hands with a laptop and a serial cable.

User Level Access Management

In the absence of some mechanism to identify individual users as they log in, the Cisco Internetworking Operating System (IOS) relies on a simple locally defined password to authenticate remote users. By default, passwords are stored unencrypted in the running configuration. This basic level of security is not recommended for use in a production network. By using an authentication scheme that uniquely defines remote users accessing the routers, Network Operators can track configuration changes made and define varying levels of access on a per user basis. The Cisco IOS provides the capability to locally define usernames and passwords in the router configuration.

Cisco also supports some of the more common authentication schemes used today in their router IOS: Terminal Access Controller Access Control System (TACACS), Remote Access Dial-in User Service (RADIUS), and Kerberos. Either TACACS or RADIUS, if not both, will be found in use at most of the major Internet service providers (ISPs). SecurID from Security Dynamics can be used with both TACACS and RADIUS. It is a random key generation technology that replaces the usual username/password pairs that are used with these types of authentication schemes. Kerberos authentication is not very widely used. In fact, the Kerberos project is still under development at MIT. There is a fundamental lack of documentation, which makes the use of Kerberos troublesome.

Local User Definition

The Cisco IOS supports the definition of multiple usernames in the running configuration. This method of user authentication is acceptable only if your network consists of a small number of routers. It is easier for Network Operators to maintain a central authentication server than to configure individual users on multiple routers, especially if there are a great number of routers in the network.

The command to enable a local user on a Cisco router is

username *name* **password** *encryption-type password*

name is the text string remote users will use to identify themselves. *encryption-type* tells the IOS that the password being supplied is either not encrypted or is encrypted, 0 or 7 respectively. *password* is obviously the password that will be used to authenticate the user. Depending on whether a 0 or 7 was specified for the *encryption-type*, the password supplied will be a clear text password or an encrypted password. The Cisco IOS expects the password supplied to be clear text. Therefore, specifying the encryption type is not necessary if you are using clear text passwords during configuration.

> **Configuring Alternate Access Methods for Redundancy**
>
> It is advisable to configure a single local username on all the routers in your network as a backdoor in case your primary authentication scheme becomes unavailable.

For instance, to define `scott` as a local user with a password of `mypassword`, the command would be

```
username scott password 0 mypassword
```

or

```
username scott password mypassword
```

To define `scott` as a local user with a password of `mypassword` that has already been encrypted, the command would be

```
username scott password 7 104310090404011C03162E
```

This functionality is included in the IOS so configurations that include encrypted passwords can be pasted into a router without error. Locally defined usernames override the other authentication schemes that might be configured on the router. The only exception to this rule is when Authentication Authorization and Accounting (AAA) authentication is configured without specifying the local database as one of the options. AAA authentication will be discussed later in this chapter in the section "AAA/TACACS+".

TACACS, Extended TACACS, and TACACS+

Terminal Access Controller Access Control System (TACACS), is one of the more commonly used user authentication schemes today. It is easily configured and the server software can be freely found on the Internet. Also, the server software runs on most of the UNIX operating systems available today. Cisco has several versions of TACACS server software available via anonymous FTP: `ftp.cisco.com/pub/netmgmt/tacacs/`.

TACACS and Extended TACACS

TACACS provides password checking, accounting, and authentication services. Extended TACACS provides information about protocol translators and router use in addition to features of TACACS.

To enable the use of a TACACS server on a Cisco router, enter the following command in global configuration mode:

```
tacacs-server host hostname or IP address
```

The `tacacs-server` host command specifies the UNIX host running the TACACS server software. If more than one `tacacs-server host` is configured, the IOS will search the list of servers until one responds.

There are a few additional commands that must be entered to make sure that total connectivity to the router is not lost if the TACACS server(s) become unavailable. This command is entered in global configuration mode:

```
tacacs-server last-resort password
```

This command tells the IOS that if the TACACS server(s) become unavailable, it should use the enable password to control access to the router.

The next step is to define which terminal lines will use TACACS authentication. Enter the following command in line configuration mode to enable TACACS authentication:

```
login tacacs
```

Now all attempts to log into the router via the access lines configured with the command above will be authenticated with the TACACS protocol.

There are other commands available in the Cisco IOS that enable the logging of accounting information to the Extended TACACS server. In order to use these Extended TACACS features, you will need a TACACS server that supports them. One is available from Cisco's FTP server. Also, Extended TACACS needs to be enabled in the IOS. To enable Extended TACACS in the Cisco IOS, enter the following command in global configuration mode:

```
tacacs-server extended
```

Extended TACACS can also be used to authenticate Point-to-Point Protocol (PPP) users. The following commands need to be entered in line configuration mode to enable TACACS authentication for PPP users:

```
ppp authentication chap or pap
ppp use-tacacs
```

The ppp authentication command specifies whether to use PAP or CHAP for password exchange.

AAA/TACACS+

If one of the main reasons you will be using TACACS as your authentication scheme is to track remote users' actions, the accounting features of Extended TACACS will probably not meet your needs. Using Authentication, Authorization, and Accounting (AAA) features in combination with TACACS+ gives the same accounting options as Extended TACACS, but with a little more control and granularity. TACACS+ is basically the features of Extended TACACS integrated with the accounting functionality of AAA. For instance, Extended TACACS only records login events, logout events, and when a user enters enable mode. With AAA/TACACS+, the Network Operator is able to record all commands as they are entered by remote users.

To enable AAA/TACACS+, enter the following commands into global configuration mode:

```
aaa new-model
tacacs-server host hostname or IP address
tacacs-server key string
```

The `aaa new-model` command enables AAA in the IOS. There is an additional command required to enable the TACACS -server host. That command is `tacacs-server key`. The ASCII key string entered in the IOS global configuration must match the key configured on the TACACS server or the router will not be able to authenticate users.

To enable user authentication using AAA/TACACS+, enter the following command in global configuration mode:

```
aaa authentication login default tacacs+ enable
```

To enable PPP user authentication using AAA/TACACS+, enter the following command in global configuration mode:

```
aaa authentication ppp default tacacs+ none
```

Now that AAA/TACACS+ is enabled for user authentication, let's explore some of the other features available. Using AAA, you can have every command entered by a user authorized before the IOS accepts it. This is the generic form of the AAA authorization command:

```
aaa authorization {network ¦ connection ¦ exec ¦ command level} methods
```

- `network`—Performs authorization for all network-related service requests, including SLIP, PPP, PPP NCPs, and ARA protocol.
- `connection`—Runs authorization for outbound Telnet and rlogin.
- `exec`—Runs authorization to determine if the user is allowed to run an EXEC shell.
- `command`—Runs authorization for all commands at the specified privilege level.

The final option to the command is a list of methods that should be tried sequentially to authenticate the user. The available options are

- `guest`—Enables guest logins. This method must be the first method listed, but can be followed by other methods if it does not succeed.
- `auth-guest`—Enables guest logins only if the user has already logged in to EXEC. This method must be the first method listed, but can be followed by other methods if it does not succeed.
- `line`—Uses the line password for authentication.
- `local`—Uses the local user database.
- `TACACS+`—Uses the defined TACACS server(s).
- `RADIUS`—Uses the defined RADIUS server(s).
- `none`—No further checking, or disabled if it is the only method listed.

The following command tells the IOS to check for authorization with the TACACS server for all shell commands up to enable level 15 and to fail if the TACACS server does not respond or authentication fails:

```
aaa authorization command 15 tacacs+ none
```

The next command tells the IOS to check the configured RADIUS server first, then the locally defined user database for authentication of outbound connection requests:

```
aaa authentication connection radius local none
```

If neither the RADIUS server nor the local database can authorize the requested command, the request is denied because of the none method defined at the end of the list.

User accounting can also be enabled tell the TACACS server to record when a user logs in, logs out, and enters a command to the IOS. Just about any AAA feature that can be enabled can be logged. All these log entries are time stamped. The importance of these log files will be discussed in Chapter 10 of this book, "Collecting Data via Other Means."

SecureID

SecureID is a product offered by Security Dynamics that replaces the password portion of the user authentication scheme with an auto-generating token. The tokens are generated every 30 or 60 seconds on a credit card sized card with an LCD display. A picture of the available token generators is Figure 8.1.

Figure 8.1   SecureID token generators.

The token is combined with a PIN number assigned to each individual user, creating a unique identifying key. This identifying key, along with the username supplied during the login process, are authenticated by server software sold by Security Dynamics. The server software is basically a modified TACACS+ server that can communicate with the Cisco IOS.

The use of a SecureID card is desirable when security is a major concern for the Network Operator. Using a randomly generated token based system rather than a static password helps protect against intruders that might be listening in on your network. Once a user has been authenticated with a specific token, that token cannot be used again. This prevents people from using a token and PIN pair even if they are able to obtain it by listening in on a TCP session.

RADIUS

Remote Access Dial In User Scheme (RADIUS) is an authentication protocol that offers an almost endless list of accounting and configuration options. RADIUS is most commonly used as the authentication scheme for large pools of dial-in users, like those found at most ISPs.

RADIUS authentication is used by dial-in ISPs because of its rich accounting features. It provides information that can be used for detailed billing and usage tracking. This information is also useful in tracking down network abusers and possible security breaches.

To configure a Cisco router to use the RADIUS authentication scheme, you first need to define the RADIUS servers. To do this, enter the following commands in the global configuration mode:

```
radius-server host hostname or IP address
radius-server key string
```

The `radius-server host` command defined the radius server to use for authenticating login requests. If more than one radius-server is defined, then the IOS will search through the list until one responds. The `radius-server host` command tells the IOS what password the RADIUS server is expecting from authenticating agents. The RADIUS server will not accept authentication requests from the router unless the radius-server key matches the key configured on the RADIUS server host.

Now that the IOS knows which RADIUS server to request authentication from, the RADIUS authentication scheme must be enabled. To enable RADIUS authentication for remote users, enter the following command in global configuration mode:

```
aaa authentication login default radius
```

All users attempting to log into a router with these commands enabled will be authenticated using the RADIUS protocol.

Kerberos

Kerberos is an authentication scheme that was developed at MIT. It is meant to be a one-time authentication service. It authenticates a user only once and then issues a DES (Digital Encryption Standard) encrypted ticket to the user. This encrypted ticket is stored in a cache on the user's host and has a limited life span. The ticket can then be used to access other devices that are using the same Kerberos Key Distribution Center (KDC) that authenticated the user in the first place. These devices do not require the user to resend a username or password. This can be an added level of security because the username and password pair are sent over the network less times than would be required with other authentication schemes.

Cisco IOS Release 11.1 supports Kerberos version 5. To enable a Cisco router to use a Kerberos KDC, enter the following commands in global configuration mode:

```
kerberos local-realm kerberos-realm
kerberos server KDC hostname or IP address
```

The *kerberos-realm* is the realm that is defined as the *default_realm* in the krb5.conf file on the UNIX host running the KDC.

Now that the router is configured to use a Kerberos KDC, it needs to be told to use Kerberos as its authentication method. To enable kerberos authentication for remote users, enter the following command:

```
aaa authentication login default krb5
```

When a user logs into a router that is configured for Kerberos authentication, the router requests a Ticket Granting Ticket (TGT) from the KDC. The router attempts to decrypt the TGT with the password supplied by the user. If the decryption succeeds, the user is granted access to the router.

If the router you are configuring for Kerberos authentication is to be used as a PPP server, then the following command must be issued in global configuration mode:

```
aaa authentication ppp default krb5
```

Because a PPP user is not authenticated to the router itself during a PPP session, the user must authenticate to the KDC directly, in order to access any other network services that are secured in the Kerberos realm.

Synchronize the Time for Kerberos

It is advisable to configure the routers in a particular Kerberos realm and the KDC for that realm to use the same NTP server because the ticket exchanges must happen within a five-minute window.

IP Filtering 101

Filtering the packets being transmitted through a router can be desirable for a number of reasons. Security is usually the first reason that comes to mind. Other reasons to place restrictions on the packets flowing through your routers are protecting your network from malicious denial of service attacks and enforcing your company's routing policies. Access–lists can be defined in one of two ways because the filtering effect has some subtle but important differences. Access–lists can be defined as either enable access, or deny access. Every access–list defined on a Cisco router has an implicit deny any at the end, whether it is configured that way or not. If CPU load on your routers is a concern, you should think a great deal about how the access–lists are configured on your router. The Cisco IOS will search an Access Control List (ACL) sequentially for matches. With this in mind, it is easy to see that you would want the most matches to your ACLs to occur in the first few lines of your ACL. Otherwise, the router has to spend a great deal of time searching the ACL for every packet that comes its way. Determining where to filter is another choice that should be given a lot of thought, specifically as to whether to filter packets as they come into your router or as they go out of your router.

The Cisco IOS supports several different types of access–lists. These access–lists are used as the basis for the filtering policies that can be defined for each router. The most commonly used access–lists on Cisco routers are basic packet filters, extended packet filters, and as–path filters. (Note: As–path filters were covered in Chapter 6, "Configuring Dynamic Routing Protocols.")

ACL Ordering Concerns

Be very careful when modifying access-lists on a router. All new access-list commands are added to the end of the existing list. If the desired action is to insert new rules into an existing access-list, copy the list to your local host via tftp or cut and paste it. Then modify the list according to the new design. Finally, remove the access-list definition from the router and paste the new list into the running configuration.

It is also very important to make sure that all references to the access-list being modified are disabled before it is removed from the running configuration. The Cisco IOS reacts differently to references to non-existent access-lists in varying situations.

Basic Packet Filters

Basic packet filters are used to restrict the propagation of packets from specified source addresses, to specified destination addresses, or a combination of both. The source and destination addresses can be MAC layer, IPX, AppleTalk, or most commonly IP addresses. Basic packet filters are also used to restrict the passing of network information on a BGP peering session, as we saw briefly in Chapter 6. The Cisco IOS defines basic IP access-lists as being numbered from 1 to 99.

Basic access-lists take the form of:

access-list <decimal number from 1-99> {**permit**¦**deny**} <source IP address> <source ⇒wildcard>

source wildcard refers to the bits that should match during the ACL check. It appears as a reverse of a normal IP subnet mask. In fact, wherever a 1 appears in the wildcard, that portion of the packet IP address being checked is ignored. The remaining portion of the packet IP address must match exactly with the corresponding portion of the source IP address. Although the IP address and source wildcard are entered in decimal form, the actual matches occur at the binary level.

Using Filters to Protect Your Routers

Basic IP filter-lists can be used to restrict access to your routers from remote locations. For instance, if you want to enable remote login access to your routers only from network hosts numbered in the 198.162.10.0/24 network block, then your configuration might look something like this:

```
access-list 1 permit 198.162.10.0 0.0.0.255
access-list 1 deny any
line vty 0 4
  access-class 1 in
```

The commands above define a basic filter-list that permits packets from the 198.162.10.0/24 network and denies all other packets. That access-list is then applied to the VTY terminal lines on the router. Routers that have an access-list defined for inbound connections will deny login requests before the user is even given a login prompt.

Access-lists can be used to restrict outbound access from a router as well. This is useful when you wish to restrict users from logging into remote systems from your routers. An example of the usefulness of this feature would be if there were a router in your network that enabled open access to anyone, such as a route server. Because this router is open to remote access from the general public with no restrictions inbound, it is important to ensure that those same users cannot access any other systems from that router.

Remember Security

Some immature individuals might even try to launch an attack from your route server on another company's network. It is very important that the filters on this type of router be strict. A good policy here is to deny everything except what you absolutely want the general public to have access to.

Basic access-lists can also be used to limit where Simple Network Management Protocol (SNMP) requests can originate. Most of the new Network Management applications on the market try to make intelligent network maps by pulling the entire route table from your routers. This action can have a detrimental effect on the performance of your routers. Restricting SNMP access to known "trusted" hosts is the safest course of action. To do this, simply define a basic access-list listing the hosts or networks that will be allowed to SNMP poll your routers. Then apply that access-list to the SNMP community string definition in the router configuration. A sample is shown below.

The ACL on the `snmp-server` command is meant only to restrict the point from which SNMP is enabled for certain community strings. Using an extended ACL is a waste of keystrokes. Because the filter is being applied to the `snmp-server community` command and not to all inbound interfaces on the router, it is not necessary to use the added features of the extended ACLs. An extended ACL would be required if we were discussing restricting SNMP requests from hitting the router.

```
access-list 5 permit 192.168.10.1 0.0.0.0
access-list 5 deny any
access-list 6 permit 192.168.10.2 0.0.0.0
access-list 6 deny any
snmp-server community public RO 5
snmp-server community private RW 6
```

Of course, access-lists can also be used to block traffic to or from certain hosts or networks. Packet filtering is configured in interface configuration mode.

Once the access-list is defined in the router configuration, all that needs to be done is to configure the appropriate interfaces to filter packets according to the access-list that you defined.

```
access-list 1 deny 192.168.0.0 0.0.0.255
access-list 1 permit any
Interface Ethernet0
  ip access-group 1 in
```

This sample configuration denies all packets coming from the 192.168.0.0/24 network into Ethernet port 0.

Distribution-Lists

Basic IP access-lists can be used to restrict certain networks from being propagated to your BGP peers. These access-lists are called distribution-lists. The Cisco IOS uses distribution-lists to remove networks from the BGP routing table before it is transmitted to a peer or accepted from a peer, depending on whether the distribution-list is configured inbound or outbound.

Filter Impact on Performance

Filtering packets *at the interface level* forces the router to process each packet at the central processor. This can bring your router to a crawl if there is a lot of traffic flowing through the router.

If an extended access-list is used in the BGP neighbor configuration, then it is possible to filter advertisements on predefined network boundaries. For instance, suppose that you wanted to only accept advertisements on /24 and above boundaries. The access-list would look like this:

```
access-list 191 deny    ip any 255.255.255.128 0.0.0.127
access-list 191 permit any any
```

Extended Packet Filters

If your requirement is to restrict IP packets at a higher granularity, then extended filter-lists might be just what you need. Extended filter-lists provide the capability to filter packets at the transport layer of the OSI model. Filtering can be done by the source port or the destination port of the packet. Also, source and destination pairs can be defined to enable finer control over the filtering of packet flows. Cisco defines extended access-lists as being numbered from 100 to 199.

Extended access-lists take the form of:

```
access-list {decimal number from 100-199} {permit¦deny} <IP based protocol>
<source IP> <source wildcard> [operator [port]] <destination IP> <destination
wildcard> [operator [port]] [established] [log]
```

The *protocol* referred to above can be either a number from 0 to 255 or the protocol name. Examples of the protocol names that can be used are IP, TCP, UDP and IGMP. The operator referred to above is a conditional in the form of eq (equal to), 1t (less than), gt (greater than), ne (not equal to), and range (inclusive). If range is specified, two port numbers must follow. The *established* keyword is only valid for TCP access-lists. The *log* keyword option at the end of the command lets you specify whether you would like matches to the access-list output to the configured syslog server.

Here is an access-list that only permits SMTP packets. The implicit deny at the end of every list blocks all other traffic:

```
access-list 100 permit tcp any eq smtp any
```

Here is an access-list that denies IP traffic from the 192.168.0.0/16 reserved address space:

```
access-list 100 deny ip 192.168.0.0 0.0.255.255 any
access-list 100 permit any any
```

Here is an access-list that enables only Web requests and logs them to a syslog server:

```
access-list 100 permit tcp any any eq www log
```

Inbound vs. Outbound Filtering

Filtering of packets can be done either as the packet enters the router or as the packet exits the router. When possible, it is better to filter on the inbound port rather than the outbound port.

Inbound filtering is done before passing the packet on to the routing process; outbound filtering is done after routing. There is no reason to waste CPU cycles on processing a packet just to have it dropped at the exit port.

Another situation where inbound filtering might be more beneficial than outbound filtering is when a number of low bandwidth interfaces are all routing traffic to one high bandwidth interface. Quite a few CPU cycles would be saved by distributing the filtering load to multiple inbound interfaces rather than having every packet run through the ACL at the one outbound interface. However, if all the inbound and outbound interfaces are similar in bandwidth and CPU load is not a grave concern, then administratively it would be easier to have just one ACL at the outbound interface.

Outbound filtering is desirable when you want to restrict the amount of information that you are passing on to another router. Examples are on BGP peering sessions or when redistributing from one routing process into another. Outbound filtering of the reserved IP address spaces should be configured for all routers that are connected to a public or private exchange point.

Using Your Router as a Firewall

By using a combination of extended access-list filtering options, a Cisco router can be configured to act as a firewall to a secure network. Let's take a look at the configuration example in Listing 8.1. In this example, the access-list assigned to the Ethernet port connecting the internal LAN segment enables TCP sessions that were established by hosts on the internal LAN to WWW servers. The Internet mail protocol (SMTP) is enabled from any host, but only to a single host, 192.168.10.10, the mail server for the company. All other traffic trying to go out the Ethernet interface is dropped.

Listing 8.1   **Example Configuration for Firewall Router**

```
interface Ethernet0
  description Internal LAN segment
  ip address 192.168.10.1 255.255.255.0
  ip access-group 100 out
!
access-list 100 permit tcp any any eq www
access-list 100 permit tcp any any established
access-list 100 permit tcp any host 192.168.10.10 eq smtp
access-list 100 deny any any
```

This, of course, is a very simplistic version of a real firewall configuration. It does, however, give you an idea of how access-lists can be used to provide a fairly robust security level with a higher performance rating than a software based firewall application can offers.

Dealing with Congestion

Congestion on network interfaces is the nightmare that all Network Operators hope they never have to face. If the routers on your network are configured properly, a pseudo early detection system can alert you when traffic levels reach certain "danger points." Chapter 9, "Collecting Data via SNMP," and Chapter 10 cover the most efficient ways to monitor the traffic levels on your routers.

The default queuing mechanism in the Cisco IOS is first in, first out (FIFO). There are several other configuration options available in the Cisco IOS that can help you to avoid congestion on your network. A couple of basic options available are priority queuing and custom queuing. Some other features available are

- Weighted Fair Queuing (WFQ)
- Weighted Random Early Detection (WRED)
- Committed Access Rate (CAR)

These features are only available in the 11.1CC, 11.3, and 12.0 strains of IOS code. They also all require that Cisco Express Forwarding (CEF) be enabled on your routers if the distributed forms of these features are to be used.

Priority Queuing

Priority queuing enables traffic to be broken up into four separate queues specifying the packet priority. Packets in the higher priority queues are serviced before those in lower priority queues. Traffic is designated into one of these four priorities though the use of **priority-list** global configuration command. The command syntax is as follows:

```
priority-list <list number> protocol <protocol> <priority> [options]
```

Congestion Management Audience

WFQ and WRED were designed to address congestion issues on networks comprised mostly of low speed lines such as T1/E1. They are not meant to be used on high-speed LAN or WAN interfaces.

list number is the IP priority list number (similar to an access-list number). Protocol can be one of the following:

- IP (Internet Protocol),
- XNS (Xerox Network Systems),
- DECnet,
- AppleTalk,
- CLNS (ISO Connectionless Network Protocol),
- Novell (keyword = IPX),
- APOLLO (Apollo Domain Routing protocol for Apollo workstations),
- VINES (Banyan VINES),
- STUN (for Serial Tunneling),
- BRIDGE (for transparent bridging traffic), or
- RSRB (for remote source-route bridged traffic)

The four priorities are high, medium, normal, and low. Options can be a combination of the following:

- **gt** (greater than) *byte-count*—Specifies a greater-than count. The priority level assigned goes into effect when a packet exceeds the value entered for the argument *byte-count*.
- **lt** (less than) *byte-count*—Specifies a less-than count. The priority level assigned goes into effect when a packet size is less than the value entered for *byte-count*.
- **tcp** *port*—Assigns the priority level defined to TCP packets originating from or destined to a specified *port*.
- **udp** *port*—Assigns the priority level defined to UDP packets originating from or destined to the specified *port*.
- **list** *list-number*—Assigns traffic priorities according to a specific list. The *list-number* argument is the IP access-list number assigned by the **access-group list** interface subcommand. (For use with the IP protocol, only.)
- **bridge list** *list-number*—Assigns the priority level to bridged traffic according to access-list number using the **bridge** and **list** keywords. The *list-number* argument is the Ethernet-type code access-list number assigned by the **access-list global** configuration command and the **access-group list** interface subcommand.

To assign all WWW traffic exiting an interface to high priority, do the following:

```
priority-list 1 protocol ip high tcp 80
interface ethernet0
  ip address 192.168.10.1 255.255.255.0
  priority-group 1
```

Custom Queuing

Custom queuing is Cisco's version of priority queuing for high-speed links. Custom queuing provides 17 separate queues for packets to be stored in (0–16). When packets exist in any of the queues, they are processed per queue in numerical order. In other words, packets in queue 0 are processed before packets in queue 1. Queue 0 is reserved for system traffic (keepalives and protocol processing). All other queues are definable by the Network Operator.

Packets are placed into queues based upon protocols. Which queue certain protocols are placed in is defined using a queue-list. The format for the queue-list command is as follows:

```
queue-list <list-number> protocol <protocol-name> <queue-number> <queue-keyword>
↪<keyword-value>
```

list-number is an arbitrary number, between 1 and 16, used to reference the defined list when it is assigned to an interface. Protocol-name is any of the options listed previously for priority queuing. Queue-number is the queue that packets matching this queue-list are to be placed in. queue-keyword and the keyword-value are optional and are used to define more specific parameters for packet matching. The options for queue-keyword are

- **gt** (greater than) byte-count—Specifies a greater-than count. The priority level assigned goes into effect when a packet exceeds the value entered for the argument byte-count.

- **lt** (less than) byte-count—Specifies a less-than count. The priority level assigned goes into effect when a packet size is less than the value entered for byte-count.

- **tcp**—Assigns the priority level defined to TCP packets originating from or destined to a specified port.

- **udp**—Assigns the priority level defined to UDP packets originating from or destined to the specified port.

- **list**—Assigns traffic priorities according to a specific list. The list-number argument is the IP access-list number assigned by the access-group list interface subcommand. (For use with the IP protocol, only.)

- **fragments**—Assigns the priority level defined to fragmented IP packets (for use with IP protocol only). More specifically, IP packets whose fragment offset field is nonzero are matched by this command. The initial fragment of a fragmented IP packet has a fragment offset of zero, so such packets are not matched by this command. Note: Packets with a nonzero fragment offset do not contain TCP or UDP headers, so other instances of this command that use the **tcp** or **udp** keyword will always fail to match such packets.

The keyword value is any supporting port number or access-list needed for the specific queue keyword. The following example assigns WWW requests to queue number 2:

```
queue-list 1 protocol ip 2 tcp 80
```

Once a queue-list has been defined, it is assigned to an interface by entering the following command in interface configuration mode:

custom-queue-list *<list number>*

Here, *list number* is the queue-list number. The following example takes our last example and assigns it to Ethernet interface 0:

```
interface Ethernet0
  custom-queue-list 1
```

Now all WWW requests that come in on interface E0 will be placed in queue number 2.

It is possible to assign all packets arriving on an interface to one queue. To accomplish this task, the following command must be entered in global configuration mode:

queue-list *<list number>* **interface** *<interface type>* *<interface number>* *<queue number>*

For example, to set all packets coming in on Ethernet interface 0 to queue number 6, enter the following command:

```
queue-list 3 interface e 0 6
```

Because the default queue used for all traffic on a Cisco router is queue number 1, it is often required that the default be changed. Use the following command to change the default queue for any packets not matching the preceding steps in a queue-list:

```
queue-list <list number> default <queue number>
```

Let's modify our WWW queue-list example from earlier to assign all other packets besides WWW requests to queue 10.

```
queue-list 1 protocol ip 2 tcp 80
queue-list 1 default 10
```

When using queue, it becomes much more important to monitor the memory usage on your router. If there are no limits to the number of packets that are queued per interface, a highly utilized router can quickly find itself without memory space to buffer packets. At that point the router will usually fail and crash. Cisco provides two mechanisms to limit the custom queuing of packets. One limits the queuing by the number of packets, and the other limits the queuing by the byte-count. Use the following command to limit a particular queue size by packet count:

queue-list *<list number>* **queue** *<queue number>* **limit** *<packet count>*

`packet count` can be any number from 0 to 32767. Specifying a value of 0 means that the queue is limitless. This should be used with extreme caution. The default packet limit per queue is 20 packets. The following command limits custom queue number 1 to 300 packets:

```
queue-list 4 queue 1 limit 300
```

Use the following command to limit a particular queue size by byte-count:

queue-list <*list number*> **queue** <*queue number*> **byte-count** <*bytes*>

The default byte limit for each custom queue is 1400. The following command limits custom queue number 15 to 100 bytes:

```
queue-list 10 queue 15 byte-count 100
```

Weighted Fair Queuing

Weighted fair queuing (WFQ) governs the amount of available transmission bandwidth that individual packet flows can use. Packet flows are defined by the Cisco IOS as packets that have the same source and destination IP address, TCP, or UDP port protocol and type of service (ToS). Each flow that is identified is assigned to a separate output queue. Each packet that arrives for that specific flow is stored in that queue. When periods of congestion occur, each active queue is granted an equal amount of bandwidth.

WFQ maintains a tally of the total number of packets in each queue as well as the total number of packets in all queues combined. When the total number of packets queued is below the aggregate limit, individual flow queues have no limit. When the total number of packets queued is greater than the aggregate limit, each interface starts to enforce the flow queue limits defined in the configuration. Any packets arriving for a flow queue that is past its limit will be dropped. Packets that are already queued, even though they might exceed the limit for that particular queue, are not dropped.

To enable WFQ for interfaces on your router, enter the following command in interface configuration mode:

```
fair-queue
```

If WFQ is enabled on an interface that resides on a Versatile Interface Card (VIP) card, *distributed weighted fair queuing (DWFQ)* is used. DWFQ behaves the same as WFQ except that all queuing is done on the VIP card rather than the Route Switching Processor (RSP).

Weighted Random Early Detection

Random early detection (RED) uses the congestion control mechanisms that are built into TCP; therefore, it works only with IP traffic. Routers configured to use RED randomly drop packets prior to interfaces becoming congested. These dropped packets cause the sending host to decrease its transmission rate. Once all transmitted packets reach their destination, the transmitting host resumes sending packets at the original rate. *Weighted random early detection* (WRED) is usually configured on the routers in the core of the network.

WRED enables you to set a different precedence for certain types of traffic. There are eight precedence values that can be set, 0-7. Precedence values are set by the Committed Access Rate (CAR) feature described in the next section. These precedence values are taken into account when the decision to drop packets is encountered. Packets with a lower precedence are dropped first. All non-IP traffic is set to a precedence of 0.

By dropping packets randomly before actual congestion of an interface is reached, a higher utilization of available bandwidth is possible. This is because no global throttling occurs. Global throttling occurs when a link becomes congested and packets are dropped. All TCP sources then decrease their transmission rate at the same time. Traffic levels drop and the congestion passes, but all the TCP sources begin transmitting at full rate again and the link becomes congested. This causes periods where the available bandwidth is under utilized and then congested repeatedly. Because TCP sources are dropped at varying times when using WRED, no global throttling occurs and hence the available bandwidth is more efficiently utilized.

Who Decides What Packets Are Dropped?

The decision to drop a packet is based on the following formula:

average_queue_size = (previous_average * (1 _ ^ n)) + (current_queue_size * _ ^ n)

(where n is the exponential weight factor) and the probability factor. The probability factor is the rate at which packets are dropped while the queue size approaches the maximum threshold. The probability factor is based on the minimum threshold, maximum threshold, and a probability denominator. The rate at which packets are dropped increases linearly until the average queue size reaches the maximum threshold. The probability denominator is a ratio of the number of packets dropped to the number of packets forwarded while the average queue size is equal to the maximum queue size. If the probability denominator is 64, one out of every 64 packets received is dropped.

When a packet is received, the average queue size is calculated. If the calculated average is less than the configured minimum threshold, then the packet is queued. If the calculated average is between the configured minimum and maximum thresholds, then the packet is either queued or dropped depending on the probability factor. When the average queue size exceeds the maximum, all packets are dropped.

To configure WRED on an interface, enter the following command in interface configuration mode:

```
random-detect
```

Committed Access Rate

Committed access rate (CAR) is a Cisco IOS feature that enables you to limit the amount of traffic coming in or going out of an interface. It also enables you to set the precedence level for IP traffic. The precedence level is used by other IOS features like WFQ and WRED. CAR is usually configured on the routers at the edge of a network to limit the amount of traffic entering or exiting and to also set precedence values.

CAR limits the traffic on an interface according to policies defined by the Network Operator. The basic form of the rate policy statements at the interface level is

```
rate-limit {input|output} <bps> <burst> <max> conform-action action exceed-action
action
```

- *bps*—the threshold in bits per second to limit traffic to. This value must be in increments of 8Kbps.
- *burst*—size of normal traffic burst allowed, in bytes. The smallest value allowed is the bps value/1000.
- *max*—size of excess traffic burst, in bytes.
- *action*—what to do with the packets matching the condition. Allowed values are
  - **continue**—proceed to the next `rate-limit` command
  - **drop**—drop the packet
  - **set-prec-continue**—set the IP precedence for the packet and evaluate the next `rate-limit` command
  - **set-prec-transmit**—set the IP precedence for the packet and then forward to next hop
  - **transmit**—forward packet to next hop

To limit the inbound traffic on an interface to 5Mbps, the configuration would look like this:

```
interface Ethernet0
  ip address 192.168.10.1 255.255.255.0
  rate-limit input 5000000 5000 5000 conform-action transmit exceed-action drop
```

Extended access-lists can be used to specify certain applications for rate limiting. To assign a higher precedence to all WWW traffic going out an interface, the configuration would look like this:

```
interface Hssi6/0/0
  ip address 192.168.11.1 255.255.255.252
  rate-limit output access-group 101 40000000 400000 400000 conform-action set-
prec-transmit 5 exceed-action set-prec-transmit 5
!
access-list 101 permit cp any any eq www
```

It is also possible to rate-limit based upon MAC address or the IP precedence of the packet. To do this, an access-list rate-limit list needs to be defined. The syntax for this list command is

access-list rate-limit *<acl-index>* {*precedence*¦*mac-address*¦**mask** *precedence-mask*}

- *acl-index*—access-list number.
- *precedence*—P precedence of the packet, 0-7.
- *mac-address*—MAC address of the packet sender.
- *precedence-mask*—a hexadecimal value to signify more than one IP precedence value. The mask is created by adding all the bit values of the IP precedence levels that are to be matched. Each IP precedence level is assigned a location in an eight bit binary string. Each bit represents an IP precedence level starting with 7 at the left end of the binary string and decreasing to the right. For instance, to match IP precedence levels 5 and 2, the binary bit string would be 00100100. The decimal total of which is 36. 36 converted to hexadecimal is 24.

Rate limiting based on a rate-limit access-list would be useful at a shared media public exchange point. It is possible to ensure that none of your peers can consume all your available bandwidth. This provides all your peers an equal chance at sending traffic to your network. Or, you can reject all traffic from non-peers. The latter is shown in Listing 8.2. The configuration shown in Listing 8.2 only enables traffic from the three MAC addresses specified in rate-limit list 100.

Default Action for CAR

If packets do not match the criteria set by the rate-limit statements on an interface that has CAR enabled, then the default action is to transmit the packet.

Listing 8.2   **Configuration to Reject Traffic from Non-Peers**

```
interface Fddi1/0
  ip address 192.168.10.1 255.255.255.0
  rate-limit input access-group rate-limit 100 90000000 90000 90000 conform-action
transmit exceed-action transmit
  rate-limit input 90000000 90000 90000 conform-action drop exceed action drop
  !
access-list rate-limit 100 00e0.34b0.7777
access-list rate-limit 100 00e0.34b0.6543
access-list rate-limit 100 00e0.34b0.8879
```

One really good use for rate-limits is to protect your network from distributed denial of service (DDoS) attacks. To do this, you apply a rate-limit sequence to all interfaces connected to the Internet directly or through an Internet service provider. Here is an example of a rate-limit that protects against the popular SMURF attack while also enabling you to track the possible origin of the attack.

```
rate-limit input access-group 199 296000 20000 20000 conform-action transmit
exceed-action continue
rate-limit input access-group 198 8000 8000 8000 conform-action transmit exceed-
action drop

access-list 198 permit icmp any any echo-reply log-input
access-list 199 permit icmp any any echo-reply
```

The first rate-limit matches all ICMP traffic up to 296Kbps. If the ICMP traffic exceeds the 20Kbps peak above 296Kbps, then the packets are passed to the second `rate-limit` command. The second rate-limit command enables only ICMP echo-replies (the packet types used in the SMURF attack) at a rate of 16Kbps. Because access-list 198 is configured to log the input packets, all matches to the `rate-limit` command that use access-list 198 are sent to the router console and syslog server if configured. This configuration enables you to withstand an attack (provided your router is powerful enough to rate-limit at large attack) while still providing necessary information for you to diagnose and track the problem.

MPLS

Multiprotocol Label Switching (MPLS) brings the traffic management features of Layer 2 ATM and Frame Relay networks to TCP/IP. MPLS integrates traffic engineering functionality into the Layer 3 routing environment. This approach streamlines the forwarding of packets in a routed network. MPLS traffic engineering routes traffic flows across a network based on the resources the traffic flow requires and the resources available in the network.

MPLS traffic engineering employs "constraint-based routing," in which the path for a traffic flow is the shortest path that meets the resource requirements (constraints) of the traffic flow. In MPLS traffic engineering, the flow has bandwidth requirements, media requirements, a priority versus other flows, and so on.

MPLS traffic engineering recovers from link or node failures that change the topology of the backbone by adapting to the new set of constraints. MPLS traffic engineering has a dynamic adaptation mechanism that provides a full solution to traffic engineering a backbone. This mechanism enables the backbone to be resistant to failures. With MPLS traffic engineering, you do not have to manually configure the network devices to set up explicit routes. Instead, you can rely on the MPLS traffic engineering functionality to understand the backbone topology and the automated signaling process. MPLS traffic engineering accounts for link bandwidth and for the size of the traffic flow when determining explicit routes across the backbone.

MPLS is available on the Cisco 7200, 7500, and 12000 series routers running IOS version 12.0 or higher. In order to implement MPLS on a Cisco router you must first have CEF enabled and be running either the IS-IS or OSPF dynamic routing protocol.

Once these conditions are met, your first task is to enable MPLS tunnels on your router. This is done with the following router configuration command:

```
router(config)# mpls traffic-eng tunnels
```

The next step in implementing MPLS on your network is to enable MPLS on the individual interfaces. The following commands accomplish this task:

```
router(config-if)# mpls traffic-eng tunnels
router(config-if)# ip rsvp bandwidth <bandwidth>
```

bandwidth is the amount of interface bandwidth to reserve for traffic engineering tunnel constraints. rsvp is the resource reservation protocol that MPLS uses to establish and maintain traffic engineering tunnels between routers.

Next, you need to enable MPLS support in your routing protocol. For OSPF, the commands are

```
router(config-router)# mpls traffic-eng area 0
router(config-router)# mpls traffic-end router-id loopback0
```

MPLS and IS-IS

Implementing MPLS on a network that currently has IS-IS running requires that the IS-IS version be changed. A new version of IS-IS that supports SPF enhancements and extensions specifically for MPLS must be enabled.

MPLS only supports traffic engineering for one area in OSPF at this time. The second command defines the interface to be used as the router ID tunnel creation and termination. In this case, it is a virtual address (loopback0). However, it can be any interface on the router. It is better to use a virtual address because it is always online as long as the router is operational, whereas physical interfaces can become unavailable in an outage situation.

The commands to enable MPLS in IS-IS are

```
router(config-router)# mpls traffic-eng level 1
router(config-router)# mpls traffic-eng router-id loopback0
router(config-router)# metric-style wide
```

MPLS only supports traffic engineering for one level in IS-IS at this time. The last command in the sequence above tells the router to send and accept the new-style type, length, and value object (TLV).

Once MPLS has been enabled in your routing protocol, the next step is to create a traffic engineering tunnel. A traffic engineering tunnel is a virtual interface on your router that is used to set your bandwidth and policy constraint options. Here are the steps to creating a traffic engineering tunnel interface:

```
router(config)# interface tunnel 1
router(config-if)# ip unnumbered loopback 0
router(config-if)# tunnel destination <destination IP address>
router(config-if)# tunnel mode mpls traffic-rng
router(config-if)# tunnel mpls traffic-eng bandwidth <bandwidth>
router(config-if)# tunnel mpls traffic-eng path-option 1 dynamic
```

The commands above create the tunnel interface, define the tunnel destination, and assign it as an MPLS traffic engineering tunnel. The last two commands enable you to define the maximum bandwidth you would like this tunnel to handle and how you would like the router to determine the path between the two tunnel end points. I used the dynamic option here. There is an explicit option, which enables you to define the physical path between the tunnel end points hop by hop. It is perfectly acceptable to assign both path option types to the same tunnel. You would simply configure a path-option 2 which would only be used if the first path-option became unavailable.

The next step is to allow the tunnel to be used by your IGP for SPF calculations. This is done by entering the following command in the tunnel interface configuration mode:

```
router(config-if)# tunnel mpls traffic-eng autoroute announce
```

The commands that you would use to verify the MPLS tunnel configuration and operation are

```
show mpls traffic-eng tunnel
show ip interface tunnel <interface number>
```

Conclusion

A lot of functionality was covered in this chapter. The information mentioned is merely the tip of the iceberg in some areas. It is easy to see that there are a great many options available to you in managing both access and traffic on your network. Hopefully, you now have enough information to determine which options deserve more evaluation and might better suit your needs. It might be a good idea to re-read portions if not all this chapter so that you have a firm grasp of the subject matter you are interested in.

As always, you should consult the specific caveats for the IOS version you are using on your routers. There might be changes to command structures or additional commands added in newer IOS releases that will change how or why you would implement some of the features covered in this chapter.

Router Monitoring

9

Collecting Data via SNMP

COLLECTING DATA FROM YOUR ROUTERS IS THE KEY to understanding the growth patterns of your network. Monitoring the usage of your network links helps in capacity planning, congestion avoidance, and budgeting forecasts. Monitoring the overall health of the routers in your network can aid in preventing crippling network outages. Several common health indicators that should be monitored are

- Environmental status such as internal and external temperature of the network device
- Internal processor performance (CPU load)
- Power supply load

The most common method used to collect data from a router is through the use of Simple Network Management Protocol, or SNMP. In this chapter, you will learn how to enable your Cisco routers for SNMP data collection as well as what uses the collected data might serve.

Management Information Base (MIB)

There are a number of commercial and publicly available applications that use SNMP to access the Management Information Base, or MIB, for an SNMP enabled device. The MIB contains a great deal of information about the device itself and each of the individual interfaces on the device. There are basically two types of data fields stored in the MIB:

- Read-only fields
- Read-write fields

Access to read-only and read-write MIB variables is controlled through the use of a password called the *community string*. The community string for the read-only variables can be different than the community string for the read-write variables. The community string to access each type of variable can be any ASCII string. Typically, SNMP enabled devices default to a read-only community string of *public* and a read-write community string of *private,* or some variation of the two. The application trying to retrieve data from an MIB must supply the correct community string for the variable type. The read-write community string can be used to access both read-only and read-write variables. Keep in mind that community strings are case sensitive.

The MIB variables are accessed via their Object Identifier, or OID. An OID is a text string that can be represented in either decimal or English notation. Every OID represents a branch on a tree. The tree begins with the root which is represented by a '.'. The root contains several branches below it. Each of these branches in turn has sub-branches beneath it. Branches at every level are labeled with a text name and an unsigned decimal identifier. See Figure 9.1 for a representation of the first few layers of the MIB tree.

Where Do MIBs Come From?

MIBs are standardized. There is a MIB for bridges, another for routers, a different one for servers, and so on. Vendors are free to add additional fields to the end of the MIBs in their devices and most of them, including Cisco, do so. The MIB standard has gone through a major revision and is now officially known as MIB-2. However, the acronym, MIB, is used to describe both MIB-1 and MIB-2 unless a particular distinction is necessary.

Write-Only Data Fields

There is also a seldom-used type of data field that is write-only, which is used to execute commands on the router via SNMP.

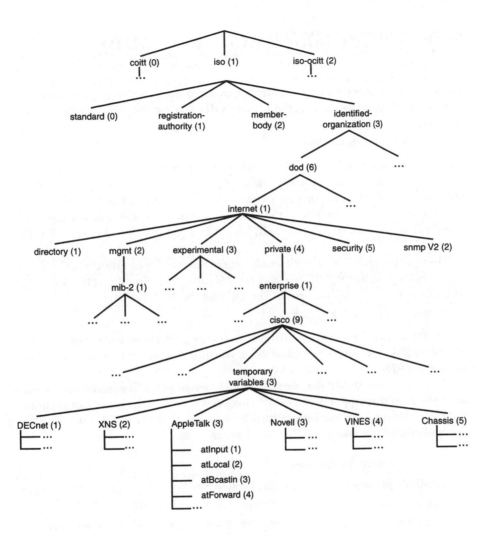

Figure 9.1   Standard MIB tree.

To access a certain variable in a MIB, the OID must be specified to the application getting the data. A complete explanation of SNMP is beyond the scope of this book. However, we will cover the basics enough for you to start collecting data today. An example of a commonly used MIB for collecting traffic data from routers is the ifInOctets variable for a specific interface. The decimal OID for this MIB is

. 1.3.6.1.2.1.2.2.1.10.<interface ifIndex>

The text equivalent of the `ifInOctets` MIB is

```
.iso.org.dod.internet.mgmt.mib.interfaces.ifTable.ifEntry.ifInOctets.<interface
➥ifIndex>
```

The interface `ifIndex` is a decimal number retrieved from another MIB variable on the router called, oddly enough, the `ifIndex` OID. The standard OID for the `ifIndex` branch is

```
.1.3.6.1.2.1.2.2.1.1.<index>
```

`index` is a decimal number between 1 and 65536. Querying this OID in sequence starting with the decimal numeral 1 and stepping forward in increments of 1 will result in a list of `ifIndexes` that are currently defined on that network device. A faster and simpler way of accomplishing this task is to use an application called snmpwalk. Snmpwalk automatically walks the MIB branch that you specify and returns all valid values.

Most people like to work with words rather than numbers. Fortunately, Cisco provides a branch inside the MIB tree that enables you to correlate the `ifIndex` number to actual port names on your router. The OID for this MIB branch is

```
.1.3.6.2.1.2.1.2.2.1.2.<ifIndex>
```

This OID is called `ifDesc`. This MIB branch is only available on certain router models. You will need to check the Cisco documentation for your specific device before using this OID.

In order to poll SNMP data from a network device, you will need to have access to an application that supports the SNMP protocol. There are several suites of applications available freely on the Internet that are very useful. Refer to Table 9.1 for a list of the applications that you are likely to find and their uses.

Table 9.1 **SNMP Applications**

SNMP Application	Application Use
snmpget	Retrieve data for a single OID
snmpgetnext	Retrieve data for the next OID in the MIB tree
snmpwalk	Retrieve data from all OIDs in the MIB tree
snmptrap	Send SNMPv1 trap to an SNMP server
snmpset	Populate an OID on a network device with a specific value
snmptest	Initiates an interactive command line session with a network device
snmptranslate	Convert the dotted decimal OID notation to text

A common set of SNMP applications can be found on the WWW at
`http://www.net.cmu.edu/groups/netdev/`.

The tasks that lay before you as the Network Operator are to enable SNMP access
to your routers, collect the desired data, and then present the data in a useful format.

Enabling SNMP Access

Each router in your network will need to be configured to enable SNMP access
before it will respond to SNMP queries. The Cisco IOS supports both SNMP version
1 and SNMP version 2. The version you need to enable depends on the management
software that you will be using. All management software available supports SNMPv1,
but not all support SNMPv2. For the purpose of collecting traffic data, SNMPv1 is
sufficient. The command syntax to enable SNMPv1 access for a Cisco router is

```
snmp-server community <community string> {RO¦RW} [access-list]
```

`community string` is an ASCII string that will be used as a sort of password for clients
trying to retrieve SNMP data from the router. The community string is case sensitive.
The `RO` and `RW` options specify whether the community string entered enables read-
only or read-write access to the MIB table. The optional argument `access-list`
is a basic IP access-list that can be used to restrict the IP hosts that can retrieve
SNMP data.

Listing 9.1 shows a sample configuration that defines a read-only community
string, a read-write community string, and limits access to one trusted host. Limited
SNMP access to your router is extremely important. It is all too easy to take over or
shutdown a router via SNMP. Always assume that your community strings are known
to everyone and limit SNMP access to only IP addresses that you know are secure.
Having access-lists also enables you to track SNMP requests from unauthorized
sources via the logging mechanisms discussed in Chapter 10, "Collecting Data via
Other Means."

Listing 9.1   **Sample Configuration for SNMPv1**

```
snmp-server community public RO 5
snmp-server community private RW 5
!
access-list 5 permit 192.168.10.10
```

Be Careful of Commercial Network Monitoring Software

Many of the commercial Network Monitoring Software (NMS) packages that are available are very useful
in discovering the network topology of your network. The reason they are so good at it is that they poll a
great deal of information from the devices on your network. This sometimes includes the routing tables
of your routers.

If you have routers connected to the Internet that carry the full global routing table, there can be a
severe performance impact to the operation of the network device as it is being polled. The option to
have the routing table retrieved from network devices can usually be disabled. Consult the documentation for any commercial NMS before running it on your network.

It is possible to configure multiple community strings for the same variable type on your Cisco devices. This is useful when changing community strings as part of a regular security precaution. It enables a sort of grace period while the various organizations in your company update the configurations for their NMS. You could have your routers configured for both the current community string, as well as, the new community string for a short period of time so that network monitoring and regular data collection is not interrupted.

To configure more than one community string on the same router, simply enter multiple snmp-server community commands into the router in global configuration mode. Here are the commands to have three read-only community strings on the same router:

```
snmp-server community public RO
snmp-server community PuBlIc RO
snmp-server community pUbLiC RO
```

Keep in mind that community strings are case sensitive. All the community strings above are different.

How to Collect the Data

There are certainly more methods for collecting SNMP data from network devices than I list here. No matter which application you use to collect your data, the underlying principles are the same. The data is pulled from the MIB variables and then stored or displayed in some fashion. Several commercially available applications enable you to collect data and might even provide reports on the data that is collected, such as the OpenView package by Hewlett-Packard. For our discussion here, we will concentrate on home grown or freely available SNMP collection utilities.

CiscoWorks

CiscoWorks is a network management application developed by Cisco to make management of complex Cisco based networks easier. CiscoWorks uses SNMP to monitor and control any SNMP based device on the network. CiscoWorks also integrated with other network management software packages, such as HP OpenView, Sun Solstice, and Tivoli. Integration with these other widely used network management applications enables Network Operators to extend and enhance the features of their currently installed software.

Some of the features that CiscoWorks offers are

- Configuration management
- Software (IOS) management
- Software (IOS) center (used for planning upgrades)
- Security management
- Device monitoring
- CiscoView (a GUI for configuring and managing Cisco devices)

Using CiscoWorks to help manage your network enables you to more easily sort through the seemingly endless list of MIBs available on each Cisco product. Also, it can be used to automate basic housekeeping tasks that are often times overlooked.

There is also an add-on application called CiscoWorks Switched Internetwork Solutions (commonly referred to as CWSI) which extends the CiscoWorks functionality to the growing line of Cisco LAN and WAN switches.

MRTG

MRTG is a freely available data collection and representation tool. It can be found at `http://ee-staff.ethz.ch/~oetiker/webtools/mrtg/mrtg.html`. This tool is widely used on the Internet for several reasons.

- **Flexibility.** MRTG can be used to collect data from any OID and graph it. It also enables data input from external sources for its graphing routines.

- **Portability.** MRTG will run on almost any workstation that supports PERL5.

- **Ease of use.** MRTG is very easy to configure and can be implemented on a large network in a matter of minutes. In fact, the MRTG distribution comes with some utilities to help in the initial configuration. Not only will these utilities generate default configuration files for network devices, they will also generate default HTML pages for your Web server.

- **Support.** Because MRTG was developed under the basic principles of the Internet culture, many individuals around the world improve upon it and there is an active mailing list that is dedicated to user support.

One of the big drawbacks to MRTG is the fact that it is bound by the disk IO of the system it runs on. What I mean by this is that if you are attempting to collect and graph data for a large number of interfaces, the corresponding reading and writing of files to the local hard disk for such an activity can be paralyzing to the system. This is a problem that is going to be addressed in the next release of MRTG.

Why Collect Data So Frequently?

You might ask why anyone would wish to subject their routers to polling at a higher interval than five minutes. It is easy to understand when you consider that the current implementation of octet counters on all routers is a 32-bit field. This means that the octets coming in and going out of an interface are accumulated in a counter which, when the limit is reached (4,294,967,296 bytes), the counter resets back to zero. This might seem like a large number, but if you consider that as networks grow in size and the backbone links approach OC3 and OC12 speeds, this number is inadequate. This can be proven by some simple mathematical calculations. Divide 4,294,967,296 by 300 (300 seconds in 5 minutes). That returns a value of 14,316,557 bytes per second. Now multiply that value by eight to convert to bits. We are now left with 114,532,461 bits per second. As you can see, the highest value that can be obtained from a 32-bit counter is around 114.5 Mbps when polling at five minute intervals. If an OC3 or higher interface in your network runs higher than that value, you have two choices: collect data more frequently, or change your collection methodology.

Cisco provides an extension to the RFC MIB specifications that enable you to poll the bits per second value directly from their router. This method limits the usefulness of the data because it is already averaged for you. If your only goal is to monitor utilization on your interfaces, it is sufficient.

Many of the newer network devices support the 64-bit interface octet counters that were recently developed. Any Cisco device that is able to run IOS 12.0 or higher supports the 64-bit counters. The only caveat to 64-bit counter support is that the NMS solution that you are using must also support 64-bit counters.

Home Grown Tools

SNMP data collection can be accomplished via what are commonly referred to as "home grown" utilities. These are generally programs or scripts, which have been written by employees of a company to accomplish a specific task that either was not available from a commercial application or was cost prohibitive. Home grown tools are also useful when a task needs to be accomplished quickly.

Listing 9.2 shows a small PERL5 program that collects the bits per second data from a Cisco router. The program reads in the interfaces and routers to collect data from a supplied configuration file. The configuration file name is supplied on the command line when executing the program. A sample format of the configuration file is shown in Listing 9.3. The SNMP modules used in the program in Listing 9.2 were borrowed from the MRTG distribution, but can also be found on the Perl WWW site (http://www.perl.com).

Listing 9.2 **Perl5 Program to Collect SNMP Data**

```
#!/usr/local/bin/perl

require 5.004;
use strict;
use SNMP_Session;
use BER;

my $DEBUG = 0;

my $intfcfg = $ARGV[0];

die unless $intfcfg;

my( %intf );

%snmpget::OIDS = (
    'sysUptime' => '1.3.6.1.2.1.1.3.0',
    'ifDescr' => '1.3.6.1.2.1.2.2.1.2',
    'ifIndex' => '1.3.6.1.2.1.2.2.1.1',
    'ifInOctets' => '1.3.6.1.4.1.9.2.2.1.1.6',
    'ifOutOctets' => '1.3.6.1.4.1.9.2.2.1.1.8',
    'ifNumber' => '1.3.6.1.2.1.2.1.0',
    # up 1, down 2, testing 3
    'ifOperStatus' => '1.3.6.1.2.1.2.2.1.8',
    'ifAdminStatus' => '1.3.6.1.2.1.2.2.1.7',
  );
```

```perl
&parse_intf_cfg();

foreach my $device  ( keys %intf ) {

  my %IFDESC;

  my $dir = '/opt/data';
  my $ip = $intf{$device}{'ip'};
  my $comm = $intf{$device}{'community'};
  my @intfs = split( /,/, $intf{$device}{'intf'} );
  my @descs = split( /,/, $intf{$device}{'descs'} );

  my ( $ifnum ) = &snmpget( $ip, $comm, $snmpget::OIDS{'ifNumber'} );

  if( $ifnum < 0 ) {
    print STDERR "SNMP Error: Unable to retreive the number of installed
    ➥interfaces from $device.\n";
    print STDERR "ifNum returned from query: $ifnum\n" if $DEBUG;
    next;
  }

  print STDERR "ifNum: $ifnum\n" if $DEBUG;
#
# Build a list of all the ifDescrs so we know which OIDs to poll
#
  for( my $i = 1; $i <= $ifnum; $i++ ) {
    my $oid = "ifDescr.$i";
    my ($ifdesc) = &snmpget( $ip, $comm, $oid );
    print STDERR "[SNMP] OID: $oid\tifDescr: $ifdesc\n" if $DEBUG;
    $IFDESC{$ifdesc} = $i;
    print STDERR "$device $ifdesc = $i\n" if $DEBUG;
  }

#
# Create the data directory if it doesn't exist
#
  unless( -e "$dir/$device" ) {
    print STDERR "Creating $dir/$device...\n";
    mkdir( "$dir/$device", 0755 );
  }

  while( defined( my $intf = pop( @intfs ) ) ) {
    my $desc = pop( @descs );

    $intf =~ s/\//-/g;

    open( DATA, ">>$cfg{'dir'}/$device/$intf" ) || die "$cfg{'dir'}/$device/$intf:
    ➥$!\n";
    $intf =~ s/-/\//g;
```

continues

Listing 9.2 **Continued**

```perl
    seek( DATA, 0, 2 );
    my $time = time();
    my $bintime = pack( "I*", $time );

    my $oid = "ifInOctets.$IFDESC{$intf}";
    print STDERR "In OID: $oid\n" if $DEBUG;
    my( $in ) = &snmpget( $ip, $comm, $oid );
    if( $in > ( 2 ** 30 ) ) {
      print STDERR "[$device]: $intf - Invalid In Data Received ($in).\n";
      $in = 0;
    }
    my $binval = pack( "I*", $in );

    syswrite( DATA, $bintime, 4 );
    syswrite( DATA, $binval, 4 );

    $oid = "ifOutOctets.$IFDESC{$intf}";
    print STDERR "Out OID: $oid\n" if $DEBUG;
    my( $out ) = &snmpget( $ip, $comm, $oid );
    if( $out > ( 2 ** 30 ) ) {
      print STDERR "[$device]: $intf - Invalid Out Data Received ($out).\n";
      $out = 0;
    }
    my $binval = pack( "I*", $out );

    syswrite( DATA, $binval, 4 );

    close( DATA );
  }
}

sub parse_intf_cfg {
  my( $device );
  open( INTF, $intfcfg ) || die "$intfcfg: $!\n";
  while( defined( my $line = <INTF> ) ) {
    chomp( $line );
    if ( $line =~ /^(.*) = \{/ ) {
      $device = $1;
      until( $line =~ /\}/ ) {
        $line = <INTF>;
        if ( $line =~ /\}/ ) { last; }
        chomp( $line );
        my( $key, $value ) = split( /=>/, $line );
        $key =~ s/\s*//g;
        $value =~ s/^\s*//g;
        $key = lc( $key );

        print STDERR "[CFG] Key: $key\tValue: $value\n" if $DEBUG;
        if ( $key =~ /intf/i ) {
          $intf{$device}{'intf'} .= $value .',';
```

```perl
        } else {
          $intf{$device}{$key} = $value;
        }
      }

      if( $intf{$device}{'ip'} !~ /\d{1,3}\.\d{1,3}\.\d{1,3}\.\d{1,3}/ ) {
        die "IP value for $device in CFG file is invalid.\n";
      }

      if( $intf{$device}{'community'} !~ /^[a-z]*/ ) {
        die "Community value for $device in CFG file is invalid.\n";
      }
    }
  }
  close( INTF );
}

sub snmpget {
  my($host,$community,@vars) = @_;
  my(@enoid, $var,$response, $bindings, $binding, $value, $inoid,$outoid,
    $upoid,$oid,@retvals);
  foreach $var (@vars) {
    if ($var =~ /^([a-z]+)/i) {
      my $oid = $snmpget::OIDS{$1};
      if ($oid) {
        $var =~ s/$1/$oid/;
      } else {
        die "Unknown SNMP var $var\n"
      }
    }
    push @enoid,  encode_oid((split /\./, $var));
  }
  srand();
  my $session;
  $session = SNMP_Session->open($host,$community,161);
  if (! defined($session)) {
    warn "SNMPGET Problem for $community\@$host\n";
    return (-1,-1);
  }

  if ($session->get_request_response(@enoid)) {
    $response = $session->pdu_buffer;
    ($bindings) = $session->decode_get_response ($response);
    $session->close ();
    while ($bindings) {
      ($binding,$bindings) = decode_sequence ($bindings);
      ($oid,$value) = decode_by_template ($binding, "%O%@");
      my $tempo = pretty_print ($value);
      $tempo=~s/\t/ /g;
      $tempo=~s/\n/ /g;
      $tempo=~s/^\s+//;
```

continues

Listing 9.2   **Continued**

```
    $tempo=~s/\s+$//;
    push @retvals, $tempo;
  }
  return (@retvals);
} else {
  return (-1,-1);
}
}
```

Listing 9.3   **Sample Configuration File for the Perl5 SNMP Collection Program**

```
mae-east = {
  ip => 192.168.10.1
  community => public
  intf => Hssi1/0/0
  intf => Fddi2/0/0
  intf => Hssi2/1/0
}
```

What is especially useful about this program is that it reads the interface indexes from the router MIB table each time it is run. A common problem with data SNMP data collection is that interfaces are assigned what is known as an ifIndex. The ifIndex is an OID that holds the key which is used to access all other interface data. The IOS numbers the interfaces in each router sequentially, starting with the number 1. When cards are installed later into a live router, the interfaces that are installed are numbered starting with the first available ifIndex. This in and of itself is not a problem. However, when the router reboots, the cards are again numbered sequentially starting with the number 1. The problem arises when the cards that were installed live precede cards that were originally in the router. Now the new interfaces are given a lower ifIndex than they were originally assigned when installed into the router live.

For instance, let's say that there is a router with an FSIP8 in Slot 1 and an EIP4 in Slot 3. The first eight serial ports are numbered 1 though 8, and the four Ethernet ports are number 9 through 12. After a few months, it is decided that another FSIP8 is needed in the router. It is decided that the new FSIP8 card will be installed into Slot 0. The eight new serial ports just installed in Slot 0 will be numbered 13 through 20. Several months later, during a routine IOS upgrade, the router is reloaded. The ifIndexes are allocated as follows: the eight serial ports in Slot 0 are number 1 through 8, the eight serial ports in Slot 1 are numbered 9 through 16, and the four Ethernet ports in Slot 3 are number 17 through 20. As you can see, ifIndex 17, which is now an Ethernet port on card 3, used to be a serial port on card 0. Figure 9.2 illustrates this phenomenon.

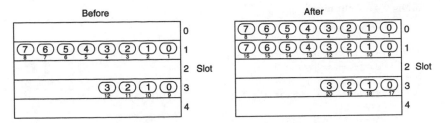

Figure 9.2 Example of `ifIndex` renumbering.

MRTG combats this problem by keeping track of which interfaces are assigned to which `ifIndexes` on each router. It outputs a warning to the console running the program when an `ifIndex` changes.

The PERL5 program in Listing 9.2 stores data based on interface name and reads the `ifIndex` during each polling cycle. This way, no human intervention is ever needed after hardware has been installed into a production system. In fact, generation of the interface configuration file can be automated as well, if the configurations from your routers are archived regularly. A simple PERL5 program can be used to convert the standard Cisco router configuration file to the format expected by this program. A sample of this conversion program is in Listing 9.4. This program assumes that the router configuration files are named config-*<router name>*.

Listing 9.4 **Cisco Router Configuration Conversion Program**

```perl
#!/usr/local/bin/perl -w

use strict;
require 5.004;

my $configdir = '/usr/local/configs';
my( $ip, $int, $IP );
my $community = 'public';

opendir( CONFS, $configdir ) || die "$configdir: $!\n";
my @configs = grep( /config-/, readdir( CONFS ) );
closedir( CONFS );
chomp( @configs );

while( defined( my $config = shift( @configs ) ) ) {
  open( CONF, "$configdir/$config" ) || print STDERR "$config: $!\n";
  $config =~ s/^config-//;
  print "$config.core = {\n";
  while( defined( my $line = <CONF> ) ) {
    chomp( $line );
    if( $line =~ /^interface (.*)$/ ) {
      $int = $1;
      if( $int =~ /(Tunnel|point-to-point|port-channel)/i ) {
```

continues

Listing 9.4 **Continued**

```
        undef( $int );
        next;
      } elsif( $int =~ /Loopback/ ) {
        my $temp = <CONF>;
        chomp( $temp );
        $temp =~ /ip address (\d{1,3}\.\d{1,3}\.\d{1,3}\.\d{1,3})/;
        $IP = $1;
        print "  ip => $IP\n";
        print "  community => $community\n";
        undef( $int );
      } elsif( $int =~ /ATM/ ) {
        $ip = '';
      }
    } elsif( $line =~ /ip address (\d{1,3}\.\d{1,3}\.\d{1,3}\.\d{1,3})/ ) {
      $ip = $1;
    }
    if( defined( $int ) && defined( $ip ) ) {
      print "  intf => $int\n";
      undef( $int );
      undef( $ip );
    }
  }
  print "}\n\n";
}
```

What to Do with the Data

Now that you have all this SNMP data taking up space on your hard disk, what do you do with it? MRTG graphs its data and makes nice HTML pages that can be served from an HTTP server. The same can be done with the data collected with our home grown application. Visual representation of the data is nice for getting a day to day idea of the traffic patterns on your network, as well as alert you when there is a problem. If one of the interfaces you are graphing suddenly drops to no traffic, that is probably an indication there is a problem with the line.

Along the same lines, if the CPU load on one of the routers in your network suddenly goes from 5 percent to 30 percent, you might be under a SMURF attack (a popular type of Denial of Service attack), or perhaps a high level debugging command was left turned on. Seemingly minor changes to a router configuration can have adverse effects on the CPU load. For instance, adding an ACL to a highly used interface will cause all packets on that interface to be process-switched rather than fast- or optimum-switched. The point is that routinely collecting and monitoring data from your network devices might help you prevent a major network event before it happens.

More than likely, when the executive team sees your data they will want more information than you might be prepared to provide. If your vice president asks you for the highest traffic day in the past three months, what do you respond with? This is when the need for a more robust system arises. Most often, executives are interested in trend analysis and growth rates. There are a number of commercial applications available that attempt to provide this information. Whether any of them will work for you depends on your needs.

Conclusion

Whatever your data collecting or reporting needs are, the Cisco product line is accommodating. Hopefully, you have learned the basic usefulness of the SNMP from this chapter. At the very least, you should be aware of the need for regular SNMP data collection as an effective network monitoring tool. Remember that a craftsman is only as good as his tool set.

10

Collecting Data via Other Means

WE HAVE LOOKED AT THE NORMAL MEANS THAT Network Operators use to collect data from their routers. Now let's explore some of the less used methods available to extract important and interesting information from Cisco routers.

There are various means with which to monitor Cisco routers, and this will by no means be an exhaustive list. We will, however, go over some less than obvious ways to collect useful information from your Cisco devices. The most basic and useful of the many options available to a Network Operator are automated telnet sessions, rsh and rcp, and the syslog facilities built into the Cisco IOS.

Automated Telnet

Scripting is a very useful tool that can be utilized by a Network Operator. Through the use of scripting, whether it is a shell script on a UNIX workstation or a full-blown Perl program, Network Operators can automate many of the basic monitoring tasks that every network requires. A sample of this type of program can be found in Listing 10.1. This program telnets into a router or list of routers and archives information about the hardware that is installed in the router. This type of information is useful for asset tracking, as well as, determining easily which cards might need memory upgrades. A sample of the output of this program is shown in Listing 10.2.

Listing 10.1   **Perl5 Program to Archive Hardware Data from Routers**

```perl
#!/usr/local/bin/perl

require 5.004;
use Net::Telnet;

my $dir = '/opt/inventory';
my $user = "userid";
my $password = "password";
my $timeout = 5;

my $routerfile = shift( @ARGV );
chomp( $routerfile );
open( IN , $routerfile ) || die "$routerfile: $!\n";
@routers = <IN>;
close( IN );
chomp( @routers );

foreach $router (@routers) {
  print STDERR "Getting hardware from $router...\n";
  @lines = &GrabHardware( $router );
  for($count=0; $count<= $#lines; $count++) {
    if( $lines[$count] =~ /^Slot (\d*)/ ) {
      $slot = $1;
      undef($PAbay);
    }
    elsif ( $lines[$count] =~ /(.*), HW rev (.*),/ ) {
      $Card{$slot}{'type'} = $1;
      $Card{$slot}{'hwrev'} = $2;
      $Card{$slot}{'type'} =~ s/^\s*//;
    }
    elsif ( $lines[$count] =~ /Serial number: (\d*)/ && ( ! $PAbay ) ) {
      $Card{$slot}{'serial'} = $1;
    }
    elsif ( $lines[$count] =~ /Insertion time: .*\((.*)\)/ ) {
      $Card{$slot}{'inserttime'} = $1;
    }
    elsif ( $lines[$count] =~ /Controller Memory Size: (.*)/ ) {
      $Card{$slot}{'memory'} = $1;
    }
    elsif ( $lines[$count] =~ /PA Bay (\d*)/ ) {
      $PAbay = "PA ".$1;
    }
    elsif ( $lines[$count] =~ /\t(.*) PA, (\d*) port/ ) {
      $Card{$slot}{$PAbay}{'Type'} = $1;
      $Card{$slot}{$PAbay}{'Ports'} = $2;
      $Card{$slot}{$PAbay}{'Type'} =~ s/^\s*//g;
    }
    elsif ( $lines[$count] =~ /\tHW rev (.*),/ ) {
      $Card{$slot}{$PAbay}{'HWrev'} = $1;
    }
    elsif ( $lines[$count] =~ /\tSerial number: (\d*).*?\bPart/ ) {
      $Card{$slot}{$PAbay}{'serial'} = $1;
```

```perl
      }
    }
  &PrintCardInfo();
  undef( %Card );
}

sub PrintCardInfo {
  open( OUT, ">$dir/$router.inv" ) || print STDERR "$router: $!\n";
  select( OUT );
  foreach $slot ( sort { $a <=> $b; } keys( %Card ) ) {
    print "\nCard Slot: $slot\n";
    print "Card Type: $Card{$slot}{'type'}\n";
    print "Card HW Revision: $Card{$slot}{'hwrev'}\n";
    print "Card Serial Number: $Card{$slot}{'serial'}\n";
    unless( $Card{$slot}{'type'} =~ /Route/ ||
            $Card{$slot}{'type'} =~ /Chassis/ ) {
      print "Card Insertion Time: $Card{$slot}{'inserttime'}\n";
      print "Card Memory: $Card{$slot}{'memory'}";
      for($i=0; $i<2; $i++) {
        $str = "PA ". $i;
        if ( exists( $Card{$slot}{$str}{'Type'} ) ) {
          print "\n  PA Bay $i: $Card{$slot}{$str}{'Type'}\n";
          print "   # of Ports on PA: $Card{$slot}{$str}{'Ports'}\n";
          print "   PA Serial #: $Card{$slot}{$str}{'serial'}\n";
          print "   PA HW Revsion: $Card{$slot}{$str}{'HWrev'}\n";
        }
      }
    }
    print "=::\n";
  }
  close( OUT );
}

sub GrabHardware {
  my( $router ) = @_;
  my $con = new Net::Telnet ( Host => "$router",
                              Timeout => 10,
                              Errmode => 'return',
                              Prompt => '/[\w\-]+[>:]$/');
  my $ok = $con->login( $user, $password );
  unless( $ok ) { print STDERR "[$router]: Login failed!\n"; next; }
  $con->timeout( $timeout );
  $con->errmode( 'return' );
  $con->max_buffer_length( '3048576' );
  $con->print( "term length 0" );
  $con->print( "sh diag" );
  while( my $return = $con->getline() ) {
    chomp( $return );
    push( @return, $return );
  }
  $con->close();
  return( @return );
}
```

Listing 10.2 **Sample Output from Hardware Archival Program**

```
Card Slot: 1
Card Type: VIP2 controller
Card HW Revision: 2.04
Card Serial Number: 06364384
Card Insertion Time: 25w0d ago
Card Memory: 32 MBytes DRAM, 2048 KBytes SRAM
  PA Bay 0: Mx HSSI-B
  # of Ports on PA: 1
  PA Serial #: 06687335
  PA HW Revsion: 1.10
=::

Card Slot: 2
Card Type: VIP2 controller
Card HW Revision: 2.04
Card Serial Number: 03713839
Card Insertion Time: 25w0d ago
Card Memory: 32 MBytes DRAM, 2048 KBytes SRAM
  PA Bay 0: FDDI
  # of Ports on PA: 1
  PA Serial #: 05103624
  PA HW Revsion: 1.13

  PA Bay 1: Mx HSSI-B
  # of Ports on PA: 1
  PA Serial #: 05878204
  PA HW Revsion: 1.00
=::

Card Slot: 3
Card Type: SSIP controller
Card HW Revision: 1.01
Card Serial Number: 04232140
Card Insertion Time: 25w0d ago
Card Memory: =::

Card Slot: 4
Card Type: Route/Switch Processor 4
Card HW Revision: 1.00
Card Serial Number: 06365106
=::

Card Slot: 31
Card Type: Chassis Interface
Card HW Revision: 1.00
Card Serial Number: 05889060
=::
```

The program in Listing 10.1 would need to be modified a little depending on the type of Cisco networking equipment that you are using. The current state of the program works well on all the Cisco 7000 and 7500 series routers.

Automated Telnet and Security

You should be cautious about the use of automated telnet scripts. They can be potential security risks if not implemented correctly. Imagine if a malicious user were to gain access to a system that had an automated telnet script on it. A few key strokes, and that person could change your script from a useful tool into a doomsday machine that rebooted all your devices. Do not be alarmed by this scenario, as it is a worst case situation. It is a good illustration as to why security should always be one of your considerations when developing or deploying network tools. There are many things that can be done to restrict access to your script even if the host on which it resides is compromised. If you are unsure how to accomplish the level of user security that is required, consult a system administrator.

RSH and RCP

Another tool available to Network Operators that can be used in scripts or programs is the RSH family of utilities which comes with every standard UNIX distribution. The two most common programs used from the RSH family of utilities are rsh and rcp. RSH stands for "remote shell" and RCP stands for "remote copy." These utilities enable a user on a UNIX workstation to execute a command or program from a trusted host on a remote system or to copy a file between two trusted hosts.

The Cisco IOS supports both RSH and RCP. Before rsh or rcp can be used to access a Cisco router, a few commands must be entered into the global configuration on the router. The first step is to enable rsh access to the router. Entering the following command in global configuration mode does this:

```
ip rcmd rsh-enable
```

Next, a trusted user on a trusted host must be allowed access to the router. Entering the following command in global configuration mode accomplishes this task:

```
ip rcmd remote-host <local username> <remote host> <remote username> [enable]
```

The enable keyword at the end is used if you want the remote user on the remote host to be allowed to execute "enable" mode commands. Enable mode commands are those IOS commands that require the user to be in enable mode before execution of those commands is allowed.

As an added security measure, it is advisable to require forward and reverse DNS name lookups for the remote host. This is because even if a would be attacker tried gaining access to your network using an IP address from your block, the attacker has no direct control over the DNS servers that are delegated authority for your companies top level domain name. Entering the following command in the global configuration mode does this:

```
ip rcmd domain-lookup
```

RSH

Now that these tasks are complete, we can proceed with completing the overall task. Listing 10.3 shows a program that monitors the status BGP sessions on a Cisco router.

Listing 10.3 **Perl5 Program to Monitor BGP Sessions Using RSH**

```perl
#!/usr/local/bin/perl

require 5.004;
use strict;

my $DEBUG = 0;

my $mail = "/usr/sbin/mailx";
my $maillist = 'noc@company.com';
my $tmp = "/tmp/bgp.temp.$$";
my $day = localtime();
```

```
my $smail=0;
my ($ip,$ver,$asn,$msgrcvd,$msgsent,$tblver,
    $inq,$outq,$updown,$state, $router, $asname,
    %Skip,
    );

$SIG {'INT'} = 'cleanup';

my $routerfile = shift( @ARGV );
chomp( $routerfile );
die &Usage unless $routerfile;
open( RTRS, $routerfile ) ¦¦ die "$routerfile: $!\n";
my @rlist = <RTRS>;
close( RTRS );
chomp(@rlist);

my $skipfile = shift( @ARGV );
chomp( $skipfile );

#
# Check to see is a previous version is running
#
if (-e "/tmp/.bgp-lock") {
  system("kill -9 `ps -efa ¦ grep bgp ¦ cut -d \" \" -f 4 ¦ sort`");
  system("rm /tmp/.bgp-lock");
  print STDERR "Lock file exists.\n";
  exit(1);
}

if ($DEBUG) { print STDERR "Creating lockfile ($$)\n"; }
open(LOCK, ">/tmp/.bgp-lock") ¦¦ print STDERR "bgp-lock: $!\n";
print LOCK "$$\n";
close(LOCK);

if ($DEBUG) { print STDERR "Creating mailfile ($tmp)\n"; }
open(MAIL, "> $tmp");

if ($DEBUG) {
  select(STDERR);
  print "Running BGP Disconnect Report at $day\n";
  print "The following BGP sessions are down:\n\n";
  $~ = "HEADER";
  write;
  select(STDOUT);
}

select(MAIL);
print "\nRunning BGP Disconnect Report at $day\n";
print "The following BGP sessions are down:\n\n";
$~ = "HEADER";
write;
```

continues

Listing 10.3 **Continued**

```perl
if( -e $skipfile ) {
  open( SKIP, $skipfile ) || die "$skipfile: $!\n";
  while( defined( my $line = <SKIP> ) ) {
    next if $line =~ /^#/;
    chomp( $line );
    my( $rtr, $as, $ip ) = split( /:/, $line );
    $Skip{$rtr}{$as} = 1;
    $Skip{$rtr}{$ip} = 1;
    if( $rtr =~ /all/i ) { $Skip{$as} = 1; $Skip{$ip} = 1; }
  }
  close( SKIP );
}

while ($router = shift(@rlist)) {
  next if $router =~ /^#/;
  if ($DEBUG) { print STDERR "Checking BGP sessions on $router...\n"; }
  my @grab = `/usr/bsd/rsh $router "sh ip bgp sum"`;
  $router =~ s/\.exodus\.net//;
  chomp(@grab);
  while (my $line = shift(@grab)) {
    next if $line !~ /^\d{1,3}\.\d{1,3}\.\d{1,3}\.\d{1,3}/;
    ($ip,$ver,$asn,$msgrcvd,$msgsent,$tblver,$inq,
     $outq,$updown,$state) = split(/\s\s*/,$line);
    next if $Skip{$router}{$asn} == 1;
    next if $Skip{$router}{$ip} == 1;
    next if $Skip{$asn} == 1;
    next if $Skip{$ip} == 1;
    my @tmp = split(" ", $line);
    if ($tblver == 0) {
      $smail = 1;
      if ($DEBUG) {
        select(STDERR);
        $~ = "LINE";
        write;
        }
      $~ = "LINE";
      write;
      }
    }
  }

select(STDOUT);
close (MAIL);

if ($smail) { `$mail -s 'BGP Disconnect Report' $maillist < $tmp` }
&cleanup();

sub cleanup {
  unlink($tmp);
```

```
    unlink("/tmp/.bgp-lock");
}

sub Usage {
    print "\nUsage: $0 <router file> [skip file]\n";
    print "\n\tExample: $0 router-file\n";
    print "\n<router file> is a text file that lists the routers that will be checked
➥for BGP session status, one per line.\n";
    print "[skip file] is optional and lists the ASNs or IP address that will be
➥ignored by this program.\n\n";
    exit( 1 );
}

format HEADER =
                                                       Time Since
Exodus Router      Peer IP address      Peer ASN       State Change Current Status
================== ================ ======================== ============ ==============
.


format LINE =
@<<<<<<<<<<<<<<<<< @<<<<<<<<<<<<<<< (@>>>>)      @<<<<<<<<<  @<<<<<<<<<
$router,$ip,$asn,$updown,$state
.
```

The program in Listing 10.3 executes the show ip bgp summary command on the list of routers provided. The output of the command is parsed to see whether the BGP table version is zero. If the BGP table version is zero, the peering session is down. Each session that is down is added to a mail file which will be emailed to the email address specified in the program. An optional skip file can be defined on the command line that tells the program to ignore certain IP addresses or autonomous system numbers, such as your own for IBGP sessions. The router file that is supplied on the command line is a simple ASCII file with one router name per line. Listing 10.4 shows a sample of the skip file.

Listing 10.4 **BGP Skip File for Program in Listing 10.3**

```
# Format: router:ASN:ip address
# the "all" keyword can be used in the router field
mae-east.core:2548:
mae-east.core::192.41.177.1
all:3967:
```

RCP

Now, what clever use can we find for RCP? How about configuration archiving? It is always good to have backups of your router configurations available both for disaster recovery and training purposes. It is much safer to have new employees weeding through ASCII configuration files than the actual configurations running on a router. The first step in this process is to enable the RCP server on the routers. Entering the following command in global configuration mode does this:

```
ip rcp-enable
```

Once the RCP server is enabled on the router, you can simply rcp the running configuration from the router to the local system. Executing the following command at the shell prompt of your UNIX workstation does this:

```
rcp <router name>:running-config <local file name>
```

A real world example of this command would be

```
rcp router1.company.com:running-config config-router1
```

This command will copy the current running configuration from router1.company.com to a file called config-router1 on the local hard disk. This task can be further simplified by automating the archival of running configurations from multiple routers. A simple shell script can be used to accomplish this task. Listing 10.5 shows an example of such a script written for the Korn shell.

Listing 10.5 **Korn Shell Script to Archive Configurations from Routers**

```
#!/sbin/ksh
ROUTERS=$1
DIR=/opt/configs
RCP=/usr/bsd/rcp
exec 4< $ROUTERS
QUIT=1

if [ $ROUTERS ]
then
        while [ $QUIT -eq 1 ]
        do
            read -u4 ROUTER
            if [ $? -eq 0 ]
            then
                echo "$RCP $ROUTER:running-config $DIR/config-$ROUTER"
            else
                QUIT=0
            fi
        done
else
        echo "Invalid command line parameters."
        echo "Usage: $0 <router file>"
        exit 1
    fi
```

SYSLOG

Syslog enables the routers to send or log messages to a specified host elsewhere on your network. These messages can be informational in nature or actual errors that would normally be seen on the system console of your network device. Syslog files give Network Engineers a place to look when a network event has occurred and a postmortem investigation is required to determine the cause of the failure. It also gives Network Operators much needed information that will help prevent network outages. Warning signs of upcoming device failures are often sent to the syslog before the event occurs. This prior notification of a potential problem can alert Network Operators early enough to take preventive action. Examples of these types of warning messages are interface line protocol flapping (quick changes between an active and inactive state), invalid OSPF packets, power supply failures, and temperature limits being exceeded.

The Cisco Technical Assistance Center (TAC) might also ask for debugging information while troubleshooting a bug report. It is monumentally easier to enable the necessary debugging on the router at the point of installation and simply cut out the debug information from your syslog files after an event occurs than to have to try to piece together information after an event has occurred. In some cases, you might even need to wait for a repeat occurrence in order to gather the information that you need. That would subject your users to a second interruption of service.

In order to utilize the syslog facilities available in the Cisco IOS, a computer that is able to run syslogd is needed. Syslogd is an application that listens for messages from other devices on the network. When a message directed for the syslog server directly is received, it is stored in a file on the UNIX host that syslogd is running on. The location and name of that file is determined by the syslogd configuration file on the UNIX host. Listing 10.6 shows a sample configuration file for a typical syslogd application. As you can see, different facilities can be sent to the same or different log files.

Listing 10.6 **Sample Syslogd Configuration File**

```
# syslog configuration file.
#
# local5
local5.debug                    /export/home/logs/local5.debug

# RSMs
local6.debug                    /export/home/logs/local6.debug

# local7 is Cisco default facility
#local7.emerg                   /export/home/logs/emergency
#local7.alert                   /export/home/logs/alert
#local7.crit                    /export/home/logs/critical
#local7.err                     /export/home/logs/err
#local7.warning                 /export/home/logs/warning
#local7.notice                  /export/home/logs/notice
```

continues

Listing 10.6 **Continued**

```
#local7.info                    /export/home/logs/info
local7.debug                    /export/home/logs/local7.debug

#mail.emerg                             /var/adm/maillog
#mail.alert                             /var/adm/maillog
#mail.crit                              /var/adm/maillog
#mail.err                               /var/adm/maillog
#mail.warning                           /var/adm/maillog
#mail.notice                            /var/adm/maillog
#mail.info                              /var/adm/maillog
mail.debug                              /var/adm/maillog
```

Syslogd comes standard with all UNIX distributions and is also available with
Windows NT. If you need help configuring your log host to run syslogd, consult your
system administrator.

After the log host is running syslogd, the routers need to be configured to send
messages to the syslog host. Before logging can be configured on your routers, several
decisions need to be made about how it will be configured. The first decision is what
logging facility will the routers use to talk to the syslog host? There are eight logging
facilities available, 0 through 7. The default is facility 7. Some of the facilities are used
by the UNIX host itself to report system messages. When two different network
devices are using the same syslog facility on the same syslog server, the messages are
combined into the same file. Next, you need to decide what condition levels you want
to log? There are eight message levels available, and they are listed in Table 10.1.

Table 10.1 **Message Levels**

Level Name	Level	Description	Syslog Definition
Emergencies	0	System unusable	SYS_EMERG
Alerts	1	Immediate action required	SYS_ALERT
Critical	2	Critical conditions	SYS_CRIT
Errors	3	Error conditions	SYS_ERR
Warnings	4	Warning conditions	SYS_WARNING
Notifications	5	Normal but significant condition	SYS_NOTICE
Informational	6	Informational messages only	SYS_INFO
Debugging	7	Debugging messages	SYS_DEBUG

Configuring SYSLOG

After all the decisions are made, the routers can be configured. The following commands need to be entered in global configuration mode:

```
logging on
logging 192.168.1.10
logging trap alerts
logging facility local6
service timestamps log
```

Once these commands have been entered in the routers, messages will start appearing in the logging files on the syslog host.

The number and type of messages will depend on the trap level that has been configured on the router. If the *debugging* trap level has been configured, every condition on the router will be logged. If the *emergency* trap level has been configured, only the severest of conditions will be logged.

There is such a thing as information overload. Be careful not to configure your routers to send too much information to your logging host. If there is a large number of routers on your network, it is very possible for the syslog files on your logging host to grow rapidly. As the amount of information being logged increases, the chances that you will miss an important piece of information increases as well.

Using SYSLOG

In a large network it is often hard to pinpoint minute problems. If there is a defective Fast Ethernet cable connecting two routers together, how do you tell? The line protocol on the interface might change from up to down for a period of a few milliseconds. This is the type of information that is useful but not readily available. The only way to see this event is through error messages reported to the system console or syslog.

Even if error messages are being exported to a syslog host, it is unlikely that there is someone watching the log files constantly waiting for an event to occur. This is where our scripting becomes valuable. It is easy to automate the task of watching the syslog files for certain predefined events. If one of these predefined events occurs, any number of notification schemes can be utilized. An email alert can be sent. Alphanumeric pages could be sent to on-call engineers. Perhaps a visual alert can be sent to an active monitoring station in a Network Operations Center. The example in Listing 10.7 watches for new events to be entered into the syslog files then sends an email when a predefined event occurs.

Why Aren't Messages Appearing?
It is often required that the syslog daemon on the log host be restarted after routers have been configured for syslogging.

Listing 10.7   **Perl5 Program to Watch Syslog Files for Predefined Events**

```perl
#!/usr/local/bin/perl -w

require 5.004;
use strict;

my $logfile = '/var/logs/critical';
my $tail = '/usr/bin/tail -f';
my $rulefile = '/var/logs/logrules';
my $mailprog = '/usr/lib/sendmail';
my $mailto = 'ncc@company.com';

open( RULES, $rulefile ) || die "$rulefile: $!\n";
my @rules = <RULES>;
close( RULES );
chomp( @rules );

open( LOG, "$tail $logfile|" ) || die "$tail $logfile: $!\n";
while( defined( my $line = <LOG> ) ) {
  chomp( $line );
  foreach my $rule ( @rules ) {
    if( $line =~ /$rule/i ) {
      &DoAlert($rule, $line);
    }
  }
}

sub DoAlert {
  my( $rule, $line ) = @_;
  open( MAIL, "|$mailprog $mailto" ) || print STDERR "$mailprog: $!\n";
  print MAIL "From: Syslog Monitor Program\n";
  print MAIL "Subject: Predefined Rule Match ($rule)\n\n";
  print MAIL "$line\n\n";
  close( MAIL );
}
```

The event file (listed as logrules in the script) is an ASCII file with one pattern per line. Each pattern is case insensitive. The event file could contain:

```
line protocol
```

This would cause an event to be triggered for all syslog messages that contained that string. An example of the kind of message that would trigger this would even be a line protocol state change.

Conclusion

Hopefully, the examples and ideas mentioned in this chapter will find a use in your network. It is likely that you will need to modify them in small ways to fit your exact needs. It is for this reason alone that commercial applications are not always the best choice for monitoring tools. I am not suggesting that professional programmed commercial applications should be replaced with home grown tools. However, I have yet to find a commercial application that has met all needs of the companies for which I have worked. I almost always find myself augmenting the purchased software with tools of my own.

IV

Router Troubleshooting

11

Troubleshooting

THERE ARE BASICALLY TWO TYPES OF NETWORK ADMINISTRATORS, the proactive type and the reactive type. A proactive Network Administrator uses monitoring tools to fix problem areas before actual trouble occurs. A reactive Network Administrator answers reports of network trouble and fixes problems after they have occurred. It is always better to be a proactive Network Administrator, but you do not always get to choose. Circumstances might dictate what role you will take. In general though, you will do yourself well to pursue proactive troubleshooting of your network rather than wait for something bad to happen. Once you become enveloped in a reactive state of troubleshooting, it is sometimes difficult to regain a proactive stance. Suppose you notice that a card in one of your routers has reset several times in the past few days. It is a much better idea to replace that card than to wait until it actually fails and perhaps crashes the whole router as well. I liken the situation to purchasing wood for my fireplace. I can buy a cord of wood in the summer, or I can buy a cord of wood in the fall. The end result is the same—I have a cord of wood to burn in my fireplace. However, I will have paid a much higher price for waiting to buy it in the fall rather than in the summer.

Troubleshooting a network problem can be a daunting task. The key to determining the origin of a problem is to use a standard troubleshooting methodology. The steps listed below form a basic outline for troubleshooting a problem. This list is by no means written in stone. It should change to fit the specific type of problem encountered. Use it to focus your train of thought on reaching your end goal, find the problem, and fix it.

1. Clearly define the trouble reported. (What exactly is the problem?)
2. Make a list of all the symptoms.
3. Make a list of all possible causes of the symptoms.
4. Define the test actions to validate or eliminate the possible causes.
5. Prioritize the list according to two metrics: items that are most likely to resolve the problem, and items that are fast and easy to test. Items on the top of both lists are tried first. Items on the bottom of both are last resorts. Those with high position on one list and lower position on another are judgment calls.
6. Execute tests to identify the actual source of the problem.
7. Generate the action required to resolve the problem.
8. Identify adverse effects the problem's resolution might have on the network.
9. Implement the fix.

It is very important to document all the steps that you take while troubleshooting a problem in your network. When trying to fix a complex problem, it becomes more likely that you will forget some of the steps which you took to reach the actual resolution. It takes a little extra time during the course of the troubleshooting procedure, but it is time well spent. The first thing that will be asked of you (usually by management) after the problem has been solved, is to provide a detailed account of the cause of the problem. In addition, you will probably be asked to provide the steps you took to resolve the problem and what steps you would take in the future to help prevent the problem from reoccurring. This should be an easy request to answer if you have documented the troubleshooting process properly.

A common practice in troubleshooting network problems is called the "Divide and Conquer" method. Simply stated, if you are having trouble isolating a problem in your network, break your network into two parts. Examine both parts individually. If one part of the network is operating normally, then you know the problem is in the other part of the network. Take the half of the network in which you have isolated the trouble, and split it into two parts. Examine each half of the troubled portion of the network. If one portion operates as expected, then you know that the problem resides somewhere in the remaining portion. Continue this process of breaking the suspected troubled portion into two parts until you have isolated the exact cause of the problem.

A Troubleshooting Example

An employee in the accounting department of your company reports that he is having trouble retrieving data stored on a network file server. After first receiving the trouble report, you contact the employee and gather some more information. Get as much information as you can. Ask if the problem occurs on a regular basis. Does it happen daily? Does it always happen at the same time of day? Is he able to connect to the file server? If he is able to connect to the file server, is he able to access other files on the server? It is far better to have too much information than to have to contact the employee again at a later date. Having to do so makes the troubleshooting process longer. Remember to document everything.

Use the information gathered to make your list of symptoms. It would be a good idea to try to recreate the problem on your own if at all possible. This can make more symptoms evident that the original employee might not have noticed. You should now have enough information to produce some possible causes of the problem. The employee might not be able to retrieve the file that he wants because he does not have permission to read the file. Or perhaps the data structure of the file itself is corrupted.

Next, develop a list of actions you can use to verify whether each of the possible causes is the actual root of the problem. Then sort that list of tests by what you believe their likelihood of success would be.

Now run through your list of tests until you reach one that verifies the cause of the problem or you exhaust the list. If you exhaust the list, you need to go back and either gather more information or generate more possible causes of the problem.

Once you have found the cause of the problem, you need to verify that implementing the fix will not affect other aspects of the system or the network that you are unaware of. A separate organization or procedure sometimes performs this function. The process of identifying the effects of one action to other aspects of a system (by system I mean a group of elements) is called Change Management.

After you have determined that the fix can be implemented without severe side effects, implement the fix. Test that the fix has indeed corrected the original problem that was reported. Then notify the person that originally reported the problem that the trouble has been resolved.

Pay Attention to Details

I once had a customer complain of a broken mouse when I was doing desktop support years ago. The mouse stopped working everyday at the same time in the morning. By the time the afternoon came the mouse would work again. I later determined that the type of mouse that he was using relied on optical sensors rather than tactile. When the sun shined through the office window in the morning it penetrated the mouse case and rendered the optical sensors useless. I never would have determined the cause of that problem had I not gathered the amount of information that I did.

Using *Ping* and *Traceroute* in the Internet

Effective troubleshooting cannot be accomplished without a good understanding of the tools used to diagnose problems. Many Network Operators use ping and traceroute to diagnose network-related problems. The problem that grows greater by the day is that the users of these tools do not clearly understand how the tools work and are therefore mislead at times by their responses. Ping and traceroute are discussed in depth in Chapter 12, "Tools of the Trade."

One of the hard things for Network Operators to understand when using ping and traceroute is that as more and more companies become multi-homed (connected to two or more exit points) for redundancy, the number of possible paths to and from a destination increases. As the number of paths increases, along with the number of Internet service providers, IP packets are forced to follow the routing policies of various different companies. That is, once the data packets leave your network and enter another, you have no control over how those packets get to their destination. They are routed through the other networks based upon the policies that the companies controlling those networks have put into place. Having multiple different exit paths for data is what enables asymmetrical routing to occur. Your outbound path is not guaranteed to be the same path that is used to return traffic to your network from that destination.

The same effect can be observed with your own network. Suppose that you have two routers that are linked by two Fast Ethernet connections (see Figure 11.1). Open Shortest Path First (OSPF) is the dynamic routing protocol used to exchange reachability information between the two routers. The path from router R1 to router R2 is via Fast Ethernet0/0/0 because the OSPF cost is lower then Fast Ethernet1/0/0. However, the path from router R2 to router R1 is via Fast Ethernet3/0/0 because the OSPF cost is lower than Fast Ethernet2/0/0.

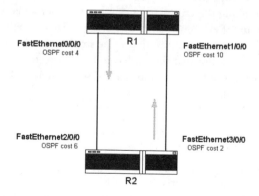

Figure 11.1   Example of asymmetric routes in a LAN.

This can be a real problem when using traceroute because the latency (delay) times displayed on the output are based on ICMP echo replies. The path back to the source for the echo replies from each host along the path to the destination might differ from the forward path; this is called *Asymmetrical Routing* (Chapter 12 discusses the workings of traceroute in more detail). The problem becomes very evident when the return packet must travel a path of ten hops when the forward path is only three. Also, if one of the links in the return path is congested, traceroute will show that hop as having high latency even though the forward path to the hop is not really congested. This is shown in Listing 11.1. The forward path goes through one Internet service provider and the return path is through another Internet service provider. The number of devices that the data packets must travel though is different in each direction. This adds more possible places for latency to occur.

Listing 11.1 **Asymmetrical Route Paths**

```
//Forward Path:
traceroute to gumby.exodus.net (207.82.177.120), 30 hops max, 40 byte packets
 1  WestEd-7513-FE11-0-0 (205.154.242.1)  1 ms  1 ms  1 ms
 2  4CNet-UUNet-GW.CSU.net (137.145.11.6)  2 ms  2 ms  2 ms
 3  33.ATM3-0-0.GW1.LAX4.ALTER.NET (157.130.226.205)  6 ms  3 ms  2 ms
 4  121.ATM3-0.XR1.LAX4.ALTER.NET (146.188.248.98)  4 ms  4 ms  3 ms
 5  193.ATM6-0.XR1.LAX2.ALTER.NET (146.188.248.145)  5 ms  3 ms  4 ms
 6  195.ATM8-0-0.GW2.LAX2.ALTER.NET (146.188.248.229)  3 ms  3 ms  3 ms
 7  uunet-px.irca-03-h1-1-0.core.exodus.net (209.1.169.93)  17 ms (ttl=248!)  21
    ➥ms (ttl=248!)  16 ms (ttl=248!)
 8  uunet-px.irca-03-h1-1-0.core.exodus.net (209.1.169.93)  21 ms  17 ms  20 ms
 9  irca-02-f1-1-0.core.exodus.net (209.185.9.221)  18 ms  18 ms  18 ms
10  irca-05-p1-0.core.exodus.net (209.185.249.22)  17 ms scca-16-p1-
    ➥0.core.exodus.net (209.185.9.81)  20 ms (ttl=245!)  25 ms (ttl=245!)
11  scca-11-p1-0-0.core.exodus.net (209.185.9.141)  20 ms (ttl=244!)  20 ms
    ➥(ttl=244!)  23 ms (ttl=244!)
12  209.185.84.198 (209.185.84.198)  20 ms (ttl=243!)  21 ms (ttl=243!)  24 ms
    ➥(ttl=243!)
gumby.exodus.net (207.82.177.120)  24 ms (ttl=242!)  24 ms (ttl=242!)  26 ms
➥(ttl=242!)


//Reverse Path:
traceroute to thor.CSU.net (130.150.20.11), 30 hops max, 40 byte packets
 1  207.82.177.3 (207.82.177.3)  2 ms  1 ms  1 ms
 2  scca-11-f5-0-0.core.exodus.net (206.79.253.2)  1 ms  1 ms  1 ms
 3  scca-15-p0-0.core.exodus.net (209.1.169.178)  1 ms  1 ms  1 ms
 4  scca-05-p0-1.core.exodus.net (209.1.169.253)  4 ms  2 ms  3 ms
 5  scca-02-p0-0-0.core.exodus.net (209.1.169.42)  3 ms (ttl=250!)  3 ms
    ➥(ttl=250!)  3 ms
 6  scca-04-f4-0-0.core.exodus.net (209.1.169.146)  3 ms  3 ms  5 ms
 7  sl-gw4-sj-6-0-0-T3.sprintlink.net (144.228.44.69)  13 ms  15 ms  13 ms
 8  sl-bb10-sj-0-3-155M.sprintlink.net (144.232.3.53)  14 ms  12 ms  9 ms
 9  sl-bb21-stk-7-0.sprintlink.net (144.232.8.194)  11 ms  8 ms  9 ms
10  sl-bb21-stk-8-0.sprintlink.net (144.232.4.113)  7 ms  9 ms  8 ms
```

continues

Listing 11.1 **Continued**

```
11  sl-gw11-stk-0-0-0.sprintlink.net (144.232.4.82)  8 ms  10 ms  9 ms
12  sl-csuhay-1-0-T3.sprintlink.net (144.228.147.14)  11 ms  11 ms  11 ms
13  WESTED-HAY-ATM.CSU.net (137.145.202.94)  21 ms (ttl=244!)  22 ms (ttl=244!)
    ➥23 ms (ttl=244!)
14  thor.csu.net (130.150.20.11)  30 ms (ttl=243!)  24 ms (ttl=243!)  28 ms
    ➥(ttl=243!)
```

The same asymmetry can be found in private corporate networks as well (see Listing 11.2).

Listing 11.2 **Corporate LAN Example of Asymmetrical Routing**

```
//Forward path:
traceroute to dcr01.jycy01.exodus.net (209.1.220.3), 30 hops max, 40 byte packets
 1  207.82.177.3 (207.82.177.3)  2 ms  1 ms  1 ms
 2  216.32.112.190 (216.32.112.190)  2 ms  1 ms  1 ms
 3  bbr02.sntc02.exodus.net (209.185.9.142)  3 ms  1 ms  1 ms
 4  bbr01.irvn01.exodus.net (209.185.9.82)  11 ms  10 ms  10 ms
 5  bbr02.irvn01.exodus.net (209.185.249.14)  10 ms  11 ms  11 ms
 6  bbr02.hrnd01.exodus.net (209.185.9.205)  92 ms  91 ms  91 ms
 7  bbr01.hrnd01.exodus.net (209.185.249.1)  175 ms (ttl=251!)  89 ms (ttl=252!)
    ➥89 ms (ttl=252!)
 8  bbr02.jycy01.exodus.net (209.185.9.202)  78 ms (ttl=249!)  79 ms (ttl=249!)
    ➥78 ms (ttl=249!)
 9  dcr01.jycy01.exodus.net (209.1.169.186)  627 ms (ttl=249!)  *  77 ms (ttl=249!)

Reverse path:
Tracing the route to gumby.exodus.net (207.82.177.120)

 1 bbr01.jycy01.exodus.net (209.1.169.193) 0 msec 0 msec 4 msec
 2 bbr02.sntc01.exodus.net (209.1.169.173) 56 msec 56 msec 60 msec
 3 bbr01.sntc01.exodus.net (209.1.169.189) 60 msec 60 msec 60 msec
 4 bbr01.sntc02.exodus.net (209.185.249.110) 80 msec 80 msec 76 msec
 5 dcr01.sntc02.exodus.net (209.1.169.177) 76 msec 80 msec 76 msec
 6 rsm-s3-a-bbone907.lan.exodus.net (206.79.253.21) 76 msec 80 msec 80 msec
 7 gumby.exodus.net (207.82.177.120) 80 msec 76 msec 80 msec
dcr01.jycy01>
```

If there were any high latency values or dropped packets reported in the forward or reverse paths (as in line 9 of the forward path in Listing 11.2), each hop along both the forward and reverse path would need to be tested individually in order to pinpoint the actual place that the problem is occurring. To do this, you need access to every router along the path of the traceroute. If the problem is within your network, this is not a problem. However, if the problem is occurring with another network that you exchange traffic with, then a little more work is required. This is where the Network Operations Center for each ISP comes into play. You will need their help in order to accomplish this task.

The basic procedure is to log in to the first host in the path and ping the next host in the path. If everything looks good, move to the next host in the path and ping the third host in the path. From the forward path example in Listing 11.1, the first host would be WestEd-7513-FE11-0-0. From there you would ping the next host in the path, which is 4CNet-UUNet-GW.CSU.net. If everything tests good between those two hosts, you move to 4CNet-UUNet-GW.CSU.net and ping to 33.ATM3-0-0.GW1.LAX4.ALTER.NET. Repeat this procedure until either the problem is found or the entire path is proven to be error free. The same is done for the reverse path.

Often times you will encounter networks that filter certain packet types on their network. Many times network diagnostic tools will appear to fail when the end host you are testing to is actually operating properly.

Cisco's Troubleshooting Mechanisms

The Cisco IOS offers a great deal of commands to aid in the troubleshooting of network problems. There are basically two types of IOS commands that can be used in troubleshooting problems:

- `Debug` set of commands
- `Show` set of commands

Specific commands from each of these families are mentioned in each of the remaining chapters of this book. Several commands from each family are introduced and their use explained.

Debug Commands

The Cisco IOS enables the output of an extreme amount of information for almost every option that can be enabled. This type of information is of critical importance when you are trying to figure out why a problem is occurring. Suppose you pinpoint a routing problem as being caused by one router. That router is running OSPF and BGP routing processes. How do you determine which protocol is causing the routing problem? You use the `show` and `debug` commands for those protocols provided in the IOS.

The text of this output is normally sent to the console port. This means that if you are connected via the Telnet ports, you will not see the `debug` output. You can fix this by redirecting the output to any of the VTY ports by executing the following command during the Telnet session:

```
terminal monitor
```

Having `debug` information output to your current terminal session is like having the various gauges on your car. There is a great deal of information available, but it is hard to look at all the gauges at once. It is best to keep the amount of debugging that is enabled at one time to a minimum. This will help you to not cause information overload on yourself. To disable the logging of `debug` information to your current session, use the following command:

```
terminal no monitor
```

Debug information is also sent to any syslog servers that might be configured as well as the internal buffer if enabled.

Use the debug ? command in the router enable mode to list all the available debugging options.

Use the show debug command to display which type of debugging, if any, are enabled. To disable debugging, use the no debug form of the command or no debug all to turn off all debugging.

Show Commands

The Cisco IOS enables the display of current system running information through its family of show commands. The current status of almost every option available to be enabled can be shown using the appropriate show command. show commands are useful in debugging as a first line of tools. They can help pinpoint a circuit or configuration problem very quickly. For instance, the show interface command will tell you whether the interface is up or down. It also shows you which configuration options are enabled and their current status. show commands display their output to the terminal in which the commands are executed. Use the show ? command in the router enable mode to list all the available options.

Debugging Caution
Debugging is CPU intensive and should be used with caution. Using the debug all command is guaranteed to bring your router to its knees.

Where Do You Find Help?
The ? IOS operator is a very powerful tool. It basically signals the IOS that you need help. It will display all the available IOS commands for the current command level you are at.

A nice feature that is available in the Cisco IOS is an internal buffer to log system messages. Following is a sample output of the show logging command:

```
Router>sh log
Syslog logging: enabled (0 messages dropped, 0 flushes, 0 overruns)
    Console logging: level debugging, 37 messages logged
    Monitor logging: level debugging, 0 messages logged
    Trap logging: level debugging, 42 message lines logged
        Logging to 192.169.10.100, 42 message lines logged
    Buffer logging: level debugging, 37 messages logged

Log Buffer (1000000 bytes):

*Oct  6 17:05:16.443 pdt: %LINEPROTO-5-UPDOWN: Line protocol on Interface  8
➥POS1/0/0, changed state to down
*Oct  6 17:05:16.443 pdt: %LINEPROTO-5-UPDOWN: Line protocol on Interface
➥FastEthernet2/0/0, changed state to down
*Oct  6 17:05:16.443 pdt: %LINEPROTO-5-UPDOWN: Line protocol on Interface
➥FastEthernet2/1/0, changed state to down
*Oct  6 17:05:16.443 pdt: %LINEPROTO-5-UPDOWN: Line protocol on Interface
➥FastEthernet5/0/0, changed state to down
*Oct  6 17:05:16.443 pdt: %LINEPROTO-5-UPDOWN: Line protocol on Interface
➥FastEthernet8/0/0, changed state to down
*Oct  6 17:05:16.443 pdt: %LINEPROTO-5-UPDOWN: Line protocol on Interface
➥Hssi8/1/0, changed state to down
```

The buffer stores messages in a stack. Older messages are displayed first with the most recent at the end of the list. As new messages are added to the bottom of the stack, older messages are pushed off of the top. This is usually the first place to look when a router has crashed unexpectedly. The final events before the router reloaded should be stored here. Some of the most common reasons for router crashes are memory errors, extremely fragmented memory on the router processor (which causes memory allocation failures), and multiple interface card resets.

Conclusion

Whether you find yourself acting in a proactive mode or a reactive mode, the steps outlined in this chapter will serve you well in correcting any problem in your network. As time goes on, the troubleshooting procedure will become almost an innate action that kicks in once a network problem is reported. If you follow the simple guidelines presented in this chapter, there is no troubleshooting challenge that you cannot meet. Remember to always document everything that you do in the course of troubleshooting and correcting a problem on your network. This documentation can be useful in training less experienced Network Operators in the future.

12

Tools of the Trade

A NUMBER OF INSTRUMENTS ARE AVAILABLE TO YOU AS THE Network Operator that will help in the troubleshooting of network problems. Because many of the problems that companies encounter today are related to Internet connectivity, this chapter will cover some of the basic tools that can be used to pinpoint network problems. Some of these tools are useful on local network segments where there is no connectivity to the Internet.

In the last chapter we learned about troubleshooting techniques. Now it is time to learn about the tools that are most often used to troubleshoot problems in the Internet and on local IP networks.

PING

PING is an application that sends packets to a specified destination. Each packet that PING sends is a request for a response from the destination node. The destination node sends a response packet to the source of the request after it receives each request.

PING uses a protocol from the TCP/IP suite of protocols called the Internet Control Messaging Protocol (ICMP). The request packets are called ICMP ECHO_REQUESTs. The response packets are called *ICMP echo replies*. There are a number of ICMP messages that can be returned when an ECHO_REQUEST is received. Table 12.1 lists the possible ICMP response messages.

Table 12.1 **ICMP Response Messages**

Message	Description
Network unreachable	Gateway has no route to destination network
Host unreachable	Gateway has no route to destination host
Protocol unreachable	Protocol is not allowed or is undefined on destination host
Port unreachable	Port is not allowed or is undefined on destination host
Fragmentation needed and do not fragment (DF) bit set	MTU of the transit path requires that the packet be fragmented but the DF bit is set in the IP header
TTL exceeded	The TTL field of the packet was decremented to 0 before it reached the destination host

PING was initially developed as an IP-based tool. In recent years, the PING application concept has been expanded to include the AppleTalk, IPX, DECnet, XNS, and Banyan VINES protocols on Cisco routers.

This is a very simple tool that can be used to test network connectivity, as well as packet loss. The PING application can keep track of how many packets it has transmitted and also how many responses it received from the destination host. Using this information, PING can determine how many request packets did not receive a response.

ICMP Message Types

RFC 792 defines the ICMP message types. All the RFCs can be found on the Internet. Merit has all the RFCs available at http://nic.merit.edu/internet/documents/rfc/INDEX.rfc

The Origin of PING

PING is said to stand for Packet Internet Groper. There are many who believe that the acronym came first, and then someone thought up words that fit. In any event, the name is now used both as a noun (the name of the program) and as a verb (the act of using the program).

PING Protocol Options

Which protocols you are allowed to use with PING depends on the version of IOS that you are running on your routers. If you are running an ISP version rather than the full Enterprise version, you would not be able to specify AppleTalk as a PING protocol. The reason for this is the ISP versions of the IOS only support IP based protocols.

For instance, suppose that you are having trouble reaching one of your favorite WWW sites. Your first step in troubleshooting this problem would be to determine if the WWW server that you are trying to reach is online. PING can be used to make this determination. If I want to see some information on the President of the United States, I would go to the White House WWW site. After typing the URL into my Web browser I get no response. My first inclination is to PING the White House WWW site to see if it is online. The following command would be used to initiate a PING to the White House WWW site:

```
test-r1>ping www.whitehouse.gov
```

By default, the Cisco PING program sends 5 ICMP_REQUEST packets to the specified host. Here is the response that you would normally expect to see:

```
Translating "www.whitehouse.gov"...domain server (209.1.221.10) [OK]

Type escape sequence to abort.
Sending 5, 100-byte ICMP Echoes to 198.137.240.92, timeout is 2 seconds:
!!!!!
Success rate is 100 percent (5/5), round-trip min/avg/max = 92/93/96 ms
test-r1>
```

In my case, I see all packets being dropped. This is shown in the following output:

```
Translating "www.whitehouse.gov"...domain server (209.1.221.10) [OK]

Type escape sequence to abort.
Sending 5, 100-byte ICMP Echoes to 198.137.240.92, timeout is 2 seconds:
.....
Success rate is 0 percent (0/5)
test-r1>
```

Having a zero percent success rate does not necessarily mean that the WWW site is down. There might be other problems prohibiting me from reaching the site. There could be a routing loop or perhaps a misconfigured filter-list on a router along the path to the WWW server. Some Internet sites purposely block ICMP traffic to their site to guard against electronic attacks. From here I would do some more investigating using other tools that are covered in this chapter, such as traceroute.

You might notice when installing new connections that the first packet of the PING series will fail, but the following four will be successful. Here is an example of output:

```
test-r1#ping 192.168.9.142

Type escape sequence to abort.
Sending 5, 100-byte ICMP Echoes to 192.168.9.142, timeout is 2 seconds:
.!!!!
Success rate is 80 percent (4/5), round-trip min/avg/max = 1/1/4 ms
test-r1#
```

The first packet is lost because the router needed to go through the ARP process for the IP address that I specified. The ICMP request timed out before the MAC address for the host that I specified could be determined. If I were to run the same PING again, all five requests would be successful.

The PING application also stores the time that each request is sent and subtracts that from the time that the response to that request was received. This delta value is called the round trip time (RTT). The RTT can be used to track latency in networks. *Latency* is a term used to express the delay between the start and end times of an ICMP response request. See Listing 12.1 for a sample output from the PING application on a UNIX workstation.

Listing 12.1   **PING Application Output**

```
PING ftp.mcp.com (206.246.150.88): 56 data bytes
64 bytes from 206.246.150.88: icmp_seq=0 ttl=245 time=69.767 ms
64 bytes from 206.246.150.88: icmp_seq=1 ttl=245 time=65.530 ms
64 bytes from 206.246.150.88: icmp_seq=2 ttl=245 time=65.494 ms
64 bytes from 206.246.150.88: icmp_seq=3 ttl=245 time=72.605 ms
64 bytes from 206.246.150.88: icmp_seq=4 ttl=245 time=70.212 ms


----ftp.mcp.com PING Statistics----
5 packets transmitted, 5 packets received, 0% packet loss
round-trip min/avg/max = 65.494/68.722/72.605 ms
```

The normal RTT for a packet originated on the west coast of the United States sent to the east coast of the United States is 65 milliseconds (ms). If you send a PING packet from a host on the west coast to a host on the east coast, and the PING output shows an RTT of 400 ms for every packet, there is something wrong somewhere in the path to the east coast host. Latency can be attributed to many things:

- The server might be overloaded.
- The local bandwidth to the server might be inadequate.
- There might be congestion problems in the path to the server.

Using PING on each router in the path to the end host can help determine where the latency is occurring. The latency values that are displayed by PING can be misleading because the path back to the originating host might not be the same as the path from the originating host.

The PING application comes standard with every IP implementation (required by the IP RFC). The PING application available in the Cisco IOS is very flexible. You can specify the packet size of the requests, the number of packets to send, and the source IP address as well as many other options. These options are available in the Cisco extended PING. Extended PING is available only in the enabled user mode. To access the extended PING features, you execute the PING application without any arguments. Listing 12.2 shows the output from a standard extended PING.

Listing 12.2   **Cisco Extended PING Output**

```
test-r1#ping
Protocol [ip]:
Target IP address: www.whitehouse.gov
Translating "www.whitehouse.gov"...domain server (209.1.221.10) [OK]

Repeat count [5]: 100
Datagram size [100]: 500
Timeout in seconds [2]:
Extended commands [n]: y
Source address or interface: 162.168.9.141
Type of service [0]: ?
Set DF bit in IP header? [no]:
Validate reply data? [no]:
Data pattern [0xABCD]: 0xFFFF
Loose, Strict, Record, Timestamp, Verbose[none]:
Sweep range of sizes [n]:
Type escape sequence to abort.
Sending 100, 500-byte ICMP Echoes to 198.137.240.92, timeout is 2 seconds:
Packet has data pattern 0xFFFF
!!!!!!!!!!!!!!!!!!!!!!!!!!!!!!!!!!!!!!!!!!!!!!!!!!!!!!!!!!!!.!!!!!!!!
!!!!!!!!!!!!!!!!!!!!!!!!!!!!!!
Success rate is 99 percent (99/100), round-trip min/avg/max = 96/104/572 ms
test-r1#
```

As you can see from Listing 12.2, extended PING lets you set the number of packets to send, the size of each packet, the source IP address of the packets, whether or not to set the DO NOT FRAGMENT bit of the IP header, and the IP data bit pattern. The IP data bit pattern is a useful option to change when testing new WAN circuits. Varying the bit pattern from all zeros to all ones can alert you to possible physical layer problems. If you see CRC or framing errors while running these types of PINGs on the circuit, you should call your telco and have them test the circuit end to end using variable bit patterns.

Listing 12.3 shows the output of an extended PING with the verbose option enabled. Verbose mode displays the RTT for each packet that is sent.

Listing 12.3   **Cisco Extended PING in Verbose Mode**

```
test-r1#ping ip
Target IP address: www.whitehouse.gov
Repeat count [5]: 20
Datagram size [100]:
Timeout in seconds [2]:
Extended commands [n]: y
Source address or interface: 192.168.9.141
Type of service [0]:
Set DF bit in IP header? [no]: y
Validate reply data? [no]:
```

continues

Listing 12.3   **Continued**

```
Data pattern [0xABCD]: 0x0000
Loose, Strict, Record, Timestamp, Verbose[none]: v
Loose, Strict, Record, Timestamp, Verbose[V]:
Sweep range of sizes [n]:
Type escape sequence to abort.
Sending 100, 100-byte ICMP Echoes to 198.137.240.92, timeout is 2 seconds:
Packet has data pattern 0x0000
Reply to request 0 (96 ms)
Reply to request 1 (92 ms)
Reply to request 2 (96 ms)
Reply to request 3 (96 ms)
Reply to request 4 (96 ms)
Reply to request 5 (96 ms)
Reply to request 6 (96 ms)
Reply to request 7 (92 ms)
Reply to request 8 (96 ms)
Reply to request 9 (96 ms)
Reply to request 10 (96 ms)
Reply to request 11 (96 ms)
Reply to request 12 (92 ms)
Reply to request 13 (96 ms)
Reply to request 14 (92 ms)
Reply to request 15 (92 ms)
Reply to request 16 (96 ms)
Reply to request 17 (96 ms)
Reply to request 18 (92 ms)
Reply to request 19 (96 ms)
Request 20 timed out
Success rate is 95 percent (19/20), round-trip min/avg/max = 92/99/380 ms
test-r1#
```

Traceroute

Traceroute is an application that works in a similar fashion as PING. Traceroute uses ICMP ECHO_REQUESTs to determine the path that packets take to get to a destination host. Traceroute does this by first sending an ICMP ECHO_REQUEST to the destination host with a time to live (TTL) of 1. The first device along the path receives the packet and decrements the TTL counter. The TTL is not zero, so the router sends back a HOST_UNREACHABLE response to the originating host. Traceroute then sends another ICMP_REQUEST with the TTL set to 2. The packet passes through the first router (which decrements the TTL to 1), and when the second router in the path receives it, the TTL is decremented by 1. The second router sees the TTL is 0 and returns a HOST_UNREACHABLE response to the originating host. This process is repeated until a packet reaches the destination host or the default maximum hop count of 30 is reached.

Traceroute sends three `ICMP_REQUEST`s during each iteration. As each response is received from the routers along the path to the destination network, traceroute outputs the IP address or DNS name of the router to your screen. This gives you a listing of the hops along a path to the destination network that you specified. An asterisk is usually displayed in the hop output if a response to a request was not received. This indicates that the packet was dropped.

Traceroute expands the capabilities of PING. It not only displays packet loss and latency information but it also gives you a road map of the path that the packet took to get to the destination host. This road map is useful in tracking down congested links and pinpointing areas of high latency and packet loss.

Along with the hop information, traceroute displays the RTT of each packet that was returned from each router along the path. See Listing 12.4 for a sample output from the traceroute application on a UNIX workstation.

Listing 12.4   **Traceroute Application Output**

```
 1  207.82.177.3 (207.82.177.3)  3 ms  24 ms  5 ms
 2  scca-11-f5-0-0.core.exodus.net (206.79.253.2)  5 ms  1 ms  1 ms
 3  scca-15-p0-0.core.exodus.net (209.1.169.178)  2 ms  1 ms  1 ms
 4  scca-12-p1-0-0.core.exodus.net (209.185.9.145)  2 ms (ttl=254!)  2 ms
    ↪(ttl=254!)  2 ms (ttl=254!)
 5  paix-h1-1-0.core.exodus.net (209.1.169.226)  3 ms (ttl=253!)  3 ms (ttl=253!)
    ↪2 ms (ttl=253!)
 6  f0.border1.pao1.genuity.net (198.32.176.10)  4 ms (ttl=252!)  3 ms (ttl=252!)
    ↪4 ms (ttl=252!)
 7  h4.core1.sjc1.genuity.net (207.240.1.249)  5 ms (ttl=250!)  4 ms (ttl=250!)  4
    ↪ms (ttl=250!)
 8  fe-6-1.core1.ord1.genuity.net (207.240.2.65)  57 ms (ttl=247!) fe-6-
    ↪0.core1.ord1.genuity.net (207.240.1.161)  58 ms (ttl=247!) fe-6-
    ↪0.core1.ord1.genuity.net (207.240.1.65)  56 ms (ttl=247!)
 9  fe-6-1.peer1.ord1.genuity.net (207.240.2.174)  56 ms (ttl=248!)  58 ms
    ↪(ttl=248!)  58 ms (ttl=248!)
10  NChicago2-core0.nap.net (207.112.249.129)  58 ms (ttl=247!)  59 ms (ttl=247!)
    ↪59 ms (ttl=247!)
11  NChicago1-core0.nap.net (207.112.247.182)  60 ms (ttl=248!)  58 ms (ttl=248!)
    ↪60 ms (ttl=248!)
12  chi-f0.iquest.net (206.54.225.250)  130 ms (ttl=247!)  158 ms (ttl=247!)  174
    ↪ms (ttl=247!)
13  204.180.50.9 (204.180.50.9)  64 ms (ttl=21!)  65 ms (ttl=21!)  63 ms (ttl=21!)
14  iq-mcp.iquest.net (206.246.190.153)  66 ms (ttl=245!)  *  65 ms (ttl=245!)
```

Listing 12.5 shows the output of a traceroute from a Cisco router to www.cisco.com.

Listing 12.5 Cisco Traceroute Output

```
test-r1>trace www.cisco.com
Translating "www.cisco.com"...domain server (209.1.221.10) [OK]

Type escape sequence to abort.
Tracing the route to cio-sys.cisco.com (192.31.7.130)

  1 scca-04-f6-0-0.core.exodus.net (209.185.9.42) 0 msec 0 msec 0 msec
  2 exodus-px.scca.bbnplanet.com (209.1.169.234) 0 msec 4 msec 4 msec
  3 p3-3.paloalto-nbr2.bbnplanet.net (4.0.1.222) [AS 1] 0 msec 4 msec 0 msec
  4 p0-0-0.paloalto-cr18.bbnplanet.net (4.0.3.86) [AS 1] 4 msec 4 msec 4 msec
  5 h1-0.cisco.bbnplanet.net (131.119.26.10) [AS 1] 4 msec 4 msec 4 msec
  6 pigpen.cisco.com (192.31.7.40) [AS 109] 4 msec 8 msec 8 msec
  7 cio-sys.cisco.com (192.31.7.130) [AS 109] 4 msec *  4 msec
test-r1>
```

As with the Cisco PING, there is an extended version of traceroute that is available in the enabled user mode. The functionality is similar to that of PING. Listing 12.6 shows the output from a Cisco extended traceroute.

Listing 12.6 Cisco Extended Traceroute Output

```
test-r1#trace
Protocol [ip]:
Target IP address: www.cisco.com
Source address: 192.168.169.177
Numeric display [n]:
Timeout in seconds [3]:
Probe count [3]: 2
Minimum Time to Live [1]:
Maximum Time to Live [30]:
Port Number [33434]:
Loose, Strict, Record, Timestamp, Verbose[none]: verbose
Loose, Strict, Record, Timestamp, Verbose[V]:
Type escape sequence to abort.
Tracing the route to cio-sys.cisco.com (192.31.7.130)

  1 scca-04-f6-0-0.core.exodus.net (209.185.9.42) 4 msec 0 msec
  2 exodus-px.scca.bbnplanet.com (209.1.169.234) 4 msec 4 msec
  3 p3-3.paloalto-nbr2.bbnplanet.net (4.0.1.222) [AS 1] 0 msec 4 msec
  4 p0-0-0.paloalto-cr18.bbnplanet.net (4.0.3.86) [AS 1] 4 msec 4 msec
  5 h1-0.cisco.bbnplanet.net (131.119.26.10) [AS 1] 4 msec 4 msec
  6 pigpen.cisco.com (192.31.7.40) [AS 109] 4 msec 8 msec
  7 cio-sys.cisco.com (192.31.7.130) [AS 109] 4 msec *
test-r1#
```

As you can see from Listing 12.6, the Cisco extended traceroute enables you to specify source address, probe count, TTL values, port numbers, and output modes.

Traceroute is often used by Network Operators to pinpoint packet loss and latency in the Internet. It is important to realize that the response packets each router sends back to the originating host are subject to processing by the router. This means the response packet might be sent to the source host via a different path than the request packet was received on. This can give the illusion of latency or packet loss at a point in the traceroute output that, in reality, is not experiencing trouble. Remember from Chapter 11, "Troubleshooting," this is called *asymmetric routing*. There is nothing that you can do to combat this problem unless you have control of the routers in the path. Then you can modify your routing policies to force symmetric routing. Otherwise, you are at the mercy of the routing policies of other companies.

It is always important to examine the forward and return path of traffic between two hosts as well as the forward and return path between each hop along the traceroute path, if it is available. This requires that you have access to the hosts on both ends of the path as well as all routers in between so that you can run traceroute from the various hosts along the path. This is not always possible especially when dealing with the Internet.

The Cisco IOS traceroute command can be used for the TCP/IP, AppleTalk, Banyan VINES, and Cisco Network Services (CNS) protocols.

The traceroute application comes with Windows 95, Windows 98, and Windows NT. There, it is called TRACERT because of the eight character filename limitation of DOS. The source code for the UNIX version can be obtained from the Lawrence Berkeley National Laboratory Network Research Group's FTP site on the Internet. The URL of the anonymous FTP site is `ftp://ftp.ee.lbl.gov/traceroute.tar.Z`. Most versions of the UNIX operating system do not include the traceroute application. It must therefore be compiled individually for each system.

Anonymous FTP

Anonymous FTP enables access to an FTP server using a generic publicly accessible userid. The userid is usually "anonymous" or "ftp". The password for anonymous FTP is your email address.

MTR

MTR stands for Matt's Traceroute or My Traceroute depending on who you talk to. I prefer the first because it gives credit to the original author of the tool. MTR was originally authored by Matt Kimball. Many developers have contributed to the design and functionality since its creation. Roger Wolff now maintains the distribution. You can find MTR on the Internet at http://www.bitwizard.nl/mtr/.

MTR combines the functionality of both the traceroute and the PING tools. As each hop in the path between the host that MTR is executed from and the destination host that you specify is discovered, a series of ICMP ECHO_REQUESTS are sent to monitor the health of the link between the originating workstation and that gateway. The tool displays a table of running statistics for each hop in the path between origin and destination host. See Figure 12.1 for a sample of the output from MTR.

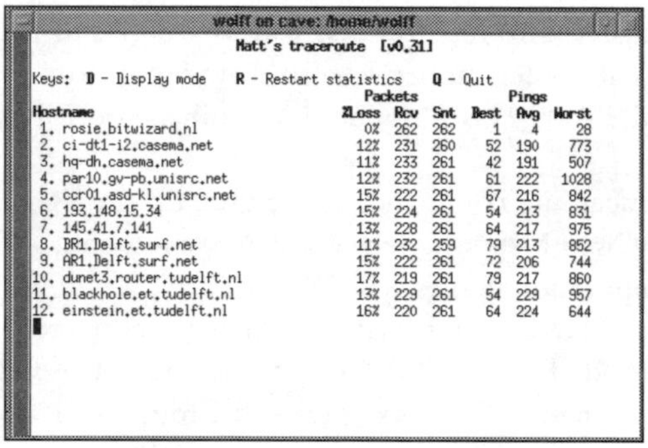

Figure 12.1   MTR output.

MTR is freely available under the GNU license. It is distributed in source format so you will need to compile it for the specific machine that you wish to run it on. You can find the GNU license at http://www.gnu.org/copyleft/gpl.html#TOC1.

MTR is a useful tool because is gives you a reasonable view of the network health in a single tool. It is becoming more and more popular with Network Operators because it enables fast and easy inquiries into trouble reports.

Cisco Discovery Protocol

The Cisco Discovery Protocol is a proprietary protocol that runs in every device that Cisco sells. It is enabled by default and works on every interface type except ATM. CDP displays a great deal of information about each neighbor. This information includes the type of Cisco device the neighbor is, its interface designation, IOS version, protocol address, and serial number. Listing 12.7 shows the output of the show cdp neighbors command:

Listing 12.7 **Sample CDP Output**

```
test-r1#sh cdp nei
Capability Codes: R - Router, T - Trans Bridge, B - Source Route Bridge
                  S - Switch, H - Host, I - IGMP, r - Repeater

Device ID          Local Intrfce    Holdtme    Capability  Platform  Port ID
069004380(sup-s3-a) Fas 5/0/0       174        T B S       WS-C5500  1/1
069004380(sup-s3-a) Fas 9/0/0       175        T B S       WS-C5500  8/1
069003074(sup-s3-b) Fas 8/0/0       129        T B S       WS-C5500  1/2
test-r1#
```

More detailed information can be retrieved using the show cdp neighbor detail command. Listing 12.8 shows a sample output from this command.

Listing 12.8 **Sample Detailed CDP Output**

```
test-r1#show cdp neighbor detail
-------------------------
Device ID: 069004380(sup-a)
Entry address(es):
  IP address: 192.168.107.139
Platform: WS-C5500,  Capabilities: Trans-Bridge Source-Route-Bridge Switch
Interface: FastEthernet5/0/0,  Port ID (outgoing port): 1/1
Holdtime : 176 sec

Version :
WS-C5500 Software, Version McpSW: 3.2(1) NmpSW: 3.2(1b)
Copyright (c) 1995-1998 by Cisco Systems


-------------------------
Device ID: 069004380(sup-a)
Entry address(es):
  IP address: 192.168.107.139
Platform: WS-C5500,  Capabilities: Trans-Bridge Source-Route-Bridge Switch
Interface: FastEthernet9/0/0,  Port ID (outgoing port): 8/1
Holdtime : 177 sec

Version :
WS-C5500 Software, Version McpSW: 3.2(1) NmpSW: 3.2(1b)
Copyright (c) 1995-1998 by Cisco Systems


-------------------------
Device ID: 069003074(sup-b)
Entry address(es):
  IP address: 192.168.107.140
Platform: WS-C5500,  Capabilities: Trans-Bridge Source-Route-Bridge Switch
Interface: FastEthernet8/0/0,  Port ID (outgoing port): 1/2
Holdtime : 129 sec
```

continues

Listing 12.8   **Continued**

```
Version :
WS-C5500 Software, Version McpSW: 3.2(1) NmpSW: 3.2(1b)
Copyright (c) 1995-1998 by Cisco Systems

test-r1#
```

Diagnosing configuration errors is made substantially easier with the use of CDP.
Mismatched protocol addresses are easily discovered. CDP is also a helpful tool in
inventory control and IOS version control. Being able to easily determine the serial
numbers and IOS versions of neighboring devices can make finding misplaced hardware a snap. Being able to determine the far end router port that a particular interface
is connected to saves a great deal of time when working with support personnel that
may be located at remote sites. Having to explain over the phone to an inexperienced
operations person how to trace a cable can take a great deal of time. I have spent many
sleepless nights trying to verify cabling between two pieces of equipment that were
not Cisco manufactured.

Pathchar

Pathchar is a recently developed tool that attempts to provide more useful information
than PING and traceroute. It enables users to find the bandwidth, delay, average
queue, and loss rate of every hop between any source and destination on the Internet.
    Pathchar can be found on the Internet at the Lawrence Berkeley National
Laboratory Network Research Group's anonymous FTP server. Currently, there are
only binaries available for Solaris, FreeBSD, Linux, NetBSD, and OSF. The source code
has not been made available yet. The program takes a great deal of time to run because
of all the mathematical calculations that need to be made for each hop along the path.

Web-based PING and Traceroute

Many companies have built WWW pages that provide access to the PING and traceroute applications for WWW clients. This enables remote users to get the output of the
PING and traceroute applications from the perspective of the remote server. This can
be a very valuable tool when you are troubleshooting routing or packet loss problems
on the Internet. If you can find a Web-based traceroute page that is on a network that
you are having problems reaching, you have a way to examine a sample of the return
path of traffic in general from that network to yours. Figure 12.2 shows a sample of
what a Web-based PING page would look like.

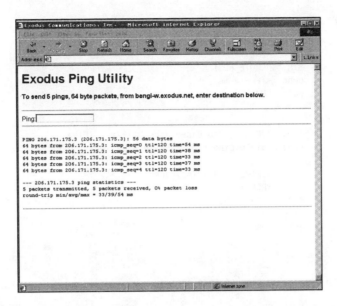

Figure 12.2   Sample Web-based PING page.

Listing 12.9 shows a sample of the program used for a Web-based PING page. It is a shell script that will run on any UNIX operating system. The Web-based traceroute program is very similar to the PING program. In fact, it is almost exactly the same. You could simply replace the TR variable definition with the path to the traceroute program rather than the PING program.

Listing 12.9   **Web-Based PING Program**

```
#!/bin/sh

TR=/usr/sbin/ping

TOP='
<HTML>
<HEAD>
<TITLE>Web Based Ping</TITLE>
</HEAD>
<BODY ALINK="FF0000" VLINK="FF0000" LINK="#FF0000" BGCOLOR="FFFFFF">
<FONT FACE="Arial">
'

if [ -x $TR ]; then
        if [ $# = 0 ]; then
                echo $TOP\<H1\>Web Based Ping Utility\</H1\>
                echo \<B\>To ping from $SERVER_NAME, enter destination
                ➝below.\</B\>
```

continues

Listing 12.9   **Continued**

```
                echo \<ISINDEX PROMPT="Ping: "\>
                echo \<PRE\>
                $TR "$REMOTE_HOST"
                echo \</PRE\>
                echo '<HR>'

        else
                echo $TOP\<H1\>Web Based Ping Utility\</H1\>
                echo \<B\>To ping from $SERVER_NAME, enter destination
➥below.\</B\>
                echo \<ISINDEX PROMPT="Traceroute: "\>
                echo \<PRE\>
                $TR "$QUERY_STRING"
                echo \</PRE\>
                echo '<HR>'

        fi
else
        echo Cannot find ping on this system.
fi
```

For example, assume you are having problems reaching a server on the Internet. Using traceroute from your workstation you determine the server is run by a company that is a customer of Sprint Internet Services. From the output of the traceroute, it appears there is packet loss inside Sprint Internet Services network. In order to verify this, you need to examine a traceroute from within Sprint's network back to your workstation. You could try calling the Sprint Service Center, or you could locate a Web-based traceroute page that is hosted by another Sprint customer. The Web-based traceroute page would enable you to see the path that packets inside Sprint's network take when trying to reach your workstation. Using a Web-based PING program would enable you to PING each hop along the return path to determine which hop, if any, is dropping the packets.

PING and traceroute both have their merits. Which program you choose to use depends on what information you are trying to gather. If you are trying to measure packet loss, PING is better suited than traceroute because you can vary the number of probe packets, as well as, the number of packets that are sent. It is better to send at least 100 probe packets when trying to determine the percentage of packet loss on a link. Losing 1 packet out of 10 shows a much higher packet loss percentage than losing 4 out of 100.

Public Route–Servers

Many Internet service providers (ISPs) have route-servers installed in their networks that are freely available to the public. These route-servers can be a simple UNIX workstation that is running the GateD software or it could be a router running BGP. The purpose of a route-server is to enable outside companies (usually other ISPs) to view the current BGP route table that exists in another network. They are usually available by telnet. Once you have connected, you can execute commands on the route-server to display information from the BGP routing table contained on it.

Route-servers can be very helpful in determining whether your BGP configuration is correct if you are peering via BGP with your ISP or another company at a public Internet exchange point. A route-server on another network can show you whether you are announcing the networks you think you are. Announcing networks in BGP is the act of your routers telling all your BGP peers you know how to get to certain networks. This is done using the `network <ip address>` netmask `<subnet mask>` command in the IOS BGP configuration mode. The network will not be announced as reachable from your ASN until there is an actual path to the network in the route table on your router. For this reason, most ISPs put static routes to the Null0 interface in their router configuration.

This is necessary because often ISPs want to announce supernets rather than individual subnets to their EBGP peers. This is done to help keep the size of the global routing table from growing too quickly. The ISP would be forced to announce the subnets individually as they are allocated to customers. Once the customer becomes active and a route to the allocated netblock exists in the ISP's route table, the netblock would then be announced to all BGP peers.

Static Routes for BGP Anchors

The static route would be entered using the `ip route <netblock> <subnet mask> <interface> <weight>` global configuration command. The weight for the route is usually set to 254 (the highest value before a route becomes invalid). This enables routes learned from other sources to take precedence over the static route. Null0 is a virtual interface on the Cisco router that is similar to /dev/null on a UNIX file system. It is basically a reference point to nothing and is often referred to as a bit bucket. The term "null routing" has been used to describe the act of routing packets to a Null0 interface on a Cisco router. Unlike other interfaces on a Cisco router, the Null0 interface does not need to be defined in the active configuration. This is opposite of the other virtual interfaces on a Cisco router, such as Tunnel and Loopback interfaces.

Supernets and Subnets

Supernet and subnet are terms used to describe netblocks that do not conform to the original IP address class boundaries. They became popular with the advent of CIDR and VLSM.

For instance, you receive an IP netblock allocation from the American Registry for Internet Numbers (ARIN). ARIN can be found on the WWW at `http://www.arin.net`. You add the netblock to the BGP configuration of one of your routers so that other ISPs on the Internet will know how to reach hosts with IP addresses from the new allocation. You could use a public route-server to verify that other ISPs are receiving the proper BGP network entry from your routers. If the route-server is a Cisco router, then you could use the `show ip bgp <netblock>` command to determine if the netblock that you are announcing is in the BGP route table. Or you could use the `show ip bgp regex ^<asn>$` command to list all routes being announced from your ASN.

Make sure that you understand the implications of deploying a publicly accessible router in your network. Telnet from the route-server should be disabled. This is done using the `transport output none` command in the VTY line configuration mode on the Cisco router. Suppose that a cracker launched an attack from a compromised host. During the investigation to determine where the cracker originally logged in from, the system logs of the compromised server showed the cracker logging in from your route-server. Also, make sure that a privileged user mode password has been set. This is done using the `enable secret <password>` global configuration command. Otherwise, remote users could gain access to the enable user mode on your router with ease. Most commands that can be used to harm other networks are not enabled in the basic user mode, but you should none the less be cautious. Just think how you would feel if someone compromised your network from a route-server that some other ISP had deployed.

Looking Glasses

Looking glasses are portals into a remote router that is not under your control. They are most often available on Web servers in ISP's networks. Looking glasses enable you to submit commands that you would like executed on a router in the remote ISP's network and then receive the output from that command. The looking glass program was first made popular by Digex. They began with access to one of their routers from their `http:///nitrous.digex.net` Web site. It now includes access to four of their routers. Digex offers the source code to their looking glass on the WWW site mentioned earlier. Theirs is a RSH based looking glass.

Caution should be used in developing and deploying publicly available looking glasses. Take extra measures to ensure that the looking glass software you use is secure and will prevent outside users from causing problems on your routers either through design or mistake. Make sure that enable mode commands are not permitted via RSH clients. This is done using the `ip rcmd remote-host` global configuration command (refer to Chapter 10, "Collecting Data via Other Means"). Also, use TACACS+ to restrict the commands that are enabled by the looking glass userid if it is a telnet based program. Refer to the documentation that accompanied your TACACS software for the correct syntax to restrict the commands enabled on a per user basis. Every piece of text submitted via a Web form should be examined for commands that you do not want executed on your routers. This is especially true if you are using looking glass software that uses telnet rather than one that uses RSH.

Other ISPs have taken the idea of the looking glass and expanded to include many more commands and routers. Most often, looking glasses enable remote users to execute PING and traceroute commands. Most also include the capability to execute some of the commands in the `show ip route` and `show ip bgp` families of commands. These commands are useful in determining the cause or source of routing problems.

Figure 12.3 shows the looking glass that I developed for Exodus Communications. This looking glass is used by the Operations Center to troubleshoot and diagnose network problems that might be reported by customers. It helps to reduce the trouble resolution time by giving the front line operations employees the tools to gather information before passing the problem off to the responsible people. The second level operations employees can then take the data gathered by the first level operations people and determine where the problem is or where to look if the problem is not obvious from the data given.

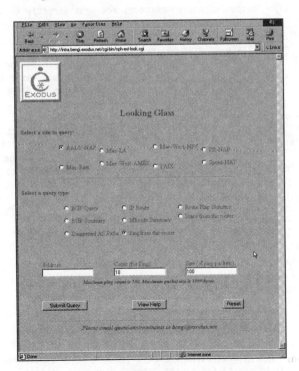

Figure 12.3 An advanced looking glass Web page.

Looking glasses are helpful because they enable other ISPs to troubleshoot problems themselves without placing a burden on your support staff. Looking glasses can also provide the functions of Web-based PING and traceroute applications as well as route-servers. Whether your looking glass is RSH-based or telnet based will depend on what functionality you want to provide the remote user. RSH is best for most applications because it is easier to implement and control. Telnet based looking glasses should be used only when the commands that you want to provide require a direct interaction with the IOS, such as extended PING or extended traceroute.

Listing 12.10 shows the Perl5 program that generates this Web page. This Perl program uses an automated telnet session to execute the commands and display the responses back to the remote user.

Listing 12.10 **Looking Glass Program Example**

```perl
#!/usr/local/bin/perl

use strict;
use Net::Telnet;
use CGI;

$| = 1; # Unbuffer output so router resonses are sent directly to browser

require 5.003;
use vars qw(@return $site $router %Sites $CMD $con);
my $company = '';                    # Company name for WWW header
my $logo = '/icons/logo.gif';        # Path to company logo (if exists)
my $timeout = '30';                  # Time to wait for remote command
                                     # ↦to respond
my $user = '';                       # User ID to login to routers
my $passwd = '';                     # Router login password
my $enable_password = "";            # Enable password for routers
                                     # ↦(used for extended ping)
my $email = 'root@localhost';        # email account to send comments
                                     # ↦to

my $default_ping_count = 10;
my $default_ping_size = 100;
my $max_ping = 100;
my $max_byte = 1000;
#my $bgcolor = 'C9C9C9';
my $bgcolor = 'C9C9C9';
#my $text_color = '007633';
my $text_color = '000000';

# Translate commands into usable router statements.
#
# Some commands are commented out because they are being phased in.
# They are ready to use as far as the program goes we just need
# to educate or NCC folk a little more :)
#
```

```perl
my %Commands = (
                ' Access List'            => 'sh ip access-list',
                ' BGP Query'              => 'sh ip bgp',
                ' BGP Summary'            => 'sh ip bgp sum',
                ' Dampened AS Paths'      => 'sh ip bgp damp',
                ' Environmental'          => 'sh env all',
                ' IP Route'               => 'sh ip route',
                ' Route Flap Statistics'  => 'sh ip bgp flap',
                ' Ping from this router'  => 'ping ip',
                ' Trace from this router' => 'trace'
                );

# The file format is a three column tab seperated list containing
# the site name in the first column and the router IP
# address in the second column. The third column holds an alternate
# description of the router. Each line contains one site entry.
# This is done not only for cleaner looking URIs,
# but for security reasons also.

open(SITES, 'looking-glass.sites') || die "Looking Glass Sites: $!\n";
while( defined( my $var = <SITES> ) ) {
  chomp( $var );
  my ($sitename, $siteip, $sitedesc) = split(/\t/, $var);
#
# Extra space is added to the begining of the string to help
# format the radio button output
#
  $Sites{" $sitename"}{'ip'} = $siteip;
  $Sites{" $sitename"}{'desc'} = $sitedesc;
  }
close(SITES);

my $q = new CGI;

$q->use_named_parameters(1);
print $q->header( "nph" => 1 );

if ($q->request_method eq 'POST') {
  &ExecCmd();
} elsif ($q->request_method eq 'GET') {
  &DisplayForm();
}

print "<HR SIZE=2 WIDTH=85%>";
print "<I><CENTER>Please email questions/comments to $email</CENTER></I>";
print $q->end_html();
exit;

sub DisplayForm {

# Some JavaScript for a help button that is displayed. I use the help window to
```

continues

Listing 12.10 **Continued**

```
# display an explaination for each of the commands listed on the web page
# as well as list pointers to Ciscos online documentation if more information
# is needed.

  print <<"Script";
<SCRIPT>
  function HelpWin() {

Win1=open('/public/look_help.html',"HelpWin","height=400,width=400,scrollbars=yes,
➥resize=yes");
    }
</SCRIPT>
Script

  print $q->start_html('title' =>"$company : Looking Glass",
                       'BGCOLOR'=>"$bgcolor",
                       'TEXT'=>"$text_color"
                      );
print "<TABLE BORDER=5 CELLPADDING=5><TR><TD BGCOLOR=FFFFFF><IMG
➥SRC=\"$logo\"></TABLE>\n";
  print "<H2><CENTER>Looking Glass</CENTER><BR></H2>\n";
  print "<H4>\n";
  print $q->start_form();

  print "Select a site to query: <BR><BR>\n";
  my @sites = sort { $a cmp $b; } keys( %Sites );
  print "<CENTER>\n";
  print $q->radio_group( 'name' => 'site',
                         'values' => \@sites,
                         'cols' => '5',
                         'linebreak' => 'true'
                       );
  print "</CENTER>\n";

  print "<CENTER><HR WIDTH=70%></CENTER><BR>\n";
  print "Select a query type:<BR><BR>\n";

  my @vals = sort { $a cmp $b; } keys( %Commands );
  print "<CENTER>\n";
  print $q->radio_group( 'name'=>'query_type',
                         'values'=> \@vals,
                         'cols'=>'3',
                         'default' => ' Ping from this router',
                         'linebreak'=>'true'
                       );
  print "<BR><BR>\n";
  print "<TABLE WIDTH=85%>\n";
  print "<TR><TD>Address:<BR> ";
  print $q->textfield( 'name'=>'address', 'size'=>'18');
  print "<TD>Count (for Ping):<BR> ";
```

```perl
      print $q->textfield( 'name'=>'count', 'size'=>'18',
    ➥'default'=>"$default_ping_count");
      print "<TD>Size (of ping packets):<BR> ";
      print $q->textfield( 'name'=>'size', 'size'=>'18',
    ➥'default'=>"$default_ping_size");
      print "</TABLE>\n";
      print "<SMALL><I>Maximun ping count is $max_ping. Maximum packet size is
    ➥$max_byte bytes.</I></SMALL>\n";
      print "</CENTER><BR><BR>\n";
      print "<TABLE WIDTH=100\%>";
      print "<TR><TD WIDTH=33\%><CENTER>", $q->submit('Submit'), "</CENTER>\n";
      print "<TD WIDTH=33\%><CENTER>";
      print "<INPUT TYPE=button NAME=but1 VALUE=\"View Help\"
    ➥onclick=\"HelpWin()\"></CENTER>\n";
      print "<TD WIDTH=33\%><CENTER>", $q->reset(), "</CENTER>\n";
      print "</TABLE>";
      print "<BR>\n";
      print $q->endform();
}


sub ExecCmd {
  my $Site = $Sites{$site}{'desc'};
  print $q->start_html( 'title'=>"$company : $Site Query Results",
                        'BGCOLOR'=>"$bgcolor",
                        'TEXT'=>"$text_color"
                      );
  print "<TABLE BORDER=5 CELLPADDING=5><TR><TD BGCOLOR=FFFFFF><IMG
➥SRC=\"$logo\"></TABLE>\n";
  my $cmd = $Commands{$q->param('query_type')};
  my $address = $q->param('address');
  my $size = $q->param( 'size' );
  my $count = $q->param( 'count' );
  $count = 10 unless $count;
  $size = 100 unless $size;
  if( $count > $max_ping ) { $count = $max_ping; }
  if( $size > $max_byte ) { $size = $max_byte; }

  unless( $q->param('query_type') eq ' Access List' ||
      $q->param('query_type') eq ' BGP Summary' ||
      $q->param('query_type') eq ' Dampened AS Paths' ||
      $q->param('query_type') eq ' Environmental' ||
      $q->param('query_type') eq ' Route Flap Statistics' ) {
    die &Usage() unless $address;
  }

  my $router = $Sites{$q->param('site')}{'ip'};
  $site = $q->param('site');

  $con = new Net::Telnet ( Host => "$router",
                           Timeout => 10,
                           Prompt => '/[\w\-]+[>:]$/');
```

continues

Listing 12.10   **Continued**

```perl
$con->login($user, $passwd);
$con->timeout($timeout);
$con->errmode('return');
$con->max_buffer_length('3048576');
unless ($con->cmd("terminal length 0")) { print "Can't set terminal length"; }

if ( ( $address ne "" ) && (
( $cmd eq 'trace' ) ||
      ( $cmd eq 'sh ip route' ) ) ) {
  print "<H2><CENTER>$Site Query Results</CENTER><BR></H2>\n";
  unless( $address =~ /^\d{1,3}\.\d{1,3}\.\d{1,3}\.\d{1,3}$/ ||
          $address =~ /^\w+\.\w+\.\w{2,3}$/i) {
     print "Invalid host specified.<BR>\n";
     return();
  }
  $CMD = "<B>$cmd $address</B>";
  print "<CENTER>$CMD</CENTER><HR WIDTH=85%>\n";
  print "<PRE>\n";
  $con->print( "$cmd $address" );
  eval {
    local $SIG{'ALRM'} = sub { die "TimeOUT\n" };
    alarm( 300 );
    while( my $ret = $con->getline( Timeout => 2  ) ) { print $ret; }
    alarm( 0 );
  };
  if( $@ eq "TimeOUT\n" ) {
    print "Command execution timed out.\n";
    die;
  }
} elsif( $q->param('query_type') eq ' BGP Query' ) {
  print "<H2><CENTER>$Site Query Results</CENTER><BR></H2>\n";
  unless( $address =~ /^\d{1,3}\.\d{1,3}\.\d{1,3}\.\d{1,3}$/ ||
          $address =~ /^\w+\.\w+\.\w{2,3}$/i) {
     print "Invalid host specified.<BR>\n";
     return();
  }
  $CMD = "<B>$cmd $address</B>";
  print "<CENTER>$CMD</CENTER><HR WIDTH=85%>\n";
  print "<PRE>\n";
  $con->print( "$cmd $address" );
  eval {
    local $SIG{'ALRM'} = sub { die "TimeOUT\n" };
    alarm( 300 );
    while( my $ret = $con->getline( Timeout => 2  ) ) { print $ret; }
    alarm( 0 );
  };
  if( $@ eq "TimeOUT\n" ) {
    print "Command execution timed out.\n";
    die;
```

```
         }
      } elsif (($address eq "") && ($q->param('query_type') eq ' BGP Query')) {

# I really don't want to kill my routers or the web server just
# because an inexperienced NOC person didn't bother to read the
# help page.

         @return = 'It is not recommended that the BGP table be queried without '.
                   'an address entry. <BR>This would cause a dump of the entire '.
                   'BGP route table (over 55,000 routes).';
      } elsif( $cmd eq 'ping ip' ) {
         unless( $address =~ /^\d{1,3}\.\d{1,3}\.\d{1,3}\.\d{1,3}$/ ||
                 $address =~ /^\w+\.\w+\.\w{2,3}$/i) {
            print "Invalid host specified.<BR>\n";
            return();
         }
         $CMD = "ping ip $address $count $size";
         print "<H2><CENTER>$Site Query Results</CENTER><BR></H2>\n";
         print "<CENTER>$CMD</CENTER><HR WIDTH=85%>\n";
         print "<PRE>\n";
         $con->print( "enable" );
         $con->waitfor( Match => '/Password: /',
                        Timeout => '1'
                      );
         $con->print( $enable_password );
         my( $prematch, $match ) = $con->waitfor( Match => '/.*\#$/',
                                                  Timeout => '1'
                                                );
         print "$prematch", "$match";
         $con->prompt( '/\b.*\#/' );
         $con->print( $cmd );
         ( $prematch, $match ) = $con->waitfor( Match => '/Target IP address: /',
                                                Timeout => '1'
                                              );
         print "$prematch", "$match";
         $con->print( $address );
         ( $prematch, $match ) = $con->waitfor( Match => '/Repeat count\[5\]: /',
                                                Timeout => '1'
                                              );
         print "$prematch", "$match";
         $con->print( $count );
         ( $prematch, $match ) = $con->waitfor( Match => '/Datagram size \[100\]: /',
                                                Timeout => '1'
                                              );
         print "$prematch", "$match";
         $con->print( $size );
         ( $prematch, $match ) = $con->waitfor( Match => '/Timeout in seconds \[2\]:
➥/',
                                                Timeout => '1'
                                              );
         print "$prematch", "$match";
```

continues

Listing 12.10 **Continued**

```
$con->print( "2" );
( $prematch, $match ) = $con->waitfor( Match => '/Extended commands \[n\]: /',
                                       Timeout => '1'
                                     );
print "$prematch", "$match";
$con->print( "n" );
( $prematch, $match ) = $con->waitfor( Match => '/Sweep range of sizes \[n\]:
➥/',
                                       Timeout => '1'
                                     );
print "$prematch", "$match";
$con->print( "n" );
( $prematch, $match ) = $con->waitfor( Match => '/seconds:/',
                                       Timeout => '1'
                                     );
print "$prematch", "$match";
my $ret = $con->get( Timeout => 1 );
print "$ret";
my $break = 0;
my $count = 0;

#
# I needed to put some text in for the ping responses because
# most browsers don't actually output data to the user until there
# is a LF/CR or some sort of tag change, ie. <PRE> or <P>
#
until( $break == 1) {
  $ret = $con->get( Timeout => 1 );
  next if $ret =~ /^\s*$/;
  $count++;
  if( $ret =~ /Success/ ) {
    print "$ret";
    $break = 1;
  } elsif( $ret =~ /\./ ) {
    print "\n\[sequence $count\] ";
    print "Packet Lost ($ret)";
  } elsif( $ret =~ /U/ ) {
    print "\n\[sequence $count\] ";
    print "Host Unreachable ($ret)";
  } elsif( $ret =~ /\!/ ) {
    print "\n\[sequence $count\] ";
    print "Ping Successful ($ret)";
  }
  undef( $ret );
}
$ret = $con->get( Timeout => 1 ); # Now that the ping is finished, let's clear
➥the buffer
print $ret;
} else {
@return = $con->cmd("$cmd");
```

```
      $CMD = "<B>$cmd</B>";
      print "<H2><CENTER>$Site Query Results</CENTER><BR></H2>\n";
      print "<CENTER>$CMD</CENTER><HR WIDTH=85%>\n";
      print "<PRE>\n";
      if ($address ne "") {
        $address =~ s/\./\\./g;
        my @lines = grep(/$address/, @return);
        @lines = 'No matches found.' unless @lines;
        unshift(@lines, "\n"); # I like things to look nice!
        my @head = splice(@return, 0, 4);
        @return = @head;
        while( defined( my $var = shift( @lines ) ) ) { push(@return, $var); }
        }
      if ($con->timed_out()) { @return = 'Command timed out'; }
      }
    $con->close;

  }

  sub Usage {
    print $q->start_html("Error");
  #   $CMD = "<B>$cmd</B>";
  #   print "<H2><CENTER>$Site Query Results</CENTER><BR></H2>\n";
  #   print "<CENTER>$CMD</CENTER><HR WIDTH=85%>\n";
    print "A valid IP address or netblock must be supplied.<BR>\n";
    print $q->end_html;
    exit;
  }
```

Instant Messaging Software

Instant messaging software is useful for communication between Network Operators within different companies. They enable quick and easy access into other networks that you might be experiencing problems with. As you increase your contacts with Network Operators within other companies, you can build a list of their screen names. Screen names are the aliases that messaging software users choose to be known by. The screen name can be the person's actual name or any other alias of their choosing.

Two well known companies offer instant messaging software; they are America Online (AOL) and Microsoft. The AOL software can be found on the Internet at http://www.aol.com/aim/. The Microsoft software can be found on the Internet at http://messenger.msn.com.

Currently, the software from both companies runs only on Windows-based machines. UNIX-based machines have an application called Internet Relay Chat (IRC). IRC is a text-based version of the AOL chat rooms. IRC client software can be found for almost all computer operating systems. A simple search on a popular Internet search engine will provide you with a current list of Internet sites where the software is available.

Related Web-based Tools

Other network troubleshooting tools are available on the Web as well as those mentioned here. There are Web interfaces for `whois` (a utility for getting contact information from IP networks that are assigned by ARIN), `nslookup` (a utility to query a DNS server for the IP address or text name of an IP host), and `dig` (Domain Information Groper, a utility to interrogate a DNS server for IP domain name information).

Whois is used to query a remote server for database information. Two public whois servers used by ISPs are whois.ra.net and whois.arin.net. The command syntax is `whois -h <server> <query object>`. Table 12.2 shows what kind of information is available from each server.

Table 12.2 **Public Whois Servers and Their Uses**

Server	Use
whois.ra.net	RADb routing information
whois.arin.net	IP address allocation information

For example, to examine the current routing policy for AS3967, you would query the Routing Arbiter Database (RADb), `whois -h whois.ra.net AS3967`. To determine what company has been assigned the use of the 209.1.0.0/16 netblock, you would query the ARIN database, `whois -h whois.arin.net 209.1.0.0`.

Nslookup is used to resolve IP addresses to their English equivalent names, if defined. It is also used to convert host names from English to dotted decimal IP format. Here is a sample of the output from the command:

```
[mtripod@gumby] nslookup www.whitehouse.gov
Server:  bengi-w.exodus.net
Address:  209.1.221.10

Name:    www.whitehouse.gov
Addresses:  198.137.240.92, 198.137.240.91

[mtripod@gumby] nslookup 198.137.240.92
Server:  bengi-w.exodus.net
Address:  209.1.221.10

Name:    www2.whitehouse.gov
Address:  198.137.240.92

[mtripod@gumby]
```

Dig is used to retrieve certain aspects of the configuration for a domain name from a DNS server. The syntax for the command is `dig @server domain query-type query-class`.

Almost any command-line tool available on the UNIX operating system can be integrated into a Web page for public use. These tools are useful in diagnosing problems that at first appear to be network related but turn out to be a system issue.

For instance, a dial-up customer calls his ISP because he cannot reach a certain WWW site. The Network Operations Center (NOC) for the ISP initially thinks that it might be a routing problem caused by a loop condition somewhere in the Internet. Routing loops occur often for very short periods of time when configuration changes are made and routing tables are rebuilt. After some investigation using `nslookup` and `dig`, the NOC engineer determines that the DNS name for the server that the remote customer is trying to reach returns an invalid IP address. The NOC engineer then uses whois to determine the administrative contact of the domain name that the server resides in and contacts that person to correct the problem.

Conclusion

This chapter introduced some applications and uses of Cisco routers that go beyond the everyday routing of packets and connecting of networks. Some of the tools listed in this chapter do not relate specifically to Cisco routers but instead point out the fact that networking is more than just routers and networks. Support systems that many functions of the Internet rely on also need to be troubleshot at times. You should now be familiar with some of the more readily used and available tools. Hopefully, some ideas have been generated in your mind for other uses for Cisco routers that are not mentioned here. In addition to presenting the most readily used and available troubleshooting tools, this chapter also introduced some simple tools available separate from the Cisco IOS that can be used to troubleshoot network problems. Table 12.3 shows a list of all the tools mentioned here and their uses. You should now be well armed to tackle any network problem that presents itself.

Table 12.3   **Troubleshooting Applications and Their Uses**

Tool	Use
PING	Determine packet loss and latency between two hosts.
Traceroute	Determine path between two hosts. Also shows packet loss and latency between each hop along path.
MTR	Determine path between two hosts and gather ongoing data for packet loss and latency between hops along the path between the two hosts.
Pathchar	Determine path between two hosts. Also shows packet loss, latency, capacity, and utilization between each hop along the path.
CDP	Determine device properties of neighboring Cisco products.
Nslookup	Resolve dotted IP address to English name and English name to dotted IP address.
Dig	Interrogate a DNS server for configuration information on a specific domain name.
Whois	Extract database information from a remote server.

13

Case Study

THIS CHAPTER INTRODUCES THE CASE STUDY AND NETWORK diagram used as the basis for the remaining three chapters. Each of the final chapters discusses a particular aspect of the network in more detail, introduces common errors, and discusses how to troubleshoot them. The main components of a network, the physical layer, the data link layer, and the network layer are covered.

Our remaining discussions are focused on a financial service company. The company maintains electronic financial records for medium-sized corporations. The network needs to be able to:

- Provide secure high-speed access to the financial data
- Support off-site employees (telecommuters)
- Provide access to the Internet
- Enable access to the development lab for all corporate employees
- Enable access to the application servers for all corporate employees

The basic layout of the company's nation-wide network is in Figure 13.1.

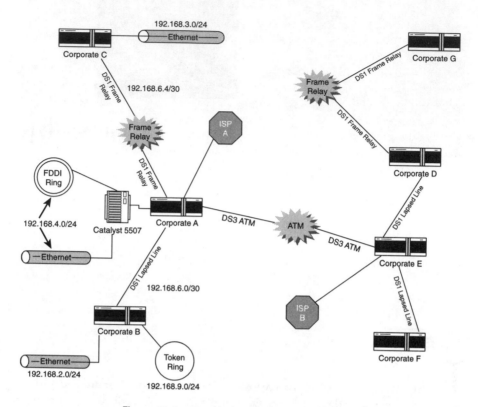

Figure 13.1 Troubleshooting network diagram.

The Network Hardware

A legacy corporate network consists of two main sites: Corporate A and Corporate E. Other remote, or satellite, sites are connected to these two main sites by a variety of different technologies. Corporate site A consists of a Cisco 7507 at the heart of the network with several types of multi-access LAN devices, such as a Cisco Catalyst 5505 and FDDI switch. This router has one HSSI interface card, one DS3 ATM interface card, one Gigabit Ethernet interface card, and two serial interface cards. There is a local connection to an ISP for connectivity to the Internet. Corporate site E is similar in design and function.

A Cisco 7507 was chosen because it provides redundant power supplies and enables the use of the most recent interface cards available from Cisco, namely the VIP2/50. The Catalyst switch provides access to a number of servers including the TACACS server, DNS server, and syslog server. The Catalyst is connected to the 7507 via a Gigabit Ethernet port.

Remote corporate site B is connected via two leased DS1 circuits (remember from Chapter 5, "Wide Area Networking," that a DS1 is the same as a T1, 1.544 Mbps). The main router in this office is a Cisco 7507 with a serial interface card, a Token Ring interface card, and an Ethernet interface card. Leased lines were chosen to connect this site to the main corporate site, rather than a switched service line, because the actual building is in the same city as corporate site A. The cost of the short distance leased lines was low enough to make them a more desirable choice than the switched service counterparts. The network designer preferred to use leased line services wherever possible because the full bandwidth of the circuit is dedicated to the company. Another reason leased lines were used is because corporate site B houses all the legacy IBM application servers, as well as, a development lab. The IBM server requires the SNA protocol and it is easier to bride SNA traffic over a leased line. In order to have connectivity to servers via the SNA protocol over an ATM network, the use of ATM LAN Emulation (LANE) is needed.

Remote site C is connected via a Frame Relay switched service line that has one 256 Kbps PVC. The physical location of corporate site C is some distance away from corporate site A and is used as a remote sales office for a traveling sales force. The main router used in this site is a Cisco 2501. The Cisco 2501 is a small access type router that has two DS1 serial ports and one Ethernet port. It is usually used to connect small sites to a WAN. Corporate sites D, F, and G are similar in design and function. Corporate site G is configured for a 56 Kbps Frame Relay PVC to corporate site D.

Table 13.1 summarizes the hardware that is deployed to each site.

Table 13.1 **Network Hardware**

	Site A	Site B	Site C
Router	7507	7507	2501
LAN Hardware	Catalyst 5500	Catalyst 5000	Ethernet Hub
Router	Serial	Serial	Serial
Interfaces	Hssi	ATM	Ethernet
	ATM	Ethernet	
	Gigabit	Token Ring	
	Ethernet		
Connected to	Site B	Site A	Site A
	Site C	Site E	
	Site E		
	ISP		
WAN Protocols	Frame Relay	HDLC	Frame Relay
	(DS1 – 256K PVC)	ATM (DS3 – 15M PVC)	(DS1 - 256K PVC)

continues

Table 13.1 **Continued**

	Site A	Site B	Site C
	ATM (DS3 – two 15M PVCs)		
	HDLC		
	PPP		
LAN Protocols	Gigabit Ethernet	Ethernet	Ethernet
	FDDI	Token Ring	
	Fast Ethernet		
	Ethernet		
Available Slots	2	2	N/A (not modular)

Telecommuters can be supported at any of the sites via the installation of a remote access server, such as a Cisco AS5300. The remote access server can be placed on the local Ethernet segment. A channelized telco circuit can be connected to the remote access server to provide the remote dial in service. Using an ISDN PRI as the channelized service enables the support of analog and digital telecommuters. This means that the telecommuters can use either a standard analog modem (33.6K or 56K) or an ISDN modem (64K or 128K).

Configuration of the Routers

The configurations for the routers in corporate sites A, B, and C are in Listings 13.1, 13.2, and 13.3 respectively. I included the full listing of the configurations to expose you to some of the commands that you might want to include in your own configurations but are not discussed in this book. Features like the Network Time Protocol (NTP) and automatically changing from daylight savings time to standard time are two specific features that you might find useful. The configurations also bring together a full picture of the pieces that I have shown you throughout the book. If you need further explanation of the use or syntax of any of the commands that are not covered in this book, consult your Cisco documentation CD-ROM or Cisco's Web page. Cisco provides the UniverCD on their Web page at http://www.cisco.com/univercd/cc/td/doc/product/software/. This is the same CD that is shipped with their routers. It also contains all the newest features and hardware supported.

Listing 13.1 **Configuration for Corporate A Router**

```
no service finger
service timestamps debug datetime msec localtime show-timezone
service timestamps log datetime msec localtime show-timezone
service password-encryption
no service udp-small-servers
no service tcp-small-servers
!
hostname corp-a-01
!
clock timezone Pacific -8
clock summer-time pdt recurring
boot system flash slot0:rsp-11.1.21CC
boot system rom
aaa new-model
aaa authentication login default tacacs+ enable
aaa authorization commands 15 tacacs+ none
aaa accounting exec start-stop tacacs+
aaa accounting commands 1 start-stop tacacs+
aaa accounting commands 15 start-stop tacacs+
aaa accounting connection start-stop tacacs+
aaa accounting system start-stop tacacs+
enable secret 5 $1$DKqO$IUvapLzulM/g.HV28FyLS1
!
ip subnet-zero
ip tftp source-interface Loopback0
ip telnet source-interface Loopback0
ip tacacs source-interface Loopback0
ip rcmd rcp-enable
ip rcmd rsh-enable
ip rcmd remote-host ruser 192.168.4.10 ruser enable
!
interface Loopback0
 ip address 172.16.220.13 255.255.255.255
 transmit-buffers backing-store
!
interface GigabitEthernet0/0/0
 description Link to Catalyst
 ip address 192.168.4.1 255.255.255.0
 ip route-cache distributed
 full-duplex
!
interface Hssi0/1/0
 description Link to ISP A
 ip address 192.168.5.2 255.255.255.252
 ip route-cache distributed
 encapsulation ppp
 hold-queue 200 in
 hold-queue 500 out
!
interface Serial1/0
```

continues

Listing 13.1 **Continued**

```
 description Leased line to corp-b-1
 ip address 192.168.6.1 255.255.255.252
!
interface Serial1/1
 description To Frame Relay cloud
 no ip address
 encapsulation frame-relay IETF
 frame-relay lmi-type ansi
!
interface Serial1/1.1 point-to-point
 description 256K PVC to corp-c-01
 ip address 192.168.7.1 255.255.255.252
 frame-relay interface-dlci 100 IETF
!
interface Serial1/2
description Leased line to corp-b-01
 ip address 192.168.6.9 255.255.255.252

!
interface Serial1/3
no ip address
 shutdown
!
interface Serial1/4
no ip address
 shutdown
!
interface Serial1/5
 no ip address
 shutdown
!
interface Serial1/6
no ip address
 shutdown
!
interface Serial1/7
no ip address
shutdown
!
interface ATM4/0
 description To ATM cloud
 no ip address
 map-group ATM-MAP
 atm ds3-scramble
!
interface ATM4/0.1 point-to-point
 description PVC for Connection to Corporate E
 ip address 192.168.8.1 255.255.255.252
 atm pvc 132 1 32 aal5snap 15000 15000
```

```
!
autonomous-system 65050
!
router ospf 100
redistribute connected subnets
network 192.168.6.0 0.0.0.3 area 0
 network 192.168.6.4 0.0.0.3 area 0
 network 192.168.6.8 0.0.0.3 area 0
 network 192.168.8.0 0.0.0.3 area 0
 default-information originate always
!
router bgp 65050
 no synchronization
 bgp always-compare-med
 bgp dampening
 bgp deterministic-med
 network 192.168.0.0 netmask 255.255.0.0 route-map community-local
 neighbor 192.168.8.1 remote-as 65020
 neighbor 192.168.8.1 send-community
 neighbor 192.168.8.1 route-map isp in
!
map-list ATM-MAP
 ip 192.168.8.2 atm-vc 132 broadcast
!
ip domain-name mcp.com
ip name-server 192.168.4.5ip classless
ip route 0.0.0.0 0.0.0.0 192.168.8.1
ip route 192.168.0.0 255.255.0.0 Null0 254
ip ospf name-lookup
logging buffered 1000000
logging trap debugging
logging source-interface Loopback0
logging 192.168.4.6
access-list 1 deny    0.0.0.0
access-list 1 deny    10.0.0.0 0.255.255.255
access-list 1 deny    172.16.0.0 0.15.255.255
access-list 1 deny    192.168.0.0 0.0.255.255
access-list 1 permit any
access-list 5 permit 192.168.4.8
access-list 99 permit 192.168.4.0 0.0.0.255
access-list 102 deny   icmp any 0.0.0.255 255.255.255.0
access-list 102 permit ip any any
!
route-map isp permit 10
 set local-preference 1000
!
tacacs-server host 192.168.4.7
tacacs-server key MyTaCkEy
!
snmp-server community private RW 5
snmp-server community public RO 5
!
```
continues

Listing 13.1 **Continued**

```
line con 0
exec-timeout 15 0
line aux 0
 modem InOut
 transport input all
line vty 0 4
 access-class 99 in
 exec-timeout 15 0
 password 7 051F1216761B1F1C1D1D
 length 0
line vty 5 12
 access-class 99 in
 exec-timeout 15 0
 password 7 051F1216761B1F1C1D1D
line vty 13 32
 access-class 99 in
 password 7 111D0D1C40465D1F0032
!
ntp clock-period 17179916
ntp update-calendar
ntp peer 204.123.2.5
end
```

Listing 13.2 **Configuration for Corporate B Router**

```
no service finger
service timestamps debug datetime msec localtime show-timezone
service timestamps log datetime msec localtime show-timezone
service password-encryption
no service udp-small-servers
no service tcp-small-servers
!
hostname corp-b-1
!
clock timezone Pacific -8
clock summer-time pdt recurring
boot system flash slot0:rsp-11.1.21CC
boot system rom
aaa new-model
aaa authentication login default tacacs+ enable
aaa authorization commands 15 tacacs+ none
aaa accounting exec start-stop tacacs+
aaa accounting commands 1 start-stop tacacs+
aaa accounting commands 15 start-stop tacacs+
aaa accounting connection start-stop tacacs+
aaa accounting system start-stop tacacs+
enable secret 5 $1$DKqO$IUvapLzulM/g.HV28FyLS1
!
```

```
ip subnet-zero
ip tftp source-interface Loopback0
ip telnet source-interface Loopback0
ip tacacs source-interface Loopback0
ip rcmd rcp-enable
ip rcmd rsh-enable
ip rcmd remote-host ruser 192.168.4.10 ruser enable
!
interface Loopback0
 ip address 172.16.220.14 255.255.255.255
 transmit-buffers backing-store
!
interface FastEthernet0/0/0
 description Link to Lab Network
 ip address 192.168.2.1 255.255.255.0
 ip route-cache distributed
 full-duplex
!
interface ATM0/1/0
 description Link to ATM cloud
 no ip address
 map-group ATM-MAP
 atm ds3-scramble
!
interface ATM0/1/0.1 point-to-point
 description PVC for Connection to Corporate E
 ip address 192.168.8.5 255.255.255.252
 atm pvc 133 1 33 aal5snap 15000 15000
!
interface TokenRing1/0
 description Link to Application Server Network
 ip address 192.168.9.1 255.255.255.252
 ring-speed 16
!
interface Serial4/0
 description Leased line to corp-a-01
ip address 192.168.6.2 255.255.255.252
!
interface Serial4/1
description Leased line to corp-a-01
 ip address 192.168.6.10 255.255.255.252
!
interface Serial4/2
no ip address
 shutdown
!
interface Serial4/3
 no ip address
 shutdown!interface Serial4/4
no ip address
 shutdown
```

continues

Listing 13.2 **Continued**

```
!
interface Serial4/5
no ip address
 shutdown
!
interface Serial4/6
no ip address
 shutdown!interface Serial4/7
no ip address
shutdown
!
router ospf 100 redistribute connected subnets
 network 192.168.6.0 0.0.0.3 area 0
 network 192.168.6.8 0.0.0.3 area 0
 network 192.169.8.4 0.0.0.3 area 0
!
map-list ATM-MAP
 ip 192.168.8.5 atm-vc 133 broadcast
!
ip domain-name mcp.com
ip name-server 192.168.4.5ip classless
ip ospf name-lookuplogging buffered 1000000
logging trap debugging
logging source-interface Loopback0logging 192.168.4.6
access-list 1 deny    0.0.0.0
access-list 1 deny    10.0.0.0 0.255.255.255
access-list 1 deny    172.16.0.0 0.15.255.255
access-list 1 deny    192.168.0.0 0.0.255.255
access-list 1 permit any
access-list 5 permit 192.168.4.8
access-list 99 permit 192.168.4.0 0.0.0.255
access-list 102 deny    icmp any 0.0.0.255 255.255.255.0
access-list 102 permit ip any any
tacacs-server host 192.168.4.7
tacacs-server key MyTaCkEy
!
snmp-server community private RW 5
snmp-server community public RO 5
!
line con 0
 exec-timeout 0 0
line aux 0
 modem InOut
 transport input all
line vty 0 4
 access-class 99 in
 exec-timeout 0 0
 password 7 051F1216761B1F1C1D1D
 length 0
line vty 5 12
```

```
 access-class 99 in
 exec-timeout 15 0
 password 7 051F1216761B1F1C1D1D
line vty 13 32
 access-class 99 in
 password 7 111D0D1C40465D1F0032
!
ntp clock-period 17179916
ntp update-calendar
ntp peer 204.123.2.5
end
```

Listing 13.3 **Configuration for Corporate C Router**

```
version 11.2
service timestamps debug datetime msec localtime show-timezone
service timestamps log datetime msec localtime show-timezone
service password-encryption
no service udp-small-servers
no service tcp-small-servers
!
hostname corp-c-01
!
aaa new-modelaaa authentication login default tacacs+ enable
aaa authorization commands 15 tacacs+ none
aaa accounting exec start-stop tacacs+
aaa accounting commands 1 start-stop tacacs+
aaa accounting commands 15 start-stop tacacs+
aaa accounting connection start-stop tacacs+
aaa accounting system start-stop tacacs+
enable secret 5 $1$SIC4$WskJ5kki3PAtGtz9hwqsK0
!
ip subnet-zero
ip host-routing
ip rcmd rcp-enableip rcmd rsh-enable
ip rcmd remote-host ruser 192.168.4.10 ruser enable
ip domain-name mcp.com
ip name-server 192.168.4.5
!
interface Ethernet0
ip address 192.168.3.0 255.255.255.0
!
interface Serial0
description To Frame Relay cloud
encapsulation frame-relay IETF
 frame-relay lmi-type ansi
!
interface Serial0.1 point-to-point
 description 256K PVC to Corporate A
```

continues

Listing 13.3 **Continued**

```
 ip address 192.168.7.2 255.255.255.252
 frame-relay interface-dlci 120 IETF
!
ip classlesslogging buffered 20000 debugging
no logging console
logging trap debugging
logging 192.168.4.6
tacacs-server host 192.168.4.7
tacacs-server timeout 30
tacacs-server key MyTaCkEy
!
line con 0line aux 0
line vty 0 4
exec-timeout 15 0
password 7 09585A104E5642400C14
!
end
```

WAN Implementation

The wide area network (WAN) consists of a combination of leased lines and switched lines. The transport speeds vary between DS0 and DS3. The protocols being used are High-Level Data Link Control (HDLC), Frame Relay, and Ansynchronous Transfer Mode (ATM). Normally, a network would not have such a wide variety of protocols for the simple reason of consistency, not to mention the fact that the less hardware you need to maintain spares for, the better. The reason they are all present in this design is because portions of the network used to exist as separate companies. The current network shown in this chapter is the result of various mergers and acquisitions.

Table 13.2 lists pointers to the specific chapters that cover the various technologies discussed here.

Table 13.2 **Pointers to Previous Chapters for Technology Topics**

Topic	Chapter
LAN Technologies	4
WAN Technologies	5
Router Configuration	3
Router Product Lines	2
Routing Protocols	6

There are also two separate connections to two different Internet service providers (ISPs). The reason the connections are high bandwidth is so the company's customers can retrieve their data files in a timely manner. These connections will be used in the BGP troubleshooting chapter. The only time that Border Gateway Control (BGP) should be used is if there are multiple paths to a destination network that is outside of your ASN. If there were only one connection to an ISP, you would simply have a default route pointing to the IP address of the ISP. The idea is that if there is no route for a certain destination in your local routing tables, the ISP should know how to get to the destination. For this reason, a dynamic routing protocol, such as BGP, is not needed.

Another consideration to think about when multiple ISP connections are used is transit. Transit is defined as using another party's network to reach destinations on a third party's network (see Figure 13.2). Normally, the use of an ISP is mainly for transit to other company's networks. However, because most ISPs have connections between themselves, it is possible to use one ISP to reach destinations on another ISP even if you have a direct connection to the second ISP (see Figure 13.3). Company X has connections to ISP A and ISP B. ISP A also has a connection to ISP B. If you are not careful in your BGP configuration, you might inadvertently force traffic destined for ISP B to go through ISP A (see Figure 13.4). This type of problem can occur because of misconfigurations on the ISP side of the connections as well.

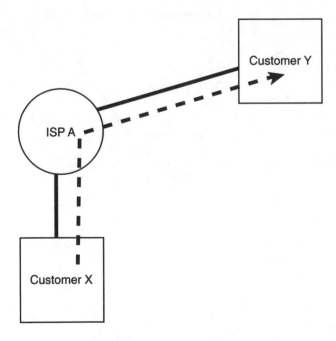

Figure 13.2   An example of transit.

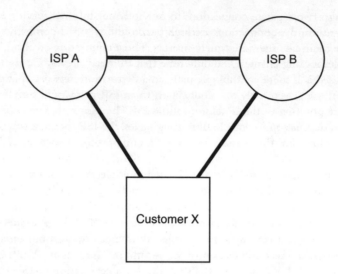

Figure 13.3   A direct connection to an ISP.

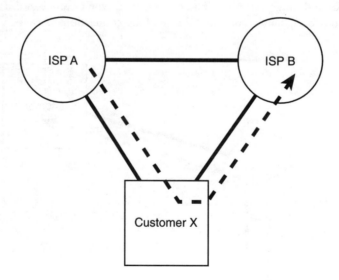

Figure 13.4   *Forcing traffic destined for an ISP to go through another ISP.*

The IGP that is used on this network is Open Shortest Path First (OSPF). In those places where there is only one WAN connection to the rest of the network, a default static route would be used rather than running a dynamic routing protocol. The reason for this is the amount of bandwidth consumed by the routing protocol updates. Assume that 3% of the bandwidth on an Ethernet is used by routing protocol updates. That is equal to 30Kbps. That is not a lot of bandwidth in comparison to the whole Ethernet segment. Consider, however, the impact of that 30Kbps of overhead on a 256Kbps Frame Relay PVC or a 56Kbps ISDN line. It becomes clear now that running a dynamic routing protocol on smaller bandwidth circuits can be more costly than the benefits it provides. There are ways to limit the amount of bandwidth that a dynamic routing protocol uses. Decreasing the update interval of the keepalive packets is one that comes to mind.

The remote offices that are close together, geographically speaking, are connected via leased lines. The reason for this is that in many cases it is almost as expensive to get a switched service connection at the same bandwidth as a leased line when the geographic distance between the two end points is small. Offices that are far apart are connected via switched service lines. An ATM service is used to connect the two main corporate sites because the company needs to be able to transfer large data files between the two sites. DS3 Frame Relay service was not available in some parts along the path so ATM was chosen instead. This also enables the company to implement video conferencing or voice over IP technology in the future should that be desired.

It is a good idea to use ATM if you plan to maintain switched service connections as you upgrade your bandwidth beyond the DS3 level. If you plan to migrate to leased lines at the OC3 level and above, it is better to use Frame Relay to save on equipment costs. Frame Relay will not run at OC3 speed, but HDLC and Point-to-Point Protocol (PPP) will. Therefore, once the physical speed of your circuit goes beyond the limits of Frame Relay, you can switch to another protocol like HDLC or PPP. This is only an option if you are using Frame Relay in a point-to-point configuration. If you know that you want a mesh type (all devices on the network connect to each other) configuration, then use ATM from the beginning and save yourself from trying to migrate from Frame Relay to ATM at a later date. If you are planning to migrate to a leased line circuit, it is better to purchase a Frame Relay initial switched service circuit and not bother buying the expensive ATM equipment. You will end up with a pile of unused ATM equipment otherwise. Table 13.3 summarizes the pros and cons of the three main transport mechanisms.

Table 13.3 **Transport Implementation Comparison**

	ATM	**Leased Line**	**Frame Relay**
Hardware Costs	High	Medium	Medium
Transmission Speed	Very High	High	Medium
Ease of Setup	Hard	Easy	Average
Support for multiple data types (video, voice, data)	High	Medium	Medium

Conclusion

Now that you have examined the overall layout of our case study network, you are ready to get into the nuts and bolts of the individual network segments. Because the scope of this book is geared toward the configuration and use of Cisco routers, we will only troubleshoot the first three layers of the OSI model. The next three chapters make reference to the network described here. You might want to leave a bookmark here to refer back to.

Cisco provides a section on their Web site for case studies of specific technology implementations. The URL for the section is `http://www.cisco.com/univercd/cc/td/doc/cisintwk/ics/index.htm`. I recommend reading all of them even if the technology does not apply to your network. The lessons learned there are invaluable, especially if you are interested in network design methodologies.

High-Speed Switch Technology

It is very likely that Frame Relay will be supported on OC3 speed circuits in the very near future. When this happens, the occurrences of high-speed long distance circuits will increase. Many people do not like ATM because of the high protocol overhead and therefore decide to use multiple lower speed connections rather than one high-speed ATM connection. ATM is a relatively new transport mechanism for transmission of data traffic. Some people are wary of using new technologies before others in the industry have had running implementations for some time. This allows you to ask the people who have deployed the technology successfully about any caveats they have encountered. The use of multiple lower speed circuits could be for redundancy as well. Circuit cost can also factor into which technology to use. Two lower speed circuits might cost less than one higher speed circuit of equal aggregate bandwidth.

14

Troubleshooting the Physical Layer

THIS CHAPTER FOCUSES ON TROUBLESHOOTING THE PHYSICAL LAYER of the Open Systems Interconnection (OSI) model. This is the first layer, the one in which the actual physical connection is defined. The physical layer defines the cabling type, connector type, and distance limitations of the transmission median use. It also defines the electrical characteristics of the signaling that are used on the various cable types. This includes the Cisco interface cards for the modular Cisco routers and the built-in interfaces of the other Cisco products. This chapter concentrates mainly on the Cisco 7000, 7500, and 12000 series router families. The same procedures and variations of the same commands can be used on any of the routers in the Cisco product line.

Some of the problems that you would expect to find that are caused by physical layer problems are

- Loss of connectivity
- Large amounts of CRC errors on the interface
- Inability to transmit data at expected rates
- Intermittent problems (due to faulty cable construction or connection)

Proactive Monitoring

Monitoring of the errors on each interface in your network will alert you to possible future problems. The error information for an interface can be obtained via several means. These can be Simple Network Management Protocol (SNMP) gathered data or the statistics made available by the hardware vendors through the user interface for the device. SNMP monitoring stations can be configured to record and report on changes in the pattern of collected data. For instance, increases in the Cyclical Redundancy Checksum (CRC) errors on an interface can trigger an alarm. Or, a decrease of the IP traffic on an interface can trigger an alarm. Several methods for monitoring and alerting are covered in Chapter 9, "Collecting Data via SNMP," and Chapter 10, "Collecting Data via Other Means." It is always best to prevent problems before they occur. The only way that you will know where problems might occur is if you gather data constantly.

Syslog is a useful tool here as well. The Internetworking Operating System (IOS) will send report messages on increased bit error rate on optical line circuits. The IOS will also report on the intermittent loss of line protocol for each interface on the router. It is important that every interface on the router be configured for keepalives (the default setting) in order for this reporting to work. The loss of line protocol can be caused by something as simple as missed keepalive packets or something as major as an installer bumping into your router, inadvertently crimping a Fast Ethernet cable, and loosening one of the pins in the modular connector. This brings up an important point it that human intervention can (and does) cause physical layer failure. This risk is especially apparent in network equipment rooms that are under constant change. If your company's business growth requires frequent addition or removal of network cabling around your network equipment, the likelihood of your network cabling being damaged is very high. Keep that in mind when you think that a cable cannot possibly have gone bad on its own (it probably didn't).

In those cases where problems have occurred and your goal is now to diagnose and fix them, Cisco provides many tools to help you accomplish your task.

Router Commands

There are several commands available in the Cisco IOS that can help in the troubleshooting of physical layer problems. All these commands reside in the show family of commands. Debug commands for the upper layer protocols can be used in conjunction with other techniques to help diagnose physical layer problems. For instance, if you are watching debug information for IP errors, and you jiggle a cable that you believe to be bad and at the same time the IOS outputs that frame errors have been encountered, it is fairly safe to correlate the two events. Jiggling a network cable while watching for errors is a technique that you just seem to pick up over time. It is a hands-on technique that is passed from experienced network professionals to new recruits.

Show Commands

The Cisco IOS enables the display of the current running status of every configurable option. Listing 14.1 shows the available show commands in the IP/VIP version of the Cisco IOS. There are two main IOS versions in each strain of the Cisco IOS:

- The Enterprise version, which contains support for all protocols including AppleTalk and IPX. This version can be obtained with or without APPN (IBM SNA) and/or Versatile Interface Processor (VIP) support.

- The ISP version, which contains support of IP only. This version can be obtained with or without VIP support.

The availability of the various show commands will depend on which version of IOS you are running on your routers. The Enterprise version will naturally have more commands available than the ISP version because more protocols are supported.

Listing 14.1 *show* Commands Available

```
test-r1#sh ?
  access-lists    List access lists
  accounting      Accounting data for active sessions
  adjacency       Adjacent nodes
  aliases         Display alias commands
  aps             APS information
  arp             ARP table
  async           Information on terminal lines used as router interfaces
  boot            Boot and related environment variable
  buffers         Buffer pool statistics
  calendar        Display the hardware calendar
  cdp             CDP information
  cef             Cisco Express Forwarding
  clns            CLNS network information
  clock           Display the system clock
  cmns            Connection-Mode networking services (CMNS) information
  compress        Show compression statistics.
  configuration   Contents of Non-Volatile memory
  context         Show context information
  controllers     Interface controller status
  debugging       State of each debugging option
  dhcp            Dynamic Host Configuration Protocol status
  diagbus         Show diagnostic bus information
  dialer          Dialer parameters and statistics
  dnsix           Shows Dnsix/DMDP information
  dxi             atm-dxi information
  environment     Environmental monitor statistics
  extended        Extended Interface Information
  file            Show a configuration file
  flash           Flash device information
  frame-relay     Frame-Relay information
  history         Display the session command history
```

continues

Listing 14.1 **continued**

```
    hosts            IP domain-name, lookup style, nameservers, and host table
    interfaces       Interface status and configuration
    ip               IP information
    ipc              Interprocess communications commands
    isis             IS-IS routing information
    key              Key information
    line             TTY line information
    llc2             IBM LLC2 circuit information
    logging          Show the contents of logging buffers
    memory           Memory statistics
    microcode        Microcode in system
    ntp              Network time protocol
    ppp              PPP parameters and statistics
    privilege        Show current privilege level
    processes        Active process statistics
    protocols        Active network routing protocols
    queue            Show queue contents
    queueing         Show queueing configuration
    registry         Function registry information
    reload           Scheduled reload information
    rhosts           Remote-host+user equivalences
    rif              RIF cache entries
    rmon             rmon statistics
    route-map        route-map information
    running-config   Current operating configuration
    sessions         Information about Telnet connections
    smds             SMDS information
    snapshot         Snapshot parameters and statistics
    snmp             snmp statistics
    sscop            SSCOP information
    stacks           Process stack utilization
    standby          Hot standby protocol information
    startup-config   Contents of startup configuration
    subsys           Show subsystem information
    tcp              Status of TCP connections
    tech-support     Show system information for Tech-Support
    terminal         Display terminal configuration parameters
    users            Display information about terminal lines
    version          System hardware and software status
    x25              X.25 information

test-r1#
```

As you can see, there are quite a few show commands available. Let's pick one and explore the functionality further. You will most likely use the show interface command the most in your monitoring and troubleshooting. Listing 14.2 shows all the sub–commands available for the show interface IOS command.

Listing 14.2 *show interface* **Commands**

```
test-r1#sh int ?
  FastEthernet    FastEthernet IEEE 802.3
  Hssi            High Speed Serial Interface
  Loopback        Loopback interface
  Null            Null interface
  POS             Packet over Sonet
  Port-channel    Ethernet Channel of interfaces
  accounting      Show interface accounting
  crb             Show interface routing/bridging info
  fair-queue      Show interface Weighted Fair Queueing (WFQ) info
  mac-accounting  Show interface MAC accounting info
  precedence      Show interface precedence accounting info
  random-detect   Show interface Weighted Random Early Detection (WRED) info
  rate-limit      Show interface rate-limit info
  |               Output modifiers
  <cr>

test-r1#
```

As you can see from Listing 14.2, not only does the Cisco IOS enable you to report on certain statistics for all interfaces on your router, it also enables you to interrogate a specific interface type. There is a great deal of useful information that can be obtained from the show interface command for a particular interface. Figure 14.1 shows the output of the show interface command for a Fast Ethernet interface.

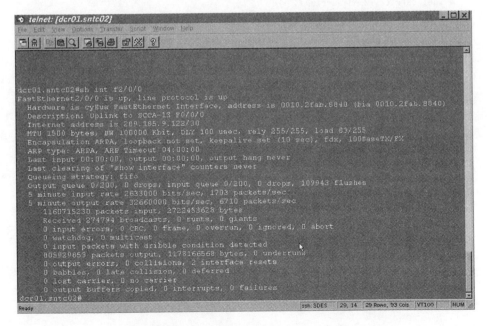

Figure 14.1 show interface command output.

This first line in the output shown in Figure 14.1 displays the interface type, name, and current status. If the line shows up, then the physical connection to the device the interface is connected to is complete. This is the first test to verify that Layer 1 connectivity has been established. The line protocol state shows whether or not the Layer 2 connection has been established. Keepalive signaling must be exchanged between the devices attached to the interface in order for the link protocol to appear in the up state. Once both the interface and the line protocol are up, the port is ready for the exchange of data traffic.

The next line shows the interface hardware type and Media Access Control (MAC) address. Next is the description of the interface that you have programmed in the configuration. Next is the Internet Protocol (IP) protocol address that has been configured for the interface. The next line shows the MTU for the interface, the bandwidth, delay, reliability and load of the interface. The reliability and load of the interface are used in the Enchanced Interior Gateway Routing Protocol (EIGRP) path calculations.

The line of real importance in determining if there is a physical layer problem is

```
0 input errors, 0 CRC, 0 frame, 0 overrun, 0 ignored, 0 abort
```

This line shows the status of the packets being sent and received on the interface. If any of these values are above zero, there is a potential physical layer problem associated with this interface. These next three lines in the show interface output are also good indicators of physical layer problems:

```
0 output errors, 0 collisions, 2 interface resets
0 babbles, 0 late collision, 0 deferred
0 lost carrier, 0 no carrier
```

These counters show collisions and carrier loss on the interface. Intermittent cabling problems will be shown in these counters. The interface counters can be reset using the clear counters command. This command must be executed from the enable user mode. It is helpful to clear the counters when you are troubleshooting interface problems so that you can get an idea at what interval errors are occurring as well as the number of errors over a specific time period.

Tracking Hardware Problems with *Show Diagbus*

Another command that is useful when tracking an interface hardware problem is the show diagbus command. This command displays information about the interface card itself. Most importantly it shows how many times, if any, the card has reset. Resets are triggered by the IOS when invalid instructions are received or there is a memory access failure. Listing 14.3 shows a sample of the output from a show diagbus command on a 7500 series router.

Listing 14.3 **Sample *show diagbus* Command Output**

```
router#sh diagbus 0
Slot 0:
        Physical slot 0, ~physical slot 0xF, logical slot 0, CBus 0
        Microcode Status 0x4
        Master Enable, LED, WCS Loaded
        Board is analyzed
        Pending I/O Status: None
        EEPROM format version 1
        VIP2 R5K controller, HW rev 2.02, board revision A0
        Serial number: 08225619  Part number: 73-2167-04
        Test history: 0x00        RMA number: 00-00-00
        Flags: cisco 7000 board; 7500 compatible

        EEPROM contents (hex):
          0x20: 01 1E 02 02 00 7D 83 53 49 08 77 04 00 00 00 00
          0x30: 50 00 00 00 00 00 00 00 00 00 00 00 00 00 00 00

        Slot database information:
        Flags: 0x4     Insertion time: 0x25D4 (8w0d ago)

        Controller Memory Size: 128 MBytes DRAM, 8192 KBytes SRAM

        PA Bay 0 Information:
                Fast-Ethernet PA, 1 ports, 100BaseTX-ISL
                EEPROM format version 1
                HW rev 1.00, Board revision A0
                Serial number: 07815491  Part number: 73-1688-04

        PA Bay 1 Information:
                Mx HSSI-B PA, 1 ports
                EEPROM format version 1
                HW rev 1.00, Board revision A0
                Serial number: 05878964  Part number: 73-2559-01

        1 crash since restart.
        Last crash context (Nov 04 1998 09:42:44):
        $0 : 00000000, AT : 00000000, v0 : 00000000, v1 : 00000000,
        a0 : 00000000, a1 : 00000000, a2 : 00000000, a3 : 00000000,
        t0 : 00000000, t1 : 00000000, t2 : 00000000, t3 : 00000000,
        t4 : 00000000, t5 : 00000000, t6 : 00000000, t7 : 00000000,
        s0 : 00000000, s1 : 00000000, s2 : 00000000, s3 : 00000000,
        s4 : 00000000, s5 : 00000000, s6 : 00000000, s7 : 00000000,
        t8 : 00000000, t9 : 00000000, k0 : 00000000, k1 : 00000000,
        gp : 00000000, sp : 00000000, s8 : 00000000, ra : 00000000,
        EPC : 0x00000000, SREG : 0x00000000, Cause : 0x00000000
        ErrorEPC : 0x00000000


        —Boot log begin—
```

continues

Listing 14.3 **Continued**

```
Cisco Internetwork Operating System Software
IOS (tm) VIP Software (SVIP-DW-M), Version 11.1(19)CC1, EARLY DEPLOYMENT RELEASE
➡SOFTWARE (fc1)
V111_19_CC_THROTTLE_BRANCH Synced to mainline version: 11.1(19)CA
Copyright (c) 1986-1998 by cisco Systems, Inc.
Compiled Mon 01-Jun-98 18:42 by richardd
Image text-base: 0x60010900, data-base: 0x601AE000


—Boot log end—

router#
```

As you can see from examining text in Listing 14.3, the card in Slot 0 has crashed once. Cisco should be able to determine the cause of the crash from the debug information listed along with the rest of the card information. It is a good idea to monitor the cards in your routers on a regular basis for resets. You will most likely be able to prevent a network outage before it happens. It is very rare that an interface card will fail completely without warning. Monitoring of this type can be automated with techniques that are discussed in Chapters 9 and 10.

The most common cause of interface card failures is defective memory chips, especially if the card is a VIP card. The VIP card moves much of the processing functions from the Route Switching Processor (RSP) to the card itself. For this reason, it is much more likely that errors will occur on the VIP card rather than the RSP. The up side to this is that problems with memory on a VIP card cause the card itself to crash rather than the whole router.

Another reason that a card might crash is that it is not seated fully in the chassis. A poor connection to the router backplane can cause communication problems between the interface card and the RSP. These communication problems can cause the card to send or receive invalid messages, which would be interpreted as a hardware failure. The Cisco IOS attempts to fix these errors by restarting the card.

The output of the show diagbus command on a Cisco 12000 series router is a little different. One difference is that the 7000 and 7500 series output shows the chassis information as Slot 31. The 12000 series routers do not show chassis information in the output. The format of the output itself is different as well. Also, the information itself is different because the 12000 series routers use a switch fabric backplane rather than the CyBus that is used on the 7000 and 7500 series routers. Listing 14.4 shows the output from the show diagbus command on the Cisco 12000 series routers.

Listing 14.4 *show diagbus* **Sample Output**

```
gsr1#sh diag 0
SLOT 0  (RP/LC 0 ): 4 Port Packet Over SONET OC-3c/STM-1 Single Mode
  MAIN: type 33,  800-2389-02 rev A0 dev 16777215
        HW config: 0x00    SW key: FF-FF-FF
  PCA:  73-2275-05 rev A0 ver 4
        HW version 1.1  S/N CAB020801ZX
  MBUS: MBUS Agent (1)  73-2146-06 rev A0 dev 0
        HW version 1.1  S/N CAB014001BY
        Test hist: 0xFF   RMA#: FF-FF-FF   RMA hist: 0xFF
  DIAG: Test count: 0xFFFFFFFF   Test results: 0xFFFFFFFF
  MBUS Agent Software version 01.35 (RAM) (ROM version is 01.33)
  Using CAN Bus A
  ROM Monitor version 00.0E
  Fabric Downloader version used 00.10 (ROM version is 00.10)
  Board is analyzed
  Board State is Line Card Enabled (IOS  RUN )
  Insertion time: 00:00:11 (4w3d ago)
  DRAM size: 134217728 bytes
  FrFab SDRAM size: 67108864 bytes
  ToFab SDRAM size: 67108864 bytes


gsr1#
```

The Cisco 12000 series router marks a big difference in software as well as hardware. On the 12000 series routers every interface card in the chassis runs a local instance of the IOS. This means that when a card is installed in the chassis it is tested for proper hardware operation. Then the processor attempts to download the IOS to the interface card. Once the IOS is downloaded to the interface card, it is loaded into memory on the card. After the IOS is running, it can then be programmed and used to pass traffic. The specific things to look for in the show diagbus output on the 12000 series routers is the Board State. This will tell you if the interface card is installed and operating properly.

Diagnosing Physical Layer Problems with *show context*

The show context IOS command is available in versions 11.1 and higher. This command displays specific as well as summary information about crashes that have already occurred. You must have enable mode access in order to execute this command. The command has different options depending on the hardware platform that it is executed on. On a 7500 series router, the command has only one output form. Listing 14.5 shows a sample of this output.

Listing 14.5   *show context* **Output on 7500 Series Router**

```
mae-west-ames#sh context
Fault History Buffer:
GS Software (RSP-PV-M), Version 11.1(23)CC, EARLY DEPLOYMENT RELEASE SOFTWARE
➥(fc1)
Compiled Fri 11-Dec-98 10:23 by jjgreen
Error EPC : C0A50C06, BadVaddr : 00000028
Signal = 10, Code = 0x8000000C, Uptime 5w0d
$0 : 00000000, AT : 601464E4, v0 : 60B65660, v1 : 60B65880
a0 : 60B65880, a1 : 60B65660, a2 : 00000083, a3 : 60B24598
t0 : 00000030, t1 : 3400E701, t2 : 34008700, t3 : FFFF00FF
t4 : 00000083, t5 : 3E840024, t6 : 00000400, t7 : 2C203120
s0 : 00000000, s1 : 00000218, s2 : 00000028, s3 : 00000001
s4 : 00000001, s5 : 00000000, s6 : 00000000, s7 : 60FE57D0
t8 : 6014492C, t9 : 00000000, k0 : 6171CC2C, k1 : 601A981C
gp : 609DB9F0, sp : 61606720, s8 : 00000002, ra : 602D8B0C
EPC : 602D8B10, SREG : 3400E703, Cause : 8000000C
Error EPC : C0A50C06, BadVaddr : 00000028

mae-west-ames#
```

The output from the show context command displays memory register information that is for the most part meaningless to you and me. The information is very useful to the Cisco development team. Providing this information to Cisco will allow them to tell you exactly the cause of the crash.

The show context command on a 12000 series router has several command specific options. The full option list is displayed in Listing 14.6.

Listing 14.6   *show context* **Options on 12000 Series Routers**

```
bbr01#sh context ?
  all      show all context info for all slots
  slot     specify a slot for which to show context information
  summary  display list of context information available
  |        Output modifiers
  <cr>

bbr01#
```

The summary display option gives you a nice quick glance at the overall health of the cards installed on your router. Listing 14.7 shows a sample output from the show context summary command.

Listing 14.7　**Sample Output from** *show context summary* **Command**

```
bbr01#sh context summ
CRASH INFO SUMMARY
  Slot 0 : 0 crashes
  Slot 1 : 0 crashes
  Slot 2 : 1 crashes
    1 - crash at 00:52:17 pst Fri Jan 14 2000
  Slot 3 : 1 crashes
    1 - crash at 20:02:19 pst Mon Nov 22 1999
  Slot 4 : 0 crashes
  Slot 5 : 0 crashes
  Slot 6 : 0 crashes
  Slot 7 : 0 crashes
bbr01#
```

As you can see, two of the cards in this router have crashed. The crash data is stored until the router itself is reloaded. From the options in Listing 14.6, you can see it is possible to investigate the individual card crashes. Let us explore the crash of the card in Slot 2 more closely. Listing 14.8 shows the output from the show context slot 2 command.

Listing 14.8　*show context slot* **Sample Output**

```
bbr01#sh context slot 2
CRASH INFO: Slot 2, Index 1, Crash at 00:52:17 pst Fri Jan 14 2000

VERSION:
GS Software (GLC1-LC-M), Version 12.0(6)S, EARLY DEPLOYMENT RELEASE SOFTWARE (fc2)
Compiled Wed 15-Sep-99 17:22 by rnapier
Card Type: 1 Port Gigabit Ethernet, S/N CAB03424Z82
System exception: sig=20, code=0xE41998E1, context=0x405AFA04

DRAM Error Status Register = 0x0
DRAM Address Exception Register = 0x0

Traceback Using RA
STACK TRACE:
-Traceback= 4023156C 40099864 40099850
CONTEXT:
$0 : 00000000, AT : 00000000, v0 : 00001FA0, v1 : 00000001
a0 : 41ACEF40, a1 : 00000000, a2 : 00000000, a3 : 00000000
t0 : 40597940, t1 : 3400BF01, t2 : 34008D00, t3 : FFFF00FF
t4 : 400B9A30, t5 : 00000000, t6 : 00000000, t7 : 00000000
s0 : 405998E0, s1 : 405932A0, s2 : 40648590, s3 : 41ACEF4A
s4 : 40590000, s5 : 41ACEF40, s6 : 000007E8, s7 : 00000000
t8 : 40A1C1E8, t9 : 40796580, k0 : 40793080, k1 : 400BB618
gp : 40549980, sp : 40B28F30, s8 : 00000000, ra : 40234A98
EPC : 0x400AA5B0, SREG : 0x3400BF05, Cause : 0x00000000
ErrorEPC : 0x40234AF0
```

continues

Listing 14.8 **Continued**

```
SLOT 2:00:00:11: %SYS-5-RESTART: System restarted —
Cisco Internetwork Operating System Software
IOS (tm) GS Software (GLC1-LC-M), Version 12.0(6)S, EARLY DEPLOYMENT RELEASE
➥SOFTWARE (fc2)
Copyright (c) 1986-1999 by cisco Systems, Inc.
Compiled Wed 15-Sep-99 17:22 by rnapier

SLOT 2:4w6d: %LCGE-6-GBIC_OIR: 1 Port Gigabit Ethernet GBIC removed from port  0

SLOT 2:4w6d: %LCGE-6-GBIC_OIR: 1 Port Gigabit Ethernet GBIC inserted in port 0

SLOT 2:4w6d: %LCGE-6-GBIC_OIR: 1 Port Gigabit Ethernet GBIC removed from port  0

SLOT 2:00:00:11: %SYS-5-RESTART: System restarted —
Cisco Internetwork Operating System Software
IOS (tm) GS Software (GLC1-LC-M), Version 12.0(6)S, EARLY DEPLOYMENT RELEASE
➥SOFTWARE (fc2)
Copyright (c) 1986-1999 by cisco Systems, Inc.
Compiled Wed 15-Sep-99 17:22 by rnapie

bbr01#
```

As you can see, not only does the command output the memory register information that we saw in Listing 14.5, it also displays information about the card type and IOS version. In addition, the syslog messages that were generated at restart are recorded and displayed.

Diagnosing Physical Layer Problems with *show controllers*

Other useful commands that can be used to help diagnose physical layer problems are the `show controllers` family of commands. Listing 14.9 shows the output of the `show controllers` command. This command shows the output of the current state of a serial interface controller.

Listing 14.9 **Sample Output from the *show controllers* Command**

```
router#show controllers serial 1/1/0
Serial1/1/0 -
   Mx T3(1) HW Revision 0x3, FW Revision 2.55
   Framing is c-bit, Clock Source is Line
   Bandwidth limit is 44210, DSU mode 0, Cable length is 50
   Data in current interval (528 seconds elapsed):
     0 Line Code Violations, 0 P-bit Coding Violation
     0 C-bit Coding Violation
     0 P-bit Err Secs, 0 P-bit Sev Err Secs
     0 Sev Err Framing Secs, 0 Unavailable Secs
     0 Line Errored Secs, 0 C-bit Errored Secs, 0 C-bit Sev Err Secs
```

```
    Total Data (last 24 hours)
      0 Line Code Violations, 0 P-bit Coding Violation,
      3 C-bit Coding Violation,
      0 P-bit Err Secs, 0 P-bit Sev Err Secs,
      0 Sev Err Framing Secs, 0 Unavailable Secs,
      3 Line Errored Secs, 3 C-bit Errored Secs, 0 C-bit Sev Err Secs

    No alarms detected.
router#show controllers serial 6/1/0
Serial6/1/0 -
    Mx T3(1) HW Revision 0x3, FW Revision 2.55
    Framing is c-bit, Clock Source is Line
    Bandwidth limit is 44210, DSU mode 0, Cable length is 50
    Data in current interval (204 seconds elapsed):
      0 Line Code Violations, 0 P-bit Coding Violation
      0 C-bit Coding Violation
      0 P-bit Err Secs, 0 P-bit Sev Err Secs
      0 Sev Err Framing Secs, 203 Unavailable Secs
      0 Line Errored Secs, 0 C-bit Errored Secs, 0 C-bit Sev Err Secs
    Total Data (last 24 hours)
      599492 Line Code Violations, 0 P-bit Coding Violation,
      0 C-bit Coding Violation,
      0 P-bit Err Secs, 0 P-bit Sev Err Secs,
      0 Sev Err Framing Secs, 0 Unavailable Secs,
      21 Line Errored Secs, 0 C-bit Errored Secs, 0 C-bit Sev Err Secs

    Transmitter is sending remote alarm.

    Receiver has loss of signal.
router#
```

As you can see by examining the text in Listing 14.9, Serial6/1/0 has been receiving errors and has a loss of signal on its receiver. This might be due to a cabling problem. It is common to see loss of signal on a circuit if the telco has not completed wiring the circuit. Usually you will see an AIS alarm on the receiver if the circuit is complete but not active yet (there is no terminating equipment on the far end). The output from the same command on a Cisco 12000 series router is different. Firstly, the format of the output is different. Also, the 12000 series routers attempt to find out the far end equipment information (similar to the show CDP command we discussed in Chapter 12, "Tools of the Trade"). This is shown in the path trace buffer. Listing 14.10 shows the output of the show controllers pos command on a Cisco 12008. In this listing I use a packet over SONET interface because the 12000 series routers do not support DS3 serial interfaces.

Listing 14.10 **Sample Output from** *show controller* **POS Command**

```
bbr01.sntc01#sh contr pos 5/0
POS5/0
SECTION
  LOF = 0           LOS = 0                          BIP(B1) = 18
LINE
  AIS = 0           RDI = 0         FEBE = 591       BIP(B2) = 287
PATH
  AIS = 9           RDI = 11        FEBE = 624       BIP(B3) = 12449354
  LOP = 0           NEWPTR = 288737   PSE = 416600     NSE = 1

Active Defects: None
Active Alarms:  None
Alarm reporting enabled for: SF SLOS SLOF B1-TCA B2-TCA PLOP B3-TCA

APS
  COAPS = 2          PSBF = 0
  State: PSBF_state = False
  ais_shut = FALSE
  Rx(K1/K2): 11/14
  S1S0 = 00, C2 = CF
CLOCK RECOVERY
  RDOOL = 0
  State: RDOOL_state = False
PATH TRACE BUFFER : STABLE
  Remote hostname : scca-15
  Remote interface: POS2/0
  Remote IP addr  : 209.185.249.110
  Remote Rx(K1/K2): 11/14  Tx(K1/K2): 00/00

BER thresholds:  SF = 10e-3  SD = 10e-6
TCA thresholds:  B1 = 10e-6  B2 = 10e-6  B3 = 10e-6

bbr01.sntc01#
```

Troubleshooting the Cable Plant

The cable plant refers to the wiring between devices in the physical layer. This includes the connectors and wiring between the user end stations and a switch or hub. It does not include the interconnect devices that may be used, such as routers, switches, hubs, or signaling repeaters. Many companies choose to make their own cables for connecting their Cisco routers to the various networking devices in use in their networks. If you do make your own cables, be sure to test the cables before deploying them into your network. Cable testers for coaxial cable, twisted-pair cable, and fiber optic cables are relatively cheap and can save your company from expensive network down time. Make sure also to use the proper terminating equipment for the cables that you are making. This includes both the hardware and the tools. You will find that an inexpensive twisted-pair crimp tool will produce far more faulty cables than the more expensive crimp tools. Save yourself the headache and wasted cable costs; purchase the best crimp tool you can find.

Twisted-pair cable comes in two types: solid copper core or stranded. The solid core cable is used for interconnect cabling on telco punch down blocks. It is also used for Ethernet patch cables. The stranded core cables are used for telephone patch cords. Each of these cable types uses different RJ-45 modular connectors.

Figure 14.2 shows the pin layout for an Ethernet RJ-45 connector.

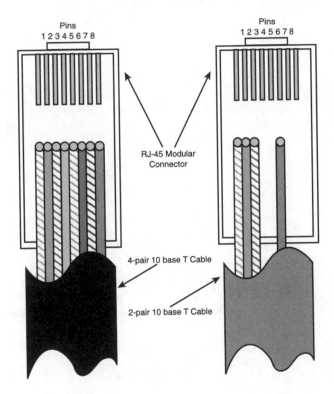

Figure 14.2 RJ-45 pin layout for Ethernet.

Ethernet Copper Connectors

RJ-45 is a telephony designation for the 8-pin modular connector on the end of a twisted-pair cable. It is very similar to the plug found on the end telephone cables. The only real difference is the layout of the individual wires in the plug and the number of individual wires.

Twisted-pair cable is usually purchased in the four pair variety. It is the most common cable type because it can be used for almost any cabling application (for example, networking and telephone wiring). Because it is so popular, cable manufacturers can produce high volumes of it, which drives the cost down.

The strands within the cable are separated into pairs and each pair is assigned a color. The standard color coding for the copper pairs within the cable is listed in Table 14.1. Each individual strand in a pair is twisted together; hence the name twisted-pair cable. The twisting of the pairs reduces the crosstalk between pairs.

Table 14.1 **Color Code for Twisted-Pair Cable**

Pair	Color
1	Blue
2	Orange
3	Green
4	Brown

Crosstalk in Copper Cabling

When many wires run along parallel paths, each wire acts as both a sending and receiving antenna. Some of the signal energy on the wire does not stay in the wire. The energy instead radiates from the wire. The adjacent wires will then pick up this radiated energy and add it to the signals that they are carrying at the time.

Shielding around each pair can be used to reduce the crosstalk that might occur.

Crosstalk can also be found on parallel traces on a printed circuit board.

Color Code Standard for Twisted-Pair Cable

The Electronics Industry Associations (EIA) has developed a standard color-coding for twisted-pair cable. The standard defines a series of five colors to be used in rotation for the distinction of individual strands within a cable. The five colors in sequence are white, red, black, yellow, and violet. These are known as the primary colors. Within each primary color there exists the five secondary colors. These secondary colors are blue, orange, green, brown, and slate (gray).

This color-coding scheme allows up to 25 pairs within one cable. To go beyond 25 pairs, each 25 pair bundle is wrapped with a primary colored band within the outside cable jacket.

The individual strands within each pair are distinguished by the primary/secondary color pattern on the strand itself. The positive strand has a primary colored coating with a secondary colored strip. The negative strand has a secondary colored coat with a primary colored strip. Because the standard twisted-pair cable for Ethernet has only four pairs, only the first four of the five secondary colors are used. The primary color for the cable is white. For instance, the positive strand in pair 1 has a white coating with a blue strip. The negative strand in pair 1 has a blue coating with a white stripe.

The outside jacket, or cover, of the twisted-pair cable can be different colors. It is a good idea to use different color cables for different networking types. You can use red cable to signify Fast Ethernet, green cable for Ethernet, and blue cable for voice wiring. This will enable you to trace cable paths more easily and quickly.

In the instances when you do not know where a cable terminates, you can use a device called a toner to trace the cable path. A toner is a small electronic box that has a modular plug, or alligator clips, which can be used to attach the device to the cable in question. The toner will emit an audible tone onto the wire. The tone cannot be heard with the naked ear. You must use a companion device referred to as a wand. The wand is inductive based, which means that is picks up electromagnetic signals by passing a metallic object through the magnetic field that is generated on the wire by the toner. It has a metal tip, which is sometimes coated in plastic to prevent inadvertent shorts on electrical circuits, that you place next to a cable to amplify the signal. The wand also has a speaker to make the tone audible to the human ear. It is not generally a good idea to place a toner on a cable that is connected to electronic equipment. You might damage the interface hardware with the signal that the toner puts on the wire. The proper procedure is to disconnect the questionable cable and then place the toner on that end of the cable. Then use the wand to determine where on your wiring board the cable terminates.

There are more advanced cable testers that have the cable tracing functionality built into them. Fluke (www.fluke.com) has been a leading manufacturer of cable testers for years. Their testers can tell you which pins in your twisted-pair jumper cables are bad. They can also tell you which strands are wired to which pin on each end of the cable. This is useful information if you think that you are testing a straight through cable and you actually have a crossover cable. A crossover cable has the transmit and receive pairs swapped on one end of the cable (see Figure 14.3). These cables are used to connect router port to router port or any Ethernet device to a router without the use of a hub or switch. These are commonly used with Virtual Private Networking (VPN) and firewall devices. Some cable testers can also be used to verify the category rating of the cable plant from end to end. You should require a report from your building cable installer that shows the results of each individual test that was run after the installation of new building wiring. The building cable installer should also provide you with a detailed cable route diagram that shows the path through the building of all the cable that was installed. This should include ceilings, riser closets, and underground conduit. This will enable you to narrow your search more quickly when attempting to find a particular cable failure. A cable route-map is also handy for reference when additional cabling is needed later. You can suggest possible routes for new cabling that parallels your current installation.

T568A Crossover

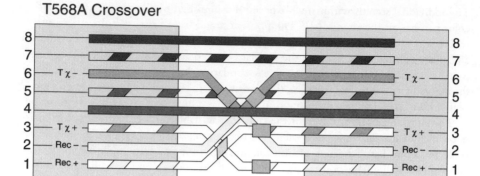

Figure 14.3 Ethernet crossover cable wiring.

Twisted-pair cabling has distance limitations for the various Ethernet versions that can be run on it. These limitations are defined to prevent signal loss to the point where the data being transmitted on the wire can no longer be distinguished from the inherent noise on the wire. Even with the use of repeaters, there is a maximum cable length. Repeaters not only boost the signal level of the data being transmitted, they increase the noise level as well. Table 14.2 lists the cable length limitations of the various Ethernet versions. The temperature of the area that they are installed in can dramatically affect cable length limits. For instance, cabling run through an attic (where it is hotter than usual) carries a signal a shorter distance than the same cabling installed in room temperature. This is a good reason to make sure that any building cabling that is installed in a dropped ceiling is tied up off of any fluorescent lights that it might cross over. Direct contact with the lighting fixture will cause the cable to heat and reduce the effective length of the cable.

Copper Data Cable and Electricity

Keep in mind that copper based data cabling should never be run in parallel to electrical wiring. This is a big danger when data cabling is installed in drop ceilings without conduit. The data cabling will pick up the 60Hz cycle of the AC power in the electrical wiring. An experienced cable installer (or tester) will recognize the sound if a wand is placed near a data cable that is carrying crosstalk from electrical wires. It sounds like a low hum.

Table 14.2 **Maximum Twisted-Pair Cable Lengths for Ethernet**

Ethernet Version	Maximum Length	Maximum Length w/Repeater
Ethernet (10Mbps)	100 meters	300 meters
Fast Ethernet (100Mbps)	150 meters	400 meters

The physical layer also includes any transceiver devices used to interface the cable plant with the actual networking device. For instance, the MAU on a Token Ring network is part of the physical layer. The transceivers used in Ethernet networks to convert one cabling type to another are also part of the physical layer. It is always a good idea to keep spares of these types of devices on hand for troubleshooting purposes. The only effective way to determine if there is a defective transceiver in your network is to attach a network test set to the interface through the transceiver. Or, you can simply verify all other parts of the cable plant and then swap the suspected transceiver with a spare. If the new transceiver works, it is a good bet that the one that was replaced is bad. I cannot count how many times I have had defective Ethernet transceivers discovered in the networks that I have worked on.

It is important that the cable plant itself be installed properly as well. Keep these ideas in mind when you are troubleshooting the cable plant:

- Fiber optic cables have specified bend radii, as well as, cable tensions. Make sure that cables are not pinched or crushed in cable trays. These types of installation methods can lead to cable plant failure at a later date.

- A separate cable tray or innerduct should be used to keep fiber optic cable from coming in direct contact with other cabling types. The reason for using a separate cable tray for fiber optic cables is to keep installation and removal of other cabling from damaging the fiber optic cables. Fiber optic cables are durable to a point. It is always better to be safe than sorry.

- Extra care should be taken when adding or removing cables from an existing cable tray to avoid damaging the installed cable plant. The friction that is caused by pulling an old cable that is buried under a pile of cable that was added later can burn through the outer jacket of other cables. This can cause the copper core of the cable strands to be exposed and even broken.

- Test all your cables before deploying them, even if they were purchased from a professional cable vendor. No one is perfect, and there is nothing more annoying than installing a new cable through all your cable management and discovering that it does not work.

Troubleshooting Cisco Hardware

All the Cisco interface cards have LED displays that show the current status of the individual ports on the interface card. The various interface cards have several LEDs that signify different things depending on the interface type. One LED that all interface cards have in common is the Enabled light. This LED signifies that the card has been recognized by the IOS and is ready for use on the router. A few things that would cause this LED to not be lit are

- Improper IOS version for the interface card. All interface cards require a specific IOS version or higher.

- The card is not seated fully in the backplane connector. Verify that the card is inserted fully and evenly and that the retaining screws are tightened.

- The card was inserted erratically. If a card is inserted partially and the IOS attempts to verify the card type and run the onboard tests but fails, the card will not be enabled. This can happen when a card is inserted far enough to cause an OIR (interrupt signal) on the backplane but not far enough for all the connector pins to make contact with the backplane. This is probably the most dangerous of all because it could cause the router to reload.

- The card itself is defective.

Use the other LEDs to determine whether the connection is active or there is a signaling problem. If a signaling problem exists, it could be due to faulty cabling.

Always be sure to wear the grounding straps provided with each interface card that Cisco sells. It is a common occurrence for the people deploying hardware in the field to forget this simple step before removing the interface cards from their static bags. The warnings that are mentioned in the installation procedures for all Cisco hardware are valid ones. Static discharges can damage sensitive components on the interface card. Besides, as I have said before, it is better to be safe than sorry.

It is good practice to keep the area around your equipment clean and free from dust, especially if you are using technology that utilizes fiber optic cabling. Dust particles on the optical transmitter and receiver of the interface card can cause intermittent signal loss. There are services available that specialize in the cleaning of raised floor areas and data communications rooms.

Conclusion

The physical layer is probably the easiest to troubleshoot. It is often not, however, the easiest to diagnose. Cabling problems and hardware degradation can cause bizarre problems that are manifested in the upper layers of the OSI model. It is always a good idea to verify all aspects of the physical layer before moving on to the layers above. It is also a good idea to keep spare hardware onsite to make the troubleshooting process move faster. Cisco will often ask that you swap interface cards when trying to determine the cause of an interface failure. Having Cisco supply replacement hardware usually takes at least a day and sometimes longer. If you have your own spare equipment onsite, you can verify that the existing hardware is good or bad much faster.

Once an interface card is installed and working, it is very rare that the hardware will fail (the router will be put out of use before you see the cards fail). You will at times encounter hardware that is dead on arrival, in which case you can call Cisco's Technical Assistance Center (TAC) and open a case for a Return Merchandise Authorization (RMA). The Cisco TAC can be contacted via several means. The three you will most likely use are the Worldwide toll-free phone number, 800-553-2447, email to tac@cisco.com, or you can open a case via the Cisco Web page at http://www.cisco.com/kobayashi/Tech_support.shtml. This last option is only available if you are a registered member of Cisco Connection Online (CCO). You can register for CCO at http://www.cisco.com/register/.

15

Troubleshooting the
Network Layer

THE NETWORK LAYER HANDLES ALL THE SOFTWARE ADDRESSES of hosts. It is responsible for making sure that packets get to the destinations for which they are intended for. These addresses can be IP, AppleTalk, IPX, or any number of other networking protocol addresses. The specific protocol that will be covered in this chapter is TCP/IP, because it is the most widely used protocol for corporate and Internet applications.

This chapter will cover troubleshooting of the network layer of the Open Systems Interconnection (OSI) model. This chapter is meant only as a guideline for troubleshooting of the network layer in general. Although specific examples are given using the Ethernet and Frame Relay data link protocols, similar methodologies and Internetworking Operating System (IOS) commands would be used no matter which data link (Layer 2 of the OSI model) protocol you are working with. For every Internet Protocol (IP) protocol specific command that is mentioned, there is a counterpart which can be used for the AppleTalk or IPX protocols. Variations of this convention are pointed out wherever applicable.

Router Commands

There are two families of commands that will be used to troubleshoot the problems introduced in this chapter. Various branches of the show tree of IOS commands will be used. Also, several branches of the debug tree of privileged user mode IOS commands will be used. The show family of commands displays information about the current status of interfaces and certain aspects of the IOS. The debug family of commands displays information about the interfaces and IOS at the packet level.

show Commands

The show interface command is a very useful command for many purposes. It displays a wide range of useful information on a per interface basis, or all interfaces on the router if no interface is specified on the command line.

Listing 15.1 shows a sample output of the show interface command on a Cisco 7500 series router. The listing shows the output for several different interface types. Notice how each interface output has basically the same format and information. This is common across all router models that run the Cisco IOS. Having the same command output structure results in a smaller learning curve when moving from one router model to another. Information specific to the interface type is displayed toward the beginning of the output. Details, such as Asynchronoos Transfer Mode (ATM) VCs configured and Fiber Distributed Data Interface (FDDI) neighbors are specific to the data link protocol (and interface type). The information that is displayed with this command which is important to you is

- The interface up/down state. The interface being up means that communication with the device on the other end of the connection has been established. The line protocol being up is dependent on the data link protocol being able to establish its connection with the remote device. This communication establishment is dependent upon line encapsulation, duplex modes, keepalives, and so on. Basically, the line status indicator shows the physical layer (OSI Layer 1) status. The line protocol status indicator shows the data link layer (OSI Layer 2) status.

- The network layer protocol address assignment(s). These can be an IP address, AppleTalk address, IPX address, and so on.

- Interface encapsulation setting. Especially important for Ethernet interfaces if the encapsulation has been changed from the default setting on the router. Both sides of the connection must be talking the same language in order to operate properly.

- Interface protocol errors (Cyclical Redundancy Checksum [CRC], overruns, ignores).

- Queuing strategy and load values. Both of these play important roles in determining when packets are dropped from an interface rather than forwarding the packets.

You would use this command to verify that all the settings you have programmed have taken effect on the correct interface. I have, on several occasions, entered interface configuration commands on the wrong interface because of a typographical error when entering the interface configuration mode. I have found that it is best to double check your typing before hitting enter at the IOS command prompt. Or, you can enter the commands that you want to enter at the IOS command prompts into your favorite text editor first. Then when you are satisfied that all the commands are correct and ready to be entered, cut the command text from the editor window and paste them into the session window that is connected to the router you are programming (this of course requires an operating system that is running a windowing environment).

Listing 15.1 **Sample Output from** *show interface* **Command**

```
router2#sh int
ATM0/0 is up, line protocol is up
  Hardware is cxBus ATM
  Description: XXX
  MTU 4470 bytes, sub MTU 4470, BW 45000 Kbit, DLY 190 usec, rely 255/255, load
  ↝107/255
  Encapsulation ATM, loopback not set, keepalive set (10 sec)
  Encapsulation(s): AAL5, PVC mode
  256 TX buffers, 256 RX buffers,
  2048 maximum active VCs, 1024 VCs per VP, 2 current VCCs
  VC idle disconnect time: 300 seconds
  Last input never, output 00:00:00, output hang never
  Last clearing of "show interface" counters 9w1d
  Queueing strategy: fifo
  Output queue 0/40, 0 drops; input queue 0/75, 0 drops
  1 minute input rate 3591000 bits/sec, 3030 packets/sec
  1 minute output rate 18894000 bits/sec, 4145 packets/sec
    3160178006 packets input, 4193341616 bytes, 21 no buffer
    Received 0 broadcasts, 0 runts, 0 giants
    14 input errors, 14 CRC, 0 frame, 0 overrun, 511 ignored, 0 abort
    1001692754 packets output, 1766977617 bytes, 0 underruns
    0 output errors, 0 collisions, 0 interface resets
    0 output buffer failures, 0 output buffers swapped out
ATM0/0.1 is up, line protocol is up
  Hardware is cxBus ATM
  Description: PVC for Transit
  Internet address is 192.168.100.1/30
  MTU 4470 bytes, BW 45000 Kbit, DLY 190 usec, rely 255/255, load 107/255
  Encapsulation ATM
FastEthernet1/0/0 is up, line protocol is up
  Hardware is cyBus FastEthernet Interface, address is 0090.5f6d.e020 (bia
  ↝0090.5f6d.e020)
  Description: Uplink
  Internet address is 192.168.200.1/30
  MTU 1500 bytes, BW 100000 Kbit, DLY 100 usec, rely 255/255, load 11/255
  Encapsulation ARPA, loopback not set, keepalive set (10 sec), fdx, 100BaseTX/FX
```

continues

Listing 15.1 **Continued**

```
ARP type: ARPA, ARP Timeout 04:00:00
Last input 00:00:00, output 00:00:00, output hang never
Last clearing of "show interface" counters 9w1d
Queueing strategy: fifo
Output queue 0/40, 0 drops; input queue 0/75, 779406 drops
5 minute input rate 21246000 bits/sec, 4263 packets/sec
5 minute output rate 4576000 bits/sec, 3939 packets/sec
   2165153188 packets input, 4096159693 bytes, 47 no buffer
   Received 1568140 broadcasts, 0 runts, 0 giants
   20 input errors, 0 CRC, 0 frame, 0 overrun, 44546 ignored, 0 abort
   0 watchdog, 0 multicast
   0 input packets with dribble condition detected
   2888580065 packets output, 130456059 bytes, 0 underruns
   0 output errors, 0 collisions, 0 interface resets
   0 babbles, 0 late collision, 0 deferred
   0 lost carrier, 0 no carrier
   0 output buffer failures, 0 output buffers swapped out
Hssi1/1/0 is up, line protocol is up
  Hardware is cyBus HSSI
  Description: XXX
  Internet address is 192.168.200.5/30
  MTU 4470 bytes, BW 45045 Kbit, DLY 200 usec, rely 255/255, load 226/255
  Encapsulation HDLC, loopback not set, keepalive set (10 sec)
  Last input 00:00:00, output 00:00:00, output hang never
  Last clearing of "show interface" counters 9w1d
  Queueing strategy: fifo
  Output queue 0/500, 0 drops; input queue 0/200, 0 drops
  1 minute input rate 4646000 bits/sec, 3657 packets/sec
  1 minute output rate 39984000 bits/sec, 7580 packets/sec
     2203466056 packets input, 172346633 bytes, 34 no buffer
     Received 0 broadcasts, 0 runts, 0 giants
              0 parity
     41 input errors, 2 CRC, 0 frame, 39 overrun, 0 ignored, 0 abort
     1651274647 packets output, 3050427333 bytes, 0 underruns
     0 output errors, 0 applique, 1 interface resets
     0 output buffer failures, 0 output buffers swapped out
     0 carrier transitions
Fddi6/0 is up, line protocol is up
  Hardware is cxBus FDDI, address is 0090.5f6d.e0c0 (bia 0090.5f6d.e0c0)
  Description: Server Network
  Internet address is 192.168.4.1/24
  MTU 4470 bytes, BW 100000 Kbit, DLY 100 usec, rely 255/255, load 31/255
  Encapsulation SNAP, loopback not set, keepalive not set
  ARP type: SNAP, ARP Timeout 04:00:00
  Phy-A state is connect, neighbor is unk, cmt signal bits 008/000, status QLS
  Phy-B state is  active, neighbor is   A, cmt signal bits 20C/008, status ILS
  ECM is in, CFM is c_wrap_b, RMT is ring_op
  Requested token rotation 5000 usec, negotiated 5000 usec
  Configured tvx is 2500 usec ring operational 15w2d
  Upstream neighbor 0080.7c0a.10d4, downstream neighbor 0080.7c0a.10d4
```

```
     Last input 00:00:00, output 00:00:00, output hang never
     Last clearing of "show interface" counters 1w2d
     Queueing strategy: fifo
     Output queue 0/500, 0 drops; input queue 0/500, 215 drops
     1 minute input rate 3680000 bits/sec, 2589 packets/sec
     1 minute output rate 12527000 bits/sec, 2668 packets/sec
        2030182056 packets input, 4061064124 bytes, 5 no buffer
        Received 1515961 broadcasts, 0 runts, 0 giants
        0 input errors, 0 CRC, 0 frame, 0 overrun, 0 ignored, 0 abort
        2134180648 packets output, 1062106127 bytes, 11 underruns
        0 output errors, 0 collisions, 0 interface resets
        0 output buffer failures, 0 output buffers swapped out
        0 transitions, 0 traces,  0 claims, 0 beacon
Loopback0 is up, line protocol is up
   Hardware is Loopback
   Internet address is 172.168.0.1/32
   MTU 1500 bytes, BW 8000000 Kbit, DLY 5000 usec, rely 255/255, load 1/255
   Encapsulation LOOPBACK, loopback not set, keepalive set (10 sec)
   Last input never, output never, output hang never
   Last clearing of "show interface" counters 9w1d
   Queueing strategy: fifo
   Output queue 0/0, 0 drops; input queue 0/75, 0 drops
   5 minute input rate 0 bits/sec, 0 packets/sec
   5 minute output rate 0 bits/sec, 0 packets/sec
      0 packets input, 0 bytes, 0 no buffer
      Received 0 broadcasts, 0 runts, 0 giants
      0 input errors, 0 CRC, 0 frame, 0 overrun, 0 ignored, 0 abort
      0 packets output, 0 bytes, 0 underruns
      0 output errors, 0 collisions, 0 interface resets
      0 output buffer failures, 0 output buffers swapped out
router2#
```

Another useful command that gives a great deal of the interface information you would usually be looking for is show ip interface brief. Listing 15.2 shows a sample output of the command from our corporate site A router. This command displays the IP addresses assigned to each interface as well as the interface and protocol up/down state. This command is good for quick looks at the major interface parameters. You do not need to wade through all the other information that is displayed with the show interface command. As the command states, the output displays information for IP configuration only.

Listing 15.2 **Sample Output from *show ip interface brief***

```
corp-a-01#sh ip int b
Interface               IP-Address      OK? Method Status            Protocol
GigabitEthernet0/0/0    192.168.4.1     YES NVRAM  up                up
Hssi0/1/0               192.168.5.2     YES NVRAM  up                up
Serial1/0               192.168.6.1     YES manual down              down
Serial1/1               unassigned      YES unset  up                up
```

continues

Listing 15.2 **Continued**

```
Serial1/1.1        192.168.7.1     YES unset   up                       up
Serial1/2          192.168.6.9     YES unset   up                       up
Serial1/3          unassigned      YES unset   administratively down down
Serial1/4          unassigned      YES unset   administratively down down
Serial1/5          unassigned      YES unset   administratively down down
Serial1/6          unassigned      YES unset   administratively down down
Serial1/7          unassigned      YES unset   administratively down down
ATM4/0             unassigned      YES unset   up                       up
ATM4/0.1           192.168.8.1     YES NVRAM   up                       up
Loopback0          172.16.220.13   YES NVRAM   up                       up
corp-a-01#
```

There are of course protocol specific show commands for AppleTalk and IPX. The command syntax for each would be as expected:

```
show appletalk interface
show ipx interface
```

Listing 15.3 shows a sample output for an AppleTalk enabled interface.

Listing 15.3 **Output from *show appletalk interface***

```
Router# show appletalk interface fddi 0
Fddi0 is up, line protocol is up
        AppleTalk cable range is 4199-4199
        AppleTalk address is 4199.82, Valid
        AppleTalk zone is "Low End SW Lab"
        AppleTalk address gleaning is disabled
        AppleTalk route cache is enabled
        Interface will not perform pre-FDDITalk compatibility
```

As with the IP specific command, the appletalk command also has a brief formatting option. Listing 15.4 shows the typical output from the show appletalk interface brief command.

Listing 15.4 **Output from *show appletalk interface brief***

```
Router# show appletalk interface brief
Interface     Address      Config        Status/Line Protocol     Atalk Protocol
TokenRing0    108.36       Extended      up                       down
TokenRing1    unassigned   not config'd  administratively down    n/a
Ethernet0     10.82        Extended      up                       up
Serial0       unassigned   not config'd  administratively down    n/a
Ethernet1     30.83        Extended      up                       up
Serial1       unassigned   not config'd  administratively down    n/a
Serial2       unassigned   not config'd  administratively down    n/a
Serial3       unassigned   not config'd  administratively down    n/a
Serial4       unassigned   not config'd  administratively down    n/a
Serial5       unassigned   not config'd  administratively down    n/a
```

```
Fddi0          50001.82     Extended        administratively down    down
Ethernet2      unassigned   not config'd    up                       n/a
Ethernet3      9993.137     Extended        up                       up
Ethernet4      40.82        Non-Extended    up                       up
Ethernet5      unassigned   not config'd    administratively down    n/a
Ethernet6      unassigned   not config'd    administratively down    n/a
Ethernet7      unassigned   not config'd    administratively down    n/a
```

As you can see, the output is very similar to the IP specific version. Listing 15.5 shows a sample output from the show interface command for an IPX enable interface.

Listing 15.5   **Output from *show ipx interface***

```
Router# show ipx interface ethernet 1
Ethernet0 is up, line protocol is up
  IPX address is E001.0000.0c02.8cf9, SAP [up] line-up, RIPPQ: 0, SAPPQ : 0
  Delay of this IPX network, in ticks is 1 throughput 0 link delay 0
  IPXWAN processing not enabled on this interface.
  IPX SAP update interval is 1 minute(s)
  IPX type 20 propagation packet forwarding is disabled
  Outgoing access list is not set
  IPX Helper access list is not set
  SAP Input filter list is not set
  SAP Output filter list is not set
  SAP Router filter list is not set
  SAP GNS output filter list is not set
  Input filter list is not set
  Output filter list is not set
  Router filter list is not set
  Netbios Input host access list is not set
  Netbios Input bytes access list is not set
  Netbios Output host access list is not set
  Netbios Output bytes access list is not set
  Update time is 60 seconds
  IPX accounting is enabled
  IPX fast switching is configured (enabled)
  IPX SSE switching is disabled
    IPX NLSP is running on primary network E001
    RIP compatibility mode is AUTO (OFF)
    SAP compatibility mode is AUTO (OFF)
    Level 1 Hello interval 20 sec
    Level 1 Designated Router Hello interval 10 sec
    Level 1 CSNP interval 30 sec
    Level 1 LSP retransmit interval 5 sec, LSP (pacing) interval 1000 mSec
    Level 1 adjacency count is 1
    Level 1 circuit ID is 0000.0C02.8CF9.02
```

Troubleshooting Frame Relay with *show* Commands

If Frame Relay is being used on your router, the show frame-relay family of commands will tell you just about everything you ever wanted to know about the current Frame Relay configuration. Refer to Figure 15.1 as a visual reference to the following discussion.

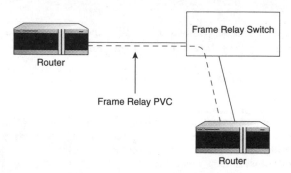

Figure 15.1   Sample Frame Relay connection.

Listing 15.6 shows the output from a show frame-relay lmi command on a Cisco 7500 series router. This command displays information about the Link Management Interface (LMI) communications between the router and the far end device. The important information here is the connection type of the router interface (DTE or DCE) and the LMI type itself. Remember from Chapter 5, "Wide Area Networking," that there are several LMI types available. If both sides of the connection are not configured for the same LMI type, the line protocol of the Frame Relay interface will not come up.

Listing 15.6   **Sample Output from the *show frame-relay lmi* Command**

```
router3#sh frame-relay lmi

LMI Statistics for interface Serial8/0/0 (Frame Relay DTE) LMI TYPE = ANSI
  Invalid Unnumbered info 0        Invalid Prot Disc 0
  Invalid dummy Call Ref 0         Invalid Msg Type 0
  Invalid Status Message 0         Invalid Lock Shift 0
  Invalid Information ID 0         Invalid Report IE Len 0
  Invalid Report Request 0         Invalid Keep IE Len 0
  Num Status Enq. Sent 213564      Num Status msgs Rcvd 213563
  Num Update Status Rcvd 0         Num Status Timeouts 2
router3#
```

Listing 15.7 shows the output from a `show frame-relay pvc` command on a Cisco 7500 series router. This command shows the per PVC statistics for every Frame Relay PVC configured on the router. You can limit the output to a single interface or PVC by adding the interface number or PVC DLCI to the command. For example, `show frame-relay pvc interface serial8/0/0` will display the PVC stats for all PVCs configured on interface Serial8/0/0. The `show frame-relay pvc 16` command will display the PVC statistics for the Frame Relay PVC with the DLCI of 16. The important information to get out of the display in Listing 15.7 is the PVC STATUS and the last time the pvc changed status. The latter information is useful if the pvc status is DELETED or INACTIVE because it can tell you when the change occurred (assuming that the PVC was ACTIVE previously). Table 15.1 shows the various PVC STATUS values and their meanings.

Listing 15.7 Sample Output from the *show frame-relay pvc* Command

```
router3#sh frame-relay pvc

PVC Statistics for interface Serial8/0/0 (Frame Relay DTE)

DLCI = 100, DLCI USAGE = LOCAL, PVC STATUS = ACTIVE, INTERFACE = Serial8/0/0.1

  input pkts 175500      output pkts 11568302    in bytes 13518389
  out bytes 1947185327   dropped pkts 0          in FECN pkts 1
  in BECN pkts 46        out FECN pkts 0         out BECN pkts 0
  in DE pkts 303         out DE pkts 0
  pvc create time 3w3d, last time pvc status changed 2w2d
router3#
```

Table 15.1 Frame Relay PVC STATUS Values and Their Meanings

PVC STATUS	Meaning
ACTIVE	The PVC is defined in the Frame Relay switch and both end devices are configured with the correct DLCIs. This PVC can pass data traffic.
INACTIVE	The PVC is defined in the Frame Relay switch. One or both ends are not configured with the correct DLCIs. This PVC cannot pass data traffic.
DELETED	The PVC is not defined in the Frame Relay switch. The PVC must be configured in the Frame Relay switch before the end point equipment configurations can be verified.

Troubleshooting ATM with *show* Commands

The Cisco IOS provides a set of commands specifically for displaying information about the operation of the ATM interfaces on your routers. The show atm family of commands is similar to the show frame-relay family of commands. Two of the commands in the show atm family that are useful in gathering information about an ATM interface are show atm map and show atm vc. Listing 15.8 shows the output from the show atm map command. This command displays the ATM map-lists defined on the router and the protocol address that is mapped to each ATM VC in that map-list. Remember from Chapter 5 that the ATM map-list is used in conjunction with the atm pvc interface command to associate a network layer (Layer 3 of the OSI model) protocol address with an ATM VPI/VCI pair (Layer 2 of the OSI model). You would use this command to verify that the current router configuration is correct.

Listing 15.8 *show ATM map* Command Output

```
corp-e-01#sh atm map
Map list CORPORATE : PERMANENT
ip 192.168.8.1 maps to VC 33
        , broadcast
ip 192.168.8.5 maps to VC 32
        , broadcast

corp-e-01#
```

The show atm vc command is useful in two forms. The first form has no ATM VC number given to the IOS on the command line. This prompts the IOS to display information for all ATM VCs defined on the router. This form of the command is useful for getting a quick look at the configuration and status of each ATM VC. Listing 15.9 shows a sample output from the show atm vc command. The display shows the VPI/VCI pair configured for each ATM PVC as well as the encapsulation type, peak, and average bandwidth limits and VC status.

Listing 15.9 *show ATM VC* Command Output

```
corp-e-01#sh atm vc
                                AAL /            Peak   Avg.  Burst
Interface   VCD  VPI  VCI Type  Encapsulation   Kbps   Kbps  Cells Status
ATM4/0.1    32   1    32  PVC   AAL5-SNAP       15000  15000    94 ACTIVE
ATM4/0.2    33   1    33  PVC   AAL5-SNAP       15000  15000    94 ACTIVE
corp-e-01#
```

The second form of the command displays information on a per VC basis. There is more information displayed and in greater detail. Listing 15.10 shows a sample output from the show atm vc 32 command. The most important statistics in this display are the traffic and error counters. This information is not available in the more concise output of the show atm vc command. You would use this command to gather data on dropped or erroneous cells.

Listing 15.10 **Output from** *show ATM VC 32*

```
corp-e-01>sh atm vc 32
ATM4/0.1: VCD: 32, VPI: 1, VCI: 32, etype:0x0, AAL5 - LLC/SNAP, Flags: 0x40830
PeakRate: 15000, Average Rate: 15000, Burst Cells: 94, VCmode: 0x0
OAM DISABLED, InARP DISABLED
InPkts: 527179206, OutPkts: 549767013, InBytes: 1487781407, OutBytes: 1495151296
InPRoc: 2551191, OutPRoc: 43148, Broadcasts: 5540473
InFast: 2619124, OutFast: 1546043, InAS: 522008891, OutAS: 542637349
InPktDrops: 0, OutPktDrops: 187854
CrcErrors: 0, SarTimeOuts: 0, OverSizedSDUs: 0
OAM F5 cells sent: 222, OAM cells received: 222
Status: ACTIVE
corp-e-01>
```

debug Commands

Several of the `debug` family of commands for data link protocols can be useful in troubleshooting network layer problems. The `debug arp` command displays information on ARP packets that are received by your router. The `debug ethernet-interface` command will display information on events that occur on all the Ethernet interfaces enabled on your router (which only works on 7000 series or higher routers). The `debug frame-relay` tree of commands enables the output of information about many of the Frame Relay specific features. There is also a `debug frame-relay detail` command that should only be used in a lab because it will bring your router to a crawl because of all the information that it displays.

Mostly you will use `debug` commands to output information on network layer protocols rather than the data link protocols. Commands from the `debug ip` family are very useful. It is a good idea to check the currently running debug modes before starting your own. You can view the currently running debug modes with the `show debug` IOS command.

Use debug Commands with Caution

Be very careful when using `debug` commands. They are very CPU intensive and can lock you out of your router if you enable too many at one time. As a general rule, you should never enable more than one debugging option at a time. The best method for turning debugging options off once they have been enabled is to use the `no debug all` command.

If you get locked out of a router because too many `debug` commands are enabled, the only easy way to recover access to the router is to reload it. Otherwise, you have to disable all communication to the router (by disconnecting all interfaces) and hope that you can get on the console port. It is usually better (and faster) to reload the router.

A very useful command to use if you are having end to end IP communication problems is debug ip packet. The debug ip packet command displays information on a per packet basis. Listing 15.11 shows a sample output of the debug ip packet command. The output shows the source and destination ip address that is stored in the packet header. The next hop gateway is also displayed. The final piece of information shows whether the packet is being forwarded to the next hop gateway or it is administratively denied via an access-list.

Listing 15.11   **Output from** *debug IP packet* **Command**

```
router# debug ip packet
IP: s=192.168.13.44 (Fddi0), d=172.125.254.1 (Serial2), g=192.168.16.2, forward
IP: s=192.168.1.57 (Ethernet4), d=172.36.125.2 (Serial2), g=192.168.16.2, forward
IP: s=192.168.1.6 (Ethernet4), d=255.255.255.255, rcvd 2
IP: s=192.168.1.55 (Ethernet4), d=172.108.2.42 (Fddi0), g=192.168.13.6, forward
IP: s=192.168.89.33 (Ethernet2), d=172.130.2.156 (Serial2), g=192.168.16.2,
↪forward
IP: s=192.168.1.27 (Ethernet4), d=172.108.43.126 (Fddi1), g=192.168.23.5, forward
IP: s=192.168.1.27 (Ethernet4), d=172.108.43.126 (Fddi0), g=192.168.13.6, forward
IP: s=192.168.20.32 (Ethernet2), d=255.255.255.255, rcvd 2
IP: s=192.168.1.57 (Ethernet4), d=172.36.125.2 (Serial2), g=192.168.16.2, access
↪denied
```

One nice feature of the debug ip packet command is that you can specify an access-list number along with the command. If the packets do not match those enabled via the access-list, then they are not displayed.

For instance, the debug ip packet 190 command with access-list 190 defined as:

```
access-list 190 permit ip 192.168.100.35 255.255.255.255 172.200.9.4
↪255.255.255.255
access-list 190 deny ip any any
```

would display IP packets that had a source IP address of 192.168.100.35 and a destination address of 172.200.9.4. This form of the command enables you to display debug information for packets traveling between two specific hosts. The capability to display only information that you are interested in seeing is quite useful, especially on a router that forwards a great deal of traffic. If you were to issue the debug command with no display limitations, you would almost certainly bury the information that you were looking for in a flood of unwanted information. That is both the power and the pitfall of the debug commands.

Ethernet Troubleshooting

Troubleshooting of an Ethernet interface is fairly straightforward. If you know that the cabling to the Ethernet interface is good, then there are only a couple of things that could cause the interface to not come up. One of these is incorrect pin wiring on the Ethernet cable. The interface would show a status of up, but the line protocol would show a status of down. For instance, use of a normal straight through cable when a crossover cable is required. This would be the case if you were connecting two routers back to back rather than through a hub or a switch. Refer back to Chapter 14, "Troubleshooting the Physical Layer," for physical layer troubleshooting.

Another problem that can be the result of human error is the manual assignment of Media Access Control (MAC) addresses to interfaces. If the MAC address that you assign to an interface is a duplicate of another machine on the same network segment, the interface will be unable to exchange packets with other stations on the network segment. You can use the `show arp` command to display which MAC addresses have been added to the local ARP table through the use of the Address Resolution Protocol (ARP). Listing 15.12 shows a sample output of the `show arp` command.

Listing 15.12   *show ARP* **Command Output**

```
router1>sh arp
Protocol  Address          Age (min)  Hardware Addr   Type  Interface
Internet  192.168.216.11        72    00e0.f9d3.4800  ARPA  FastEthernet10/0/0
Internet  192.168.216.12        72    00e0.f9d3.4800  ARPA  FastEthernet10/0/0
Internet  192.168.216.13        72    00e0.f9d3.4800  ARPA  FastEthernet10/0/0
Internet  192.168.216.14        72    00e0.f9d3.4800  ARPA  FastEthernet10/0/0
Internet  192.168.71.40          0    0010.1fc0.0000  ARPA  FastEthernet12/0/0
Internet  192.168.71.39          -    00e0.8f0d.e980  ARPA  FastEthernet12/0/0
Internet  192.168.71.38         94    00e0.f9ce.8800  ARPA  FastEthernet12/0/0
```

Once the interface is operational, there are a few things that could cause degraded performance. Having mismatched duplex settings on interfaces on the same LAN segment would cause CRC errors and possibly misalignment errors. On the Cisco 4000 series routers, the Ethernet modules have both AUI and RJ45 connector types. You need to tell the IOS which connector type you will be using. This is done with either of the following two commands:

```
media-type aui
media-type 10baset
```

If every other aspect of the Ethernet segment is verified to be operating normally and you are still seeing errors or poor performance, try replacing the interface processor if the router is one from the modular series (Cisco 4000 and higher model numbers). This can mean moving the connection to another Ethernet port on the same card, moving the connection to another Ethernet port on a different card installed in the same router, or removing the Ethernet interface processor card and replacing it with a new one. If this does not solve your problem, you will need to place a protocol analyzer on the LAN segment and collect data to determine the source of the errors. A protocol analyzer captures packets from a network segment and displays their contents. They are mostly used to verify that the data link headers are formatted correctly for each packet and that the packet headers contain the correct bit patterns. They are used heavily in the development stages of new hardware. You will rarely have need for one unless you are participating in an early field trial of a new hardware product.

It is important to make sure that all hosts on a shared media network segment have consistent network layer addressing. For example, you cannot have two hosts on an Ethernet segment with IP addresses out of different IP netblocks. If one station were to be addressed with 192.168.4.1 with a subnet mask of 255.255.255.0, and the other host were to be addressed with 192.168.8.167 with a subnet mask of 255.255.255.128, there would be two problems. The first problem is that both hosts are configured for different netblocks. The first host is in netblock 192.168.4.0/24, and the second host is in netblock 192.168.8.128/25. Only one netblock can exist on a segment at a time (except when secondary addresses are used). Secondly, even if both hosts were configured for the same netblock, the subnet masks would need to be the same. Otherwise, each host would have a different idea about what the network address was and what the broadcast address was. This can be a problem because what one host thinks is a unicast (single station) address might be a broadcast (all stations) address to another host.

For example, the netblock 206.11.100.0/24 has a broadcast address of 206.11.100.255. The netblock 206.11.100.0/25 has a broadcast address of 206.11.100.127. Now if two stations were on the same network segment, one with an IP address of 206.11.100.127 and a subnet mask of 255.255.255.0, the other with an IP address of 206.11.100.5 with a subnet mask of 255.255.255.128, there would be a communication problem (see Figure 15.2). Host A would send packets to Host B with no problems at all. Host B on the other hand would send packets destined to Host A to all stations on the LAN segment. The reason for this is the IP address of 206.11.100.127 is the broadcast address for the network as far as Host B is concerned. This IP address would be translated into a broadcast MAC address in the packet header. This would cause frequent broadcast storms and a higher number of collisions on your Ethernet segment than normal.

Secondary IP Addresses

The Cisco IOS enables the configuration of secondary IP addresses on interfaces. This enables two separate IP netblocks to exist on the same network segment at the same time. The interface configuration command used to configure a secondary IP address is

```
ip address <address> <subnet mask> secondary
```

This command is useful when renumbering hosts on LAN segments because both hosts with the new IP addresses and hosts with the old IP addresses can access the network at the same time. Once the renumbering of the hosts has been completed, you can remove the secondary address from the LAN interface.

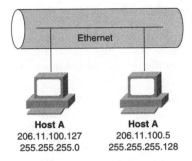

Host A
206.11.100.127
255.255.255.0

Host A
206.11.100.5
255.255.255.128

Figure 15.2   Mismatched subnet masking on IP networks.

FDDI Troubleshooting

FDDI network segments are just as easy to troubleshoot as Ethernet LAN segments, simply because most FDDI installations use FDDI concentrators to connect all their FDDI devices to the ring. Remember from Chapter 4, "Local Area Networking," that FDDI concentrators provide the "ring" portion of the topology. When concentrators are used, the physical layout of the wiring of FDDI stations is a star topology. FDDI stations communicate to other FDDI stations via the concentrator. When FDDI concentrators are used, there is only one device associated with each FDDI port on your Cisco router.

Most FDDI networks are fairly straightforward. Two things that could cause an FDDI station to not operate properly would be defective cabling or incorrectly attaching the ports of a dual-attached station to a concentrator. Once these possibilities have been ruled out, the next step to repairing a failed FDDI port would be to replace the interface processor in the Cisco router. If this does not solve the problem, you should look to the concentrator as the source of the fault. The concentrator might be programmed to support multiple FDDI rings on the same device. Perhaps the port to which your router is connected is segregated from the rest of the ports on the FDDI concentrator. You can verify that all FDDI stations are on the same FDDI ring via the user interface for the concentrator.

After connectivity to the FDDI ring has been established, you can configure and test the network layer protocol. The procedure for this is the same for almost all the LAN interfaces on the Cisco router. Refer back to Chapter 4 for the steps to configure network layer protocols on LAN interfaces.

Frame Relay Troubleshooting

Several things need to operate in order for a Frame Relay connection to become active. The circuit must be installed and connected to the routers on both ends, the PVC needs to be provisioned in the telco Frame Relay switches, and the routers need to be configured on both ends.

Most often the serial interface itself will be operating properly but the Frame Relay PVC will not become active. The first thing to do is make sure that the LMI type on the router is configured for the same type as your telco's Frame Relay switch. The default LMI type on Cisco routers used to be American National Standards Institute (ANSI), but has recently changed to CISCO. You should check which version of IOS you are using to determine which default is used. The easiest way to be sure your router is configured for the correct type is to ignore the default and manually configure the LMI type at all times. If the PVC is still not active, make sure the LMI timers are set correctly. The default settings should work, but I have needed to adjust mine on more than one occasion because of problems with the telco's Frame Relay switch. See Table 15.2 for the Frame Relay settings that need to be configured for proper operation of a Frame Relay PVC.

Table 15.2   **Frame Relay Configuration Options**

Options	Values
Encapsulation	Cisco
	IETF (ANSI)
LMI Type	ANSI
	Cisco
	q933a
LMI Keepalive Timer	0–32767 seconds (Default: 10)

After the PVC is active, you might still be unable to transmit traffic to the other end of the PVC. This is common if there are multiple PVCs on one Frame Relay interface. One side of the PVC might be configured for a DLCI that is defined in the Frame Relay switch but does not map to the end point that you are trying to connect to. Verify that the DLCI is set correctly on both ends and that the Frame Relay PVC is mapped to those DLCIs. This can be done by contacting the service center of your telco.

After verifying the telco portion, make sure that the Frame Relay encapsulation type is compatible on both ends. If the far end of the PVC is not a Cisco router, you will need to make sure that the IETF (ANSI) Frame Relay encapsulation is configured on your router.

Frame Relay Auto-Detect

Frame Relay switches from certain vendors offer an auto-detect feature for the LMI type. I have run into situations where this auto-detect feature did not operate correctly. It is best to verify that the Frame Relay switch that your telco uses is specifically set to a certain LMI type and not any kind of auto-detect.

When the Frame Relay PVC shows active, you are ready to configure and test your network layer protocol. From this point on, configuration and troubleshooting of the network layer protocols are basically the same as the other interface types.

Conclusion

You should now have a good idea of which types of commands are available in the Cisco IOS that can be used for troubleshooting data link and network layer problems. The commands covered in this chapter apply to more than the interface types presented here. If you are not sure if the command that you want to use is available in the IOS for the particular interface type that you are troubleshooting, use the online help operator (the ?). The online help features of the IOS are very useful when troubleshooting and debugging problems.

To recap the steps to take in troubleshooting network problems:

- Verify physical layer connectivity. This will be indicated by the interface up/down state. Things to look for here are cabling problems and hardware failures.
- Verify line protocol is up for the interface you are working with. Check the encapsulation type for the interface. Also verify any necessary keepalive timer settings and duplex modes for the interface time.
- Verify network layer protocol functionality. Check IP netblock assignments for all devices on the same network segment. Verify the IP subnet mask configuration for all hosts on the network segment. Make sure that duplex modes are the same on all stations.

Table 15.3 shows a quick reference of which command to use for certain troubleshooting situations.

Table 15.3 **Which IOS Command to Use When**

To find...	Use...
The current operational state of an interface	`show interface`
	`show ip interface brief`
The current state of Frame Relay PVCs	`show frame-relay pvc`
The current state of ATM VCs	`show atm vc`
Packet errors on an interface	`show interface`
Network address to ATM VC mappings	`show atm map-list`
Network address to Frame Relay mappings	`show frame-relay map`
Frame Relay Link Management Interface status	`show frame-relay lmi`
MAC addresses for Ethernet interfaces	`show arp`
The current IP options enabled on an interface	`show ip interface`

16

Troubleshooting Routing Protocols

Routing problems are often easy to diagnose but difficult to correct. The difficulty comes in the fact that understanding why a routing problem is occurring is often times not easy. You might run into a situation where you have exhausted every avenue available to you and a solution has still not presented itself. Perhaps your router configuration is correct but the IOS software is not operating properly. This chapter explains the commands you need for retrieving information from the router IOS and provides suggestions on how to work with your hardware manufacturer to solve network problems.

To effectively diagnose a routing problem, you must be able to retrieve information on the interworkings of the Internetworking Operating System (IOS) from the router. The Cisco IOS offers a great deal of commands to extract this type information.

Router Commands

As mentioned in Chapter 15, "Troubleshooting the Network Layer," there are two types of IOS commands to help you diagnose problems with the operation of your Cisco router. These are the show family of commands and the debug family of commands. The show commands display information in a formatted output and give a high to medium level of information. The debug commands display information about the actual interworkings of the IOS. This information can be about the packets that the router is processing or the actual IOS operation.

show Commands

There are numerous commands in the show family that can be used to diagnose routing problems. Because the IOS commands exist in a hierarchical nature, there are many individual commands that are useful. This book concentrates on IP network troubleshooting, so the commands that are discussed exist in the show ip branch of IOS commands. Below the show ip branch there are several other branches of commands that are specific to the various IP features supported in the IOS. Among these are

- OSPF
- BGP
- RIP
- IGRP
- EIGRP
- IS-IS
- Static routing

For each of these IP features that are supported, there are sub branches of the IOS command tree. Listing 16.1 shows a complete list of the available command options in the 11.1CC strain of the Cisco IOS.

Listing 16.1   *show ip* **Command Branches Available**

```
corp-a-01#sh ip ?
  access-lists        List IP access lists
  accounting          The active IP accounting database
  aliases             IP alias table
  arp                 IP ARP table
  as-path-access-list List AS path access lists
  bgp                 BGP information
  cache               IP fast-switching route cache
  cef                 Cisco Express Forwarding
  community-list      List community-list
  drp                 Director response protocol
  dvmrp               DVMRP information
  egp                 EGP connections and statistics
  eigrp               IP-EIGRP show commands
  flow                NetFlow switching
  igmp                IGMP information
  interface           IP interface status and configuration
  irdp                ICMP Router Discovery Protocol
  local               IP local options
  masks               Masks associated with a network
  mbgp                BGP multicast RIB information
  mcache              IP multicast fast-switching cache
  mds                 Distributed multicast
  mpacket             Display possible duplicate multicast packets
  mroute              IP multicast routing table
```

```
nhrp              NHRP information
ospf              OSPF information
pim               PIM information
policy            Policy routing
prefix-list       List IP prefix lists
protocols         IP routing protocol process parameters and statistics
redirects         IP redirects
route             IP routing table
rpf               Display RPF information for multicast source
sdr               Session Directory (SDPv2) cache
sockets           Open IP sockets
spd               SPD statistics
tcp               TCP/IP header-compression statistics
traffic           IP protocol statistics
wccp              WCCP information

corp-a-01#
```

The show ip route command is used heavily in debugging routing problems in IP networks.

There are corresponding commands for other network layer protocols, like the AppleTalk Routing Protocol and several of the IPX routing protocols. As you would expect, the command syntax is similar. To display information for the IPX protocol, the IOS command is show ipx. To display information for the AppleTalk protocol, the IOS command is show appletalk.

The actual commands that are available to you can vary depending on the version of IOS that you are running on your routers. We will discuss only the basic commands that are available in most recent versions of the 11.1 strain of IOS and above.

debug Commands

As I am sure you have come to learn, the debug command tree structure is similar to the show command tree structure. Cisco did this for a reason. The easier the user inter-face is to use, the more likable the product is. The main IOS command in the debug family that will be introduced in this chapter is debug ip. There are several branches of commands below the debug ip command that display information on a number of different aspects of the specific protocol's operation or current status. Listing 16.2 shows the available command branches below the debug ip command. The commands listed are not dissimilar from those found in Listing 16.1.

Listing 16.2 *debug ip* **Command Branches Available**

```
corp-a-01#debug ip ?
  bgp        BGP information
  cache      IP cache operations
  cef        IP CEF operations
  cgmp       CGMP protocol activity
  drp        Director response protocol
  dvmrp      DVMRP protocol activity
  egp        EGP information
  eigrp      IP-EIGRP information
  error      IP error debugging
  ftp        FTP dialogue
  http       HTTP connections
  icmp       ICMP transactions
  igmp       IGMP protocol activity
  igrp       IGRP information
  mbgp       MBGP information
  mcache     IP multicast cache operations
  mds        IP Distributed Multicast information
  mobile     Mobility protocols
  mpacket    IP multicast packet debugging
  mrouting   IP multicast routing table activity
  ospf       OSPF information
  packet     General IP debugging and IPSO security transactions
  peer       IP peer address activity
  pim        PIM protocol activity
  policy     Policy routing
  rip        RIP protocol transactions
  routing    Routing table events
  sd         Session Directory (SD)
  security   IP security options
  tcp        TCP information
  udp        UDP based transactions
  wccp       WCCP information

corp-a-01#
```

As with the show commands, the actual commands that are available can vary depending on the version of IOS that you are running on your routers. We will discuss only the basic commands that are available in most of the recent versions of the 11.1 strain of IOS and above.

Troubleshooting Routing Problems with *show ip route*

The command most used to troubleshoot IP routing problems is by far show ip route. This command displays the contents of the routing table that exists on your router. Using the command with no arguments will dump the entire routing table to your screen. Usually, you use the command in conjunction with an IP netblock that you are troubleshooting. For example, if you want to know the next hop the router is using for the forwarding of IP packets to the destination network 198.32.128.0, you would execute the following command at the IOS command prompt of your router:

```
show ip route 198.32.128.0
```

Here is the output you might see on your router:

```
corp-a-01#sh ip route 198.32.128.0
Routing entry for 198.32.128.0/24, 4 known subnets
  Variably subnetted with 2 masks, Hash 578
  Redistributing via ospf 3967

O E2    198.32.128.67/32 [110/20] via 192.186.169.178, 05:08:26, POS12/0/0
O E2    198.32.128.0/24 [110/20] via 192.168.169.178, 05:08:26, POS12/0/0
O E2    198.32.128.130/32 [110/20] via 192.168.169.178, 05:08:26, POS12/0/0
O E2    198.32.128.131/32 [110/20] via 192.168.169.178, 05:08:26, POS12/0/0
corp-a-01#
```

Of the four networks listed, three have the same subnet mask. If you wanted information on the one netblock with the different subnet mask, you could add the subnet mask to the preceding command. The output would then look like this:

```
corp-a-01#sh ip route 198.32.128.0  255.255.255.0
Routing entry for 198.32.128.0/24
  Known via "ospf 3967", distance 110, metric 20, type extern 2, forward metric 9
  Redistributing via ospf 3967
  Last update from 192.168.169.178 on POS12/0/0, 05:11:15 ago
  Routing Descriptor Blocks:
  * 192.168.169.178, from 172.16.220.41, 05:11:15 ago, via POS12/0/0
      Route metric is 20, traffic share count is 1

corp-a-01#
```

This information is a little more useful because it shows you where the route was learned from, the metrics associated with the route, and how old the route announcement is.

Even if there were routes learned from different IP routing protocols on your router, the show ip route command will tell you definitively which protocol was chosen as the best route to the destination network. The Cisco IOS determines which IP routing protocols are better than the others by an administrative distance system. Each IP routing protocol is assigned a default administrative distance in the IOS. The routing protocol with the lowest distance is chosen first. These administrative weights can be altered using IOS distance commands. Table 16.1 shows the default administrative distance values for the various IP routing protocols.

Table 16.1   **Default Administrative Distance Values for IP Routing Protocols**

IP routing protocol	Default Administrative Distance
Connected network	0
Static Route	1
EIGRP Summary Route	5
EBGP	20
EIGRP	90
IGRP	100
OSPF	110
IS-IS	115
RIP	120
EGP (Exterior Gateway Protocol)	140
IBGP	200
Unknown	255

Administrative Distance for Static Routes

Remember back to the BGP anchor routes discussed in Chapter 6, "Configuring Dynamic Routing Protocols." A static route is placed in the router configuration to keep the BGP network announcement to EBGP peers from flapping (changing states continually). The static route is also used to initiate the EBGP route announcement when a route does not exist for the network in your IGP. A 254 value was placed at the end of the static route command. That 254 value is actually an administrative distance that you set for that static route. By setting the value to 254 you told the IOS to believe all other sources of routing information for that network before the static route, which pointed to the Null0 interface. Obviously you want real network reachability information to be believed before the static route that you entered. Otherwise all packets destined for that network would be dropped.

OSPF Troubleshooting

Let's examine a typical routing problem. A problem exists on one of the serial leased line between corp-a-01 and corp-b-01. One side of the leased line connected to Serial 1/0 on corp-a-01 and Serial 4/0 on corp-b-01 is assigned to a different OSPF area then the other side. Let's refer back to our case study network that was introduced in chapter 12 (see figure 12.1) To recap, the configuration for the serial interface on corp-a-01 is as follows:

```
interface Serial1/0
 description Leased line to corp-b-1
 ip address 192.168.6.1 255.255.255.252
```

The interface configuration for serial4/0 on corp-b-01 is as follows:

```
interface Serial4/0
 description Leased line to corp-a-1
 ip address 192.168.6.2 255.255.255.252
```

The OSPF configuration for corp-a-01 is as follows:

```
router ospf 100
 redistribute connected subnets
 network 192.168.6.0 0.0.0.3 area 0
```

The OSPF configuration for corp-b-01 is as follows:

```
router ospf 100
 redistribute connected subnets
 network 192.168.6.0 0.0.0.3 area 10
```

Assuming that you are unaware that one side of the serial leased line is configured for the wrong OSPF area, let's walk though the troubleshooting steps you would take to resolve the problem. Remembering the troubleshooting steps outlined in chapter 10, "Collecting Data via Other Means," you would first clearly define the problem. In this case the problem is that the OSPF adjacency between corp-a-01 and corp-b-01 is not being established. The next step is to make a list of the possible causes of the problem. Following is a few of the possible reasons that the OSPF adjacency would not be formed:

- Serial interface is down
- OSPF is not enabled
- Serial interface network is not configured in the OSPF process
- The OSPF areas defined on each side of the link are not the same

Now that the possible causes are known you need to develop ways of testing each to either validate or invalidate it as the cause of the problem. Table 16.2 shows the IOS command that you could use to verify each of the causes listed.

Table 16.2 **Commands to Test OSPF Problem Causes**

Cause	Test command
Serial interface is down	show interface
OSPF is not enabled	show ip ospf
Serial interface network is not configured in the OSPF process	show ip ospf interface
OSPF areas defined on each router are different	show ip ospf interface

Now you must prioritize your list of test actions depending on which causes are most likely and are easiest to test. In this case each of the tests are equally easy to execute because each only requires one command. I would sort the likelihood of each cause as follows:

- Serial interface is down
- Serial interface network is not configured in the OSPF process
- The OSPF areas defined on each router are different
- OSPF is not enabled on the routers

The reason I sort the list this way is because of experience. I know that interface problems are common. I also know that OSPF is running on the other serial leased line between the routers, so the process is configured.

Troubleshooting OSPF Problems with *show* Commands

Next, you need to execute your tests in order until you find the cause of the problem or have exhausted all your tests.

First is `show interface serial1/0` on corp–a–01:

```
corp-a-01#show interface serial1/0
Serial1/0 is up, line protocol is up
  Hardware is cxBus Serial
  Description: DS1 to corp-b-01
  Internet address is 192.168.6/1/30
  MTU 1500 bytes, BW 1544 Kbit, DLY 20000 usec, rely 255/255, load 1/255
  Encapsulation HDLC, loopback not set, keepalive set (10 sec)
  Last input 00:00:00, output 00:00:01, output hang never
  Last clearing of "show interface" counters never
  Input queue: 0/75/85 (size/max/drops); Total output drops: 67227
  Queueing strategy: weighted fair
  Output queue: 0/64/67227 (size/threshold/drops)
     Conversations  0/256 (active/max active)
     Reserved Conversations 0/0 (allocated/max allocated)
  5 minute input rate 8000 bits/sec, 12 packets/sec
  5 minute output rate 9000 bits/sec, 11 packets/sec
     71932872 packets input, 1601711700 bytes, 24 no buffer
     Received 0 broadcasts, 0 runts, 0 giants
     5 input errors, 4 CRC, 0 frame, 0 overrun, 0 ignored, 1 abort
```

```
       89588815 packets output, 2797659158 bytes, 0 underruns
       0 output errors, 0 collisions, 105 interface resets
       0 output buffer failures, 676223 output buffers swapped out
       5 carrier transitions
       RTS up, CTS up, DTR up, DCD up, DSR up
   corp-a-01#
```

You can tell from the first line of the output from that command that the serial interface is online. Record which test you ran and the outcome, then move to the next test. You use the `show ip ospf interface s1/0` on corp-a-01 to determine whether the IP network assigned to interface serial1/0 has been enabled in the OSPF process configuration for corp-a-01. Examining the first line of the output from this command, you probably notice that this same command could have been used to test the up/down status of the interface as well. The Cisco `show` commands are very good about giving you all the information you might need in the output of each command. This makes gathering information easier and faster.

```
   corp-a-01#sh ip ospf int serial1/0
   Serial1/0 is up, line protocol is up
     Internet Address 192.168.6.1/30, Area 0
     Process ID 100, Router ID 192.168.6.1, Network Type BROADCAST, Cost: 20
     Transmit Delay is 1 sec, State DR, Priority 1
     Designated Router (ID) 192.168.6.1, Interface address 192.168.6.1
     No backup designated router on this network
     Timer intervals configured, Hello 10, Dead 40, Wait 40, Retransmit 5
       Hello due in 00:00:03
     Neighbor Count is 0, Adjacent neighbor count is 0
     Suppress hello for 0 neighbor(s)
   corp-a-01#
```

The output from the last command shows that the Internet Protocol (IP) network is indeed configured in the OSPF process for the router. Record the test that was run and the outcome. Because the IP network for the serial interface is configured in OSPF, you know that OSPF is enabled on the router. Looking forward, this test invalidates the last cause in your prioritized list. All that remains is to verify the OSPF area configurations on both sides of the serial leased line. The output from the last command on corp-a-01 shows that serial1/0 is in OSPF area 0 (end of the second output line). All you need to do is execute the same command on corp-b-01 for serial interface 4/0.

```
   corp-b-01#sh ip ospf int serial4/0
   Serial4/0 is up, line protocol is up
     Internet Address 192.168.6.2/30, Area 10
     Process ID 100, Router ID 192.168.6.2, Network Type BROADCAST, Cost: 20
     Transmit Delay is 1 sec, State DR, Priority 1
     Designated Router (ID) 192.168.6.2, Interface address 192.168.6.2
     No backup designated router on this network
     Timer intervals configured, Hello 10, Dead 40, Wait 40, Retransmit 5
       Hello due in 00:00:03
     Neighbor Count is 0, Adjacent neighbor count is 0
     Suppress hello for 0 neighbor(s)
   corp-b-01#
```

Looking back at the output from the show ip ospf interface s1/0/0 command on corp-a-01, you see that the interface is in OSPF area 0. The output from the show ip ospf interface serial4/0 command on corp-b-01 shows that interface in OSPF area 10. You have now found the cause of the problem. One side of the DS1 connection is configured for OSPF area 0, whereas the other side is configured for area 10. A simple change in the network statement for the IP network assigned to serial4/0 on corp-b-01 in the OSPF configuration will fix the problem. The old configuration was

```
router ospf 100
 redistribute connected subnets
 network 192.168.6.0 0.0.0.3 area 10
```

The new configuration should be

```
router ospf 100
 redistribute connected subnets
 network 192.168.6.0 0.0.0.3 area 0
```

The series of commands that you would use to make this change are

```
corp-b-01#conf t
corp-b-01(config)#router ospf 100
corp-b-01(config-router)#no network 192.168.6.0 0.0.0.3 area 10
corp-b-01(config-router)#network 192.168.6.0 0.0.0.3 area 0
corp-b-01(config-router)#^Z
corp-b-01#
```

You need to remove the old network statement from the OSPF configuration and then add the correct network statement. The Cisco IOS will not allow you to simply change the area ID by issuing a new network statement. The override will not be effective.

Troubleshooting OSPF Problems with *debug ip ospf* Events

Another Cisco IOS command that is useful in tracking down OSPF problems is debug ip ospf events. Using this command, the previous problem could have been easily caught without any testing. First make sure that the output of debug commands is displayed to your current VTY session on the router. The terminal monitor command is used to accomplish this.

Next, use the debug ip ospf events command on corp-a-01. Here is a sample of the output that would have been seen during the previously described problem:

```
OSPF: Rcv pkt from 192.168.0.1, Serial4/0, area 0.0.0.10
      mismatch area 0.0.0.0 in the header
```

OSPF Area ID Display

The Cisco IOS displays the OSPF area ID in dotted IP notation. For instance, if the area configured for an interface is area 500, the debug information would display that area as 0.0.1.244. To convert the integer area ID to a dotted IP format, simply convert the decimal integer number to binary and then split the binary number into four sets of eight-bit groups (filling the bit positions to the left with 0 until all 32-bit positions are present). Each eight-bit group from left to right is then converted back to decimals individually to create the dotted IP address version of the area ID.

What this message means is that a packet was received from the router with the OSPF ID of 192.168.0.1, which is corp-a-01. The OSPF area that the local router expects to see is area 10. What is sent in the OSPF hello packet is area 0.

With this information, it is now a simple matter to change the network statement in the OSPF configuration on corp-b-01 to reflect the correct area ID.

BGP Troubleshooting

In this section, we cover the diagnosis of a few BGP related problems on the Cisco router. Because of the flexibility of the BGP protocol, there are a great many problems that can be encountered when using BGP to exchange routing information between autonomous systems. Most BGP problems you will run into will be routing policy implementation errors. This means that the configurations of the routers in your network do not implement the routing policy that you defined correctly. We will cover some of the more common problems here.

Referring to the network diagram in the case study introduced in Chapter 13, "Case Study," you can see that there is a connection to an Internet service provider (ISP) on corp-a-01. The connection is a DS3 HSSI running PPP encapsulation. Because there is another connection to a different ISP on corp-e-01, corp-a-01 exchanges routes with ISP A via BGP4. The following is the interface configuration for the DS3 HSSI interface on corp-a-01 that connects to ISP A:

```
interface Hssi0/1/0
 description DS3 connection to ISP A
 ip address 192.168.5.2 255.255.255.252
```

The following is the configuration for the BGP session with ISP A from corp-a-01:

```
router bgp 65050
 no synchronization
 bgp always-compare-med
 bgp dampening
 bgp deterministic-med
 neighbor 192.168.5.1 remote-as 65020
 neighbor 192.168.5.1 distribute-list 1 in
 neighbor 192.168.5.1 distribute-list 1 out
 neighbor 192.168.5.1 route-map isp-a in
 neighbor 192.168.5.1 filter-list 1 out
```

The preceding configuration makes use of an IP filter-list and an AS-Path filter-list. Following is the definition of these two filter-lists:

```
ip as-path access-list 1 deny _65051_
ip as-path access-list 1 permit ^$
!
access-list 1 deny   10.0.0.0 0.255.255.255
access-list 1 deny   172.16.0.0 0.15.255.255
access-list 1 deny   192.168.0.0 0.0.255.255
```

AS-path 1 enables the announcement of networks from ASN 65050 only. It specifically denies the announcement of routes from ASN 65051. Access-list 1 prevents the
acceptance or announcement of reserved IP address space. Refer to Chapter 6,
"Configuring Dynamic Routing Protocols," and Chapter 8, "Access and Traffic
Management," for the use of as-path lists and access-lists. There is also a route-map
used to set certain attributes on updates coming in from ISP A. The following is the
definition of route-map isp-a:

```
route-map isp-a permit 10
 set local-preference 1000
```

The route-map is fairly basic. It sets the local preference value of all routes that are
learned from ISP A to 1000.

Now that the entire BGP configuration has been established, let us examine a
problem that exists. The remote IP address of the ISP is reachable but the BGP session
will not establish. This is shown by the output of the show ip bgp summary command
on corp-a-01, which is listed here:

```
corp-a-01#sh ip bgp sum
BGP table version is 1, main routing table version 1

Neighbor        V    AS MsgRcvd MsgSent   TblVer  InQ OutQ Up/Down  State
192.168.5.1     4 65020       0       0        0    0    0 never    Idle
corp-a-01#
```

You can tell the session is not established because the table version is 0, the up/down
state is never, and the communication state is idle. Your first task, in our troubleshooting methodology, is to clearly define the problem. The BGP session is not active.

Next, you determine possible causes for the BGP session not being active. The
cause of this could be any number of reasons.

- The interface connected to the ISP could be down.
- The BGP session could not be configured on either router.
- The remote ASN could be incorrectly configured on either your router or the
  ISP's router.
- The neighbor IP address could be unreachable.
- There could be an auto-negotiation bug in the IOS. I encountered this problem
  when implementing a version of the Cisco IOS that supported the new multi-
  cast BGP (MBGP or BGP4+) extensions. Cisco fixed the problem by adding a
  configuration command to stop auto-negotiation. The BGP neighbor command
  is dont-capability-negotiate.

Now you need to define test actions for each of these possible causes. Table 16.3 lists
the test actions for each cause.

Table 16.3 **Test Actions for Possible Problem Causes**

Cause to test	Command used to test
The Hssi interface is down	`show interface`
The BGP session is not configured	`show ip bgp neighbor` `write terminal`

Remote ASN is configured wrong	`show ip bgp summary`
	`show ip bgp neighbor`
	`write terminal`

Neighbor IP address is unreachable	`ping`
MBPG auto-negotiation not operating	N/A (try disabling the feature)

Now the list needs to be prioritized by the ease of the testing and the likelihood of the cause. You always want to check the simple causes first, so the list gets sorted as follows:

- The interface is down.
- The remote IP address is unreachable.
- BGP is not configured on either router.
- The remote ASN is incorrectly configured.
- MBGP auto-negotiation is enabled.

Troubleshooting BGP with *show* Commands

I stated earlier that the remote IP address of the ISP connection is reachable. This fact negates the need to test whether the interface is up or if the remote IP is reachable. Had you needed to test these possible causes, the procedure would have been the same as the one used in the OSPF section. The commands are the same, as are the outputs. We know that the BGP session is configured on our router. You need to contact an engineer at the ISP to verify that their side is configured.

Verification of the correct Abstract Syntax Representation (ASN) configuration is done by visually checking the current router configuration. If none of the possible causes have been validated, then try disabling the MBGP auto-negotiation feature.

Once the BGP session has been established, you should see an output from the `show ip bgp summary` command that looks like this:

```
corp-a-01#sh ip bgp sum
BGP table version is 1, main routing table version 1

Neighbor        V    AS MsgRcvd MsgSent   TblVer  InQ OutQ Up/Down  State
192.168.5.1     4 65020   45350   45350  7634267    0    0  2d10h
corp-a-01#
```

The messages received (MsgRcvd) and messages sent (MsgSent) counters show the number of messages that have been exchanged between the two BGP peers. The table version (TblVer) is used by the BGP process to make sure that all BGP peers are synchronized. The table version of all BGP peers should be the same number when all updates have been processed. The in queue (InQ) and out queue (OutQ) counters show how many messages have been received or sent that have not been processed. The up/down column shows the amount of time that the BGP session has been in its current state. The state column shows the current state of the BGP session. This column will be blank if the session is up. It will show active with a table version of 0 when the BGP session is down. If the BGP session was never established since configuration, the state column will show never.

To gather more detailed information about a particular BGP neighbor, use the show ip bgp neighbor *<ip address>* command. Here is a sample output from that command on our BGP peer that is currently down:

```
corp-a-01>sh ip bgp nei 192.168.5.1
BGP neighbor is 192.168.5.1,  remote AS 65020, internal link
 Index 0, Offset 0, Mask 0x0
  NEXT_HOP is always this router
  BGP version 4, remote router ID 0.0.0.0
  BGP state = Active, table version = 0
  Last read 18:54:51, hold time is 180, keepalive interval is 60 seconds
  Minimum time between advertisement runs is 5 seconds
  Received 1532 messages, 0 notifications, 0 in queue
  Sent 1549 messages, 0 notifications, 0 in queue
  Incoming update network filter list is 98
  Connections established 4; dropped 4
  No active TCP connection
corp-a-01>
```

Once the BGP session has been established, the output from the show ip bgp neighbor command changes. Here is what the output looks like for an established peer:

```
corp-a-01#sh ip bgp nei 192.168.5.1
BGP neighbor is 12.168.5.1, remote AS 65020, external link
 Index 3, Offset 0, Mask 0x8
  Inbound soft reconfiguration allowed
  BGP version 4, remote router ID 192.168.5.1
  BGP state = Established, table version = 6555518, up for 2d12h
  Last read 00:00:10, hold time is 180, keepalive interval is 60 seconds
  Minimum time between advertisement runs is 30 seconds
  Received 138854 messages, 0 notifications, 0 in queue
  Sent 90247 messages, 0 notifications, 0 in queue
  Inbound path policy configured
  Outbound path policy configured
  Incoming update network filter list is 1
  Outgoing update network filter list is 1
  Outgoing update AS path filter list is 1
  Route map for incoming advertisements is isp-a
```

```
       Connections established 29; dropped 28
       Last reset 2d12h, due to Peer closing down the session
       No. of prefix received 425
       No. of prefix received but not used 0
     Connection state is ESTAB, I/O status: 1, unread input bytes: 0
     Local host: 192.168.5.2, Local port: 179
     Foreign host: 192.168.5.1, Foreign port: 41740

     Enqueued packets for retransmit: 0, input: 0, saved: 0

     Event Timers (current time is 0x1212E0F48):
     Timer          Starts    Wakeups         Next
     Retrans          3708         6           0x0
     TimeWait            0         0           0x0
     AckHold          8188      8006           0x0
     SendWnd             0         0           0x0
     KeepAlive           0         0           0x0
     GiveUp              0         0           0x0
     PmtuAger            0         0           0x0

     iss: 2048809659  snduna: 2048887469  sndnxt: 2048887469     sndwnd:   14066
     irs: 2041569949  rcvnxt: 2041841810  rcvwnd:         15876  delrcvwnd:   508

     SRTT: 333 ms, RTTO: 1022 ms, RTV: 178 ms, KRTT: 0 ms
     minRTT: 0 ms, maxRTT: 1044 ms, ACK hold: 300 ms
     Flags: passive open, nagle, gen tcbs

     Datagrams (max data segment is 4430 bytes):
     Rcvd: 11866 (out of order: 0), with data: 8189, total data bytes: 271860
     Sent: 11773 (retransmit: 6), with data: 3701, total data bytes: 77809
     corp-a-01#
```

Most BGP problems occur while the peering sessions are up and operating properly. The problems, which you will encounter, will be from routing policy configurations. Examples of some the problems that you might encounter are

- BGP peering sessions being dropped due to link congestion.

- Configuration changes being made without resetting the BGP sessions. In order for some changes to fully take effect, like route-map changes, the corresponding BGP session needs to be reset. This is done with the clear ip bgp command.

- Routing policy changes not being implemented on all routers in your network. If some routers prefer destination routes from ISP A while all the other routers in your network prefer destination routes from ISP B, there is a good chance that routing loops will occur. There could also be occasion for traffic to go to an ISP that you did not intend.

Commands Available in Different User Modes

As you can see by the command prompts from the last few examples, many of the show ip bgp commands are available in both basic user mode and enable mode. Remember that the basic user mode command prompt ends in a > whereas the enabled user mode command prompt ends in a #.

Working with Your Hardware Vendor

It might be that your router configuration is correct but the IOS software is not operating properly. This is when a bug ID must be opened with the hardware vendor. A *bug ID* is a reference number that Cisco assigns to known problems which are discovered in the IOS. This bug ID is used to reference any other reports that might come in regarding similar problems from other Cisco customers.

In the case of Cisco, getting a bug ID can be done simply by calling their Technical Assistance Center (TAC). They will gather some information from you, assign a case number, and then forward you to a Cisco engineer. Cisco will usually collect data on the problem and, if needed, commit a fix for the bug to the next interim release of IOS. If it is a major problem, they might even produce a fix and compile a special IOS image just for you until the patch can be applied to the mainstream IOS release. The special image is basically the most recent IOS version in the strain that you are running on your routers with the patch applied. These types of IOS versions are considered experimental and go through very little testing. These are used only in rare cases.

The types of information that Cisco might ask you for are

- The output from a `show tech-support` command.
- Any syslog data you might have.
- Recent configuration changes to the router.
- Data output from various `show` and `debug` commands.
- Access to your router in order to gather data over time.

Conclusion

Hopefully, from this chapter you have gained a good understanding of how to go about troubleshooting problems with OSPF and BGP. You can take the ideas introduced here and apply them to any of the routing protocols available in the Cisco IOS. All the command formats are similar no matter which protocol you are trying to troubleshoot.

Also, you should have gained a firm grasp on the overall troubleshooting methodology that was first introduced in Chapter 10. By applying the ideas given in the text of Chapter 10 to the real-world examples provided here, you should be able to tackle problems in your own network even if they are not similar to the ones covered here. It is also my hope that you have gained knowledge of some common pitfalls that you should avoid when configuring your routers. It is always a good idea to double-check your configurations, as many of the problems that you will encounter will be configuration errors. Errors also can be introduced by typographical mistakes or plain and simple omissions. Double checking your configurations is usually done by simply displaying the running configuration of the router to your terminal and verifying visually that the commands displayed are correct. To display the current configuration to your terminal use the `write terminal` enable mode command. To recap this chapter, Table 16.4 shows which IOS commands to use for specific situations.

Table 16.4 **Which IOS Command to Use When**

To do this...	You use this command...
Display routing table entry for an IP network	`show ip route <network>`
Display OSPF database entry for an IP network	`show ip ospf database external <network>`
Display BGP table entry for an IP network	`show ip bgp <network>`

Index

Symbols

B

F

I

J-K

T

W-Z

Windows 2000 Answers

This is the updated edition of New Riders' best-selling *Inside Windows NT Server 4*. Taking the author-driven, no-nonsense approach that we pioneered with our *Landmark* books, New Riders proudly offers something unique for Windows 2000 administrators—an interesting and discriminating book on Windows 2000 Server, written by someone in the trenches who can anticipate your situation and provide answers you can trust.

INSIDE Windows 2000 Server

William Boswell

ISBN: 1-56205-929-7

Windows 2000 ESSENTIAL REFERENCE

Steven Tate, et al.

Architected to be the most navigable, useful, and value-packed reference for Windows 2000, this book uses a creative "telescoping" design that you can adapt to your style of learning. It's a concise, focused, and quick reference for Windows 2000, providing the kind of practical advice, tips, procedures, and additional resources that every administrator will need.

ISBN: 0-7357-0869-X

Windows 2000 Active Directory is just one of several new Windows 2000 titles from New Riders' acclaimed *Landmark Series*. Perfect for network architects and administrators, this book describes the intricacies of Active Directory while keeping real-world systems and constraints in mind. It's a detailed, solution-oriented book which addresses the need for a single work to planning, deploying, and managing Active Directory in an enterprise setting.

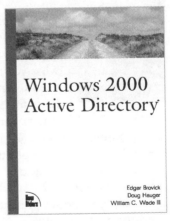

Windows 2000 Active Directory

Edgar Brovick
Doug Hauger
William C. Wade III

ISBN: 0-7357-0870-3

Advanced Information on
Networking Technologies

New Riders Books Offer Advice and Experience

LANDMARK

Rethinking Computer Books

We know how important it is to have access to detailed, solution-oriented information on core technologies. *Landmark* books contain the essential information you need to solve technical problems. Written by experts and subjected to rigorous peer and technical reviews, our *Landmark* books are hard-core resources for practitioners like you.

ESSENTIAL REFERENCE
Smart, Like You

The *Essential Reference* series from New Riders provides answers when you know what you want to do but need to know how to do it. Each title skips extraneous material and assumes a strong base of knowledge. These are indispensable books for the practitioner who wants to find specific features of a technology quickly and efficiently. Avoiding fluff and basic material, these books present solutions in an innovative, clean format—and at a great value.

MCSE CERTIFICATION
Engineered for
Test Success

New Riders offers a complete line of test preparation materials to help you achieve your certification. With books like the *MCSE Training Guide*, and software like the acclaimed *MCSE Complete* and the revolutionary *ExamGear*, New Riders offers comprehensive products built by experienced professionals who have passed the exams and instructed hundreds of candidates.

New Riders \ Books for Networking Professionals

Windows NT/2000 Titles

Windows 2000 TCP/IP

Windows 2000 TCP/IP
By Karanjit Siyan, Ph.D.
2nd Edition
700 pages, $34.99
ISBN: 0-7357-0992-0

Windows 2000 TCP/IP cuts through the complexities and provides the most informative and complex reference book on Windows 2000–based TCP/IP topics. The book is a tutorial-reference hybrid, focusing on how Microsoft TCP/IP works, using hands-on tutorials and practical examples. Concepts essential to TCP/IP administration are explained thoroughly, and are then related to the practical use of Microsoft TCP/IP in a serious networking environment.

Windows 2000 DNS

Windows 2000 DNS
By Roger Abell, Herman Knief, Andrew Daniels, and Jeffrey Graham
2nd Edition
450 pages, $39.99
ISBN: 0-7357-0973-4

The Domain Name System is a directory of registered computer names and IP addresses that can be instantly located. Without proper design and administration of DNS, computers wouldn't be able to locate each other on the network, and applications like email and Web browsing wouldn't be feasible. Administrators need this information to make their networks work. *Windows 2000 DNS* provides a technical overview of DNS and WINS, and how to design and administer them for optimal performance in a Windows 2000 environment.

Windows 2000 Registry

Windows 2000 Registry
By Sandra Osborrne
2nd Edition
550 pages, $34.99
ISBN: 0-7357-0944-0

Windows 2000 Registry is a powerful tool for accomplishing many important administration tasks, but little information is available on registry settings and how they can be edited to accomplish these tasks. This title offers unique insight into using registry settings to software or configure client systems in a Windows 2000 environment. The approach of the book is that of revealing the GUI through the registry, allowing system administrators to edit the registry settings to efficiently accomplish critical tasks such as configuration, installation, and management.

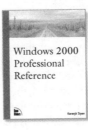

Windows 2000 Professional Reference

Windows 2000 Professional Reference
By Karanjit Siyan, Ph.D.
3rd Edition
1800 pages, $75.00
ISBN: 0-7357-0952-1

Windows 2000 Professional Reference is the benchmark of references available for Windows 2000. Although other titles take you through the setup and implementation phase of the product, no other book provides the user with detailed answers to day-to-day administration problems and tasks. Real-world implementations are key to help administrators discover the most viable solutions for their particular environments. Solid content shows administrators how to manage, troubleshoot, and fix problems that are specific to heterogeneous Windows networks, as well as Internet features and functionality.

Windows 2000 Professional
By Jerry Honeycutt
350 pages, $34.99 US
ISBN: 0-7357-0950-5

Windows 2000 Professional explores the power available to the Windows workstation user on the corporate network and Internet. The book is aimed directly at the power user who values the security, stability, and networking capabilities of NT alongside the ease and familiarity of the Windows 95/98 user interface. This book covers both user and administration topics, with a dose of networking content added for connectivity.

Windows NT Power Toolkit
By Stu Sjouwerman and Ed Tittel
1st Edition
800 pages, $49.99
ISBN: 0-7357-0922-X

This book covers the analysis, tuning, optimization, automation, enhancement, maintenance, and troubleshooting of Windows NT Server 4.0 and Windows NT Workstation 4.0. In most cases, the two operating systems overlap completely. Where the two systems diverge, each platform is covered separately. This advanced title comprises a task-oriented treatment of the Windows NT 4.0 environment. By concentrating on the use of operating system tools and utilities, resource kit

elements, and selected third-party tuning, analysis, optimization, and productivity tools, this book will show you how to carry out everyday and advanced tasks.

Windows 2000 User Management
By Lori Sanders
300 pages, $34.99
ISBN: 1-56205-886-X

With the dawn of Windows 2000, it has become even more difficult to draw a clear line between managing the user and managing the user's environment and desktop. This book, written by a noted trainer and consultant, provides a comprehensive, practical advice to managing users and their desktop environments with Windows 2000.

Windows 2000 Deployment & Desktop Management
By Jeffrey A. Ferris, MCSE
1st Edition
400 pages, $34.99
ISBN: 0-7357-0975-0

More than a simple overview of new features and tools, *Windows 2000 Deployment & Desktop Management* is a thorough reference to deploying Windows 2000 Professional to corporate workstations. Incorporating real-world advice and detailed excercises, this book is a one-stop resource for any system administrator, integrator, engineer, or other IT professional.

Planning for Windows 2000

By Eric K. Cone, Jon Boggs, and Sergio Perez
1st Edition
400 pages, $29.99
ISBN: 0-7357-0048-6

Windows 2000 is poised to be one of the largest and most important software releases of the next decade, and you are charged with planning, testing, and deploying it in your enterprise. Are you ready? With this book, you will be. *Planning for Windows 2000* lets you know what the upgrade hurdles will be, informs you of how to clear them, guides you through effective Active Directory design, and presents you with detailed rollout procedures. Eric K. Cone, Jon Boggs, and Sergio Perez give you the benefit of their extensive experiences as Windows 2000 Rapid Deployment Program members by sharing problems and solutions they've encountered on the job.

Inside Windows 2000 Server

By William Boswell
2nd Edition
1533 pages, $49.99
ISBN: 1-56205-929-7

Finally, a totally new edition of New Riders' best-selling *Inside Windows NT Server 4*. Taking the author-driven, no-nonsense approach pioneered with the *Landmark* books, New Riders proudly offers something unique for Windows 2000 administrators—an interesting, discriminating book on Windows 2000 Server written by someone who can anticipate your situation and give you workarounds that won't leave a system unstable or sluggish.

BackOffice Titles

Implementing Exchange Server

By Doug Hauger, Marywynne Leon, and William C. Wade III
1st Edition
400 pages, $29.99
ISBN: 1-56205-931-9

If you're interested in connectivity and maintenance issues for Exchange Server, this book is for you. Exchange's power lies in its capability to be connected to multiple email subsystems to create a "universal email backbone." It's not unusual to have several different and complex systems all connected via email gateways, including Lotus Notes or cc:Mail, Microsoft Mail, legacy mainframe systems, and Internet mail. This book covers all of the problems and issues associated with getting an integrated system running smoothly, and it addresses troubleshooting and diagnosis of email problems with an eye toward prevention and best practices.

Exchange System Administration

By Janice Rice Howd
1st Edition
300 pages, $34.99
ISBN: 0-7357-0081-8

Your Exchange server is installed and connected—now what? Email administration is one of the most critical networking jobs, and Exchange can be particularly troublesome in large, heterogeneous environments. Janice Howd, a noted consultant and teacher with more than a decade of email administration experience, has put together this advanced, concise handbook for daily, periodic, and emergency administration. With in-depth coverage of topics like managing disk resources, replication, and disaster recovery, this is the one reference every Exchange administrator needs.

SQL Server System Administration

By Sean Baird,
Chris Miller, et al.
1st Edition
352 pages, $29.99
ISBN: 1-56205-955-6

How often does your SQL Server go down during the day when everyone wants to access the data? Do you spend most of your time being a "report monkey" for your coworkers and bosses? *SQL Server System Administration* helps you keep data consistently available to your users. This book omits introductory information. The authors don't spend time explaining queries and how they work. Instead, they focus on the information you can't get anywhere else, like how to choose the correct replication topology and achieve high availability of information.

Internet Information Services Administration

By Kelli Adam
1st Edition,
200 pages, $29.99
ISBN: 0-7357-0022-2

Are the new Internet technologies in Internet Information Services giving you headaches? Does protecting security on the Web take up all of your time? Then this is the book for you. With hands-on configuration training, advanced study of the new protocols, the most recent version of IIS, and detailed instructions on authenticating users with the new Certificate Server and implementing and managing the new e-commerce features, *Internet Information Services Administration* gives you the real-life solutions you need. This definitive resource prepares you for upgrading to Windows 2000 by giving you detailed advice on working with Microsoft Management Console, which was first used by IIS.

SMS 2 Administration

By Michael Lubanski
and Darshan Doshi
1st Edition
350 pages, $39.99
ISBN: 0-7357-0082-6

Microsoft's new version of its Systems Management Server (SMS) is starting to turn heads. Although complex, it allows administrators to lower their total cost of ownership and more efficiently manage clients, applications, and support operations. If your organization is using or implementing SMS, you'll need some expert advice. Michael Lubanski and Darshan Doshi can help you get the most bang for your buck with insight, expert tips, and real-world examples. Michael and Darshan are consultants specializing in SMS and have worked with Microsoft on one of the most complex SMS rollouts in the world, involving 32 countries, 15 languages, and thousands of clients.

SQL Server Essential Reference

By Sharon Dooley
1stEdition
$35.00 US
ISBN: 0-7357-0864-9

SQL Server Essential Reference is a comprehensive reference of advanced how-tos and techniques for SQL Server 7 administrators. This book provides solid grounding in fundamental SQL Server 7 administrative tasks to help you tame your SQL Server environment. With coverage ranging from installation, monitoring, troubleshooting security and backup and recovery plans, this book breaks down SQL Server into its key conceptual areas and functions. This easy to use reference is a must-have for any SQL Server administrator.

UNIX/Linux Titles

Solaris Essential Reference
By John P. Mulligan
1st Edition
300 pages, $24.95
ISBN: 0-7357-0023-0

Looking for the fastest and easiest way to find the Solaris command you need? Need a few pointers on shell scripting? How about advanced administration tips and sound, practical expertise on security issues? Are you looking for trustworthy information about available third-party software packages that will enhance your operating system? Author John Mulligan—creator of the popular "Unofficial Guide to The Solaris™ Operating Environment" Web site (sun.icsnet.com)—delivers all that and more in one attractive, easy-to-use reference book. With clear and concise instructions on how to perform important administration and management tasks, and key information on powerful commands and advanced topics, *Solaris Essential Reference* is the book you need when you know what you want to do and only need to know how.

Linux System Administration
By M. Carling, Stephen Degler, and James Dennis
1st Edition
450 pages, $29.99
ISBN: 1-56205-934-3

As an administrator, you probably feel that most of your time and energy is spent in endless firefighting. If your network has become a fragile quilt of temporary patches and work-arounds, this book is for you. Have you had trouble sending or receiving email lately? Are you looking for a way to keep your network running smoothly with enhanced performance? Are your users always hankering for more storage, services, and speed? *Linux System Administration* advises you on the many intricacies of maintaining a secure, stable system. In this definitive work, the authors address all the issues related to system administration, from adding users and managing file permissions, to Internet services and Web hosting, to recovery planning and security. This book fulfills the need for expert advice that will ensure a trouble-free Linux environment.

GTK+/Gnome Application Development
By Havoc Pennington
1st Edition
492 pages, $39.99
ISBN: 0-7357-0078-8

This title is for the reader who is conversant with the C programming language and UNIX/Linux development. It provides detailed and solution-oriented information designed to meet the needs of programmers and application developers using the GTK+/Gnome libraries. Coverage complements existing GTK+/Gnome documentation, going into more depth on pivotal issues such as uncovering the GTK+ object system, working with the event loop, managing the Gdk substrate, writing custom widgets, and mastering GnomeCanvas.

Developing Linux Applications with GTK+ and GDK
By Eric Harlow
1st Edition
490 pages, $34.99
ISBN: 0-7357-0021-4

We all know that Linux is one of the most powerful and solid operating systems in existence. And as the success of Linux grows, there is an increasing interest in developing applications with graphical user interfaces that take advantage of the power of Linux. In this book, software developer Eric Harlow gives you an indispensable development handbook focusing on the GTK+ toolkit. More than an overview of the elements of application or GUI design, this is a hands-on book that delves into the technology. With in-depth material on the various GUI programming tools and loads of examples, this book's unique focus will give you the information you need to design and launch professional-quality applications.

Linux Essential Reference
By Ed Petron
1st Edition
350 pages, $24.95
ISBN: 0-7357-0852-5

This book is all about getting things done as quickly and efficiently as possible by providing a structured organization for the plethora of available Linux information. We can sum it up in one word—value. This book has it all: concise instructions

on how to perform key administration tasks, advanced information on configuration, shell scripting, hardware management, systems management, data tasks, automation, and tons of other useful information. This book truly provides groundbreaking information for the growing community of advanced Linux professionals.

Lotus Notes and Domino Titles

Domino System Administration
By Rob Kirkland, CLP, CLI
1st Edition
850 pages, $49.99
ISBN: 1-56205-948-3

Your boss has just announced that you will be upgrading to the newest version of Notes and Domino when it ships. How are you supposed to get this new system installed, configured, and rolled out to all of your end users? You understand how Lotus Notes works—you've been administering it for years. What you need is a concise, practical explanation of the new features and how to make some of the advanced stuff work smoothly by someone like you, who has worked with the product for years and understands what you need to know. *Domino System Administration* is the answer—the first book on Domino that attacks the technology at the professional level with practical, hands-on assistance to get Domino running in your organization.

Lotus Notes & Domino Essential Reference

By Tim Bankes, CLP
and Dave Hatter, CLP, MCP
1st Edition
650 pages, $45.00
ISBN: 0-7357-0007-9

You're in a bind because you've been asked to design and program a new database in Notes for an important client who will keep track of and itemize a myriad of inventory and shipping data. The client wants a user-friendly interface that won't sacrifice speed or functionality. You are experienced (and could develop this application in your sleep), but feel you need something to facilitate your creative and technical abilities—something to perfect your programming skills. The answer is waiting for you: *Lotus Notes & Domino Essential Reference*. It's compact and simply designed. It's loaded with information. All of the objects, classes, functions, and methods are listed. It shows you the object hierarchy and the relationship between each one. It's perfect for you. Problem solved.

detection specialists, security analysts, and consultants responsible for setting up and maintaining an effective defense against network security attacks.

Understanding Data Communications, Sixth Edition

By Gilbert Held
Sixth Edition
600 pages, $39.99
ISBN: 0-7357-0036-2

Updated from the highly successful fifth edition, this book explains how data communications systems and their various hardware and software components work. More than an entry-level book, it approaches the material in textbook format, addressing the complex issues involved in internetworking today. A great reference book for the experienced networking professional that is written by the noted networking authority, Gilbert Held.

Networking Titles

Network Intrusion Detection: An Analyst's Handbook

By Stephen Northcutt
1st Edition
267 pages, $39.99
ISBN: 0-7357-0868-1

Get answers and solutions from someone who has been in the trenches. The author, Stephen Northcutt, original developer of the Shadow intrusion detection system and former director of the United States Navy's Information System Security Office at the Naval Security Warfare Center, gives his expertise to intrusion

Other Books By New Riders

We Want to Know What You Think

To better serve you, we would like your opinion on the content and quality of this book. Please complete this card, and mail it to us or fax it to 317-581-4663.

Name _____

Address _____

City_____State_____Zip _____

Phone _____

Email Address _____

Occupation _____

Operating system(s) that you use _____

What influenced your purchase of this book?
- ❏ Recommendation
- ❏ Table of Contents
- ❏ Magazine Review
- ❏ New Riders' Reputation
- ❏ Cover Design
- ❏ Index
- ❏ Advertisement
- ❏ Author Name

How would you rate the contents of this book?
- ❏ Excellent
- ❏ Good
- ❏ Below Average
- ❏ Very Good
- ❏ Fair
- ❏ Poor

How do you plan to use this book?
- ❏ Quick Reference
- ❏ Classroom
- ❏ Self-Training
- ❏ Other

What do you like most about this book?
Check all that apply.
- ❏ Content
- ❏ Accuracy
- ❏ Listings
- ❏ Index
- ❏ Price
- ❏ Writing Style
- ❏ Examples
- ❏ Design
- ❏ Page Count
- ❏ Illustrations

What do you like least about this book?
Check all that apply.
- ❏ Content
- ❏ Accuracy
- ❏ Listings
- ❏ Index
- ❏ Price
- ❏ Writing Style
- ❏ Examples
- ❏ Design
- ❏ Page Count
- ❏ Illustrations

What would be a useful follow-up book for you? _____

Where did you purchase this book?_____

_____

Can you name a similar book that you like better than this one, or one that is as good? Why?

_____

_____

How many New Riders books do you own? _____

What are your favorite computer books?_____

_____

What other titles would you like to see us develop? _____

_____

Any comments for us? _____

_____

_____

_____

Cisco Router Configuration & Troubleshooting,
Second Edition:
0-7357-0999-8

www.newriders.com • Fax 317-581-4663

Fold here and tape to mail

New Riders Publishing
201 W. 103rd St.
Indianapolis, IN 46290

# How to Contact Us

Visit Our Web Site

`www.newriders.com`

On our Web site you'll find information about our other books, authors, tables of contents, indexes, and book errata.

Email Us

Contact us at this address:

`nrfeedback@newriders.com`

- If you have comments or questions about this book
- To report errors that you have found in this book
- If you have a book proposal to submit or are interested in writing for New Riders
- If you would like to have an author kit sent to you
- If you are an expert in a computer topic or technology and are interested in being a technical editor who reviews manuscripts for technical accuracy

`nrfeedback@newriders.com`

- To find a distributor in your area, please contact our international department at this address.

`nrmedia@newriders.com`

- For instructors from educational institutions who want to preview New Riders books for classroom use. Email should include your name, title, school, department, address, phone number, office days/hours, text in use, and enrollment, along with your request for desk/examination copies and/or additional information.
- For members of the media who are interested in reviewing copies of New Riders books. Send your name, mailing address, and email address, along with the name of the publication or Web site you work for.

Write to Us

New Riders Publishing

201 W. 103rd St.

Indianapolis, IN 46290-1097

Call Us

Toll-free (800) 571-5840 + 9 + 4511

If outside U.S. (317) 581-3500. Ask for New Riders.

Fax Us

(317) 581-4663